CRITICAL INSIGHTS

Kurt Vonnegut

CRITICAL INSIGHTS

Kurt Vonnegut

Editor

Robert T. Tally Jr.

Texas State University

SALEM PRESS
A Division of EBSCO Publishing

Ipswich, Massachusetts

GREY HOUSE PUBLISHING

Library of Congress Cataloging-in-Publication Data

Kurt Vonnegut / editor, Rob Tally.
      pages cm. -- (Critical Insights)
  Includes bibliographical references and index.
  ISBN 978-1-4298-3832-0 (hardcover)
  1. Vonnegut, Kurt. I. Tally, Robert T.
  PS3572.O5Z7536 2013
  813'.54--dc23

                                                                      2012050603

ebook ISBN: 978-1-4298-3848-1

Contents_____

About This Volume, Robert T. Tally Jr.   vii

Career, Life, and Influence

On Kurt Vonnegut, Robert T. Tally Jr.   3
Biography of Kurt Vonnegut, Charles J. Shields   18

Critical Context

Tralfamadore is America: Cultural History in *Slaughterhouse-Five,*
    Darryl Hattenhauer   27
The Curious Reception of Kurt Vonnegut, Donald E. Morse   42
Worlds of Wordcraft: The Metafiction of Kurt Vonnegut, Ralph Clare   60
Walker Percy: Kurt Vonnegut for Adults, Henry L. Carrigan, Jr.   78

Critical Readings

"Instructions for Use": The Opening Chapter of *Slaughterhouse-Five*
    and the Reader of Historiographical Metafictions, Peter Freese   95
Looking for Vonnegut: Confronting Genre and the Author/Narrator
    Divide, P. L. Thomas   118
Vonnegut and Religion: Daydreaming about God, Susan E. Farrell   141
Another "Atheist's Bible": Knowledge Defeats *Hocus Pocus,*
    Lara Narcisi   163
Anthropology across the Universe: Folk Societies in the Early
    Novels of Kurt Vonnegut, Shiela Ellen Pardee   185
The Myth of the Two Monsters in *Breakfast of Champions,*
    Gilbert McInnis   206
Time, Transformation, and the Reading Process in Vonnegut,
    Sharon Lynn Sieber   228
Can a Machine Be a Gentleman?: Machine Ethics and Ethical
    Machines, Ádám T. Bogár   248
Humane Harmony: Environmentalism and Culture in Vonnegut's
    Writings, Said Mentak   269

Resources

Chronology of Kurt Vonnegut's Life 293

Works by Kurt Vonnegut 299

Bibliography 301

About the Editor 305

Contributors 307

Index 311

About This Volume_____

Robert T. Tally Jr.

During the earlier part of his career, Kurt Vonnegut struggled to find an audience and was virtually unknown to most literary critics and academic scholars. By the late 1960s, and especially with the overwhelming popularity of *Slaughterhouse-Five*, Vonnegut began to be taken seriously. Soon, a large body of secondary material on the novelist emerged. Since his death in 2007, even more scholarly articles and books have appeared. This *Critical Insights* volume itself represents the cutting edge of research on Vonnegut's life and writings. The contributors include leading figures in Vonnegut studies, as well as emerging scholars in contemporary American literature. The result is an important resource for students, scholars, and critics.

The volume begins with my own overview of Vonnegut's career in "On Kurt Vonnegut," where I discuss his development as a writer: his early work as an author of magazine fiction and of what seemed to be science fiction, through his most famous novels of the 1960s and his popularity in the 1970s and 1980s when he became something of a cultural icon, and to his late-in-life role as a curmudgeonly voice of humor and social critique. I also discuss the context of post-war American literature and culture as a way of illustrating both Vonnegut's own influences and his role in shaping the culture around him. Then, biographer Charles J. Shields provides a brief essay on Vonnegut's eventful life. Shields is the author of *And So It Goes: Kurt Vonnegut, A Life*, the first scholarly Vonnegut biography. In researching and writing his book, Shields interviewed dozens of Vonnegut's friends and associates, and he consulted thousands of letters and other unpublished writings. As such, Shields's biography goes well beyond the seemingly autobiographical content of Vonnegut's novels and nonfiction. The resulting information provides a more fully fleshed-out, more wholly human figure—one that inevitably takes the bad with the good—but is also the most realistic and fascinating portrait of the author.

Four essays make up the "Critical Contexts" section of this volume. First, in "Tralfamadore is America: Cultural History in *Slaughterhouse-Five*," Darryl L. Hattenhauer places Vonnegut's most famous novel in its historical and cultural contexts. Early studies of *Slaughterhouse-Five* read it as Vonnegut's testament of acceptance, but Vonnegut holds that there is meaning and purpose to the critique of contemporary American society. Vonnegut finds that militarism, consumerism, and the unequal distribution of income are absurd. Hattenhauer argues that Tralfamadore is not a blissful utopia but a futuristic dystopia that parodies the dominant American culture of the 1960s.

Donald E. Morse, one of the world's leading scholars and critics of Vonnegut's work, then examines the critical reception of the author and his oeuvre. Moving from Vonnegut's relative obscurity in the 1950s and early 1960s to the celebrity of the immediate post–*Slaughterhouse-Five* years and on to the more nuanced and complex criticism of recent decades, Morse shows a mastery of the relevant Vonnegut criticism while providing a helpful survey of secondary literature.

In "Worlds of Wordcraft: The Metafiction of Kurt Vonnegut," Ralph Clare opens a critical lens for viewing Vonnegut's work by looking especially at his most famous technique, metafiction. Drawing on recent criticism and theory, Clare first establishes a working definition of metafiction along with a basic contextualization of the rise of American literary metafiction in the 1960s and 1970s, its cultural expansion, and its lasting influence as evidenced in today's television and popular culture. Clare explores how Vonnegut's metafiction can be understood in three different, yet overlapping, ways: in the creation of a self-aware fictional universe populated by recurring characters who sometimes suspect they are fictional creations; by the fact that so much of "reality" in Vonnegut's stories turns out to be "a lie," or a kind of script that people have been living by, which underscores the textual nature of reality as well as the way in which narratives bring order, structure, and meaning to the chaos of experience, for good and ill; and through the suggestion that even history itself is textual and that its competing narratives are constructed often with the help of fictional devices.

Next, in "Walker Percy: Kurt Vonnegut for Adults," Henry L. Carrigan, Jr. presents a comparison and contrast between the two contemporary writers. Carrigan demonstrates the ways in which both Percy and Vonnegut addressed the same cultural and social issues, often in similar ways but leading to sometimes rather different conclusions. Starting with a critic's remark that Walker Percy was "the adult's Kurt Vonnegut," Carrigan shows how the two writers resemble one another, each using satire to reveal the gaping holes between reality and illusion in the worlds of their characters and, by extension, of course our own world. Percy and Vonnegut each explore themes of alienation, loss, and despair through characters attempting to make some sense of life in a world gone somehow awry and to restore some dignity, wholeness, and hope to this world. Yet, despite both writers' pessimism about the human condition, each sees glimmers of hope for the future of humankind shining through the tatters of this world. This essay explores these differences and similarities by comparing and contrasting the ways that the works of each writer approach madness, alienation, despair, loss, love, hope, and redemption.

The nine essays included in the "Critical Readings" section explore a range of scholarly approaches to a variety of works by Vonnegut. For example, Peter Freese, the imminent German literary scholar and author of the monumental study *The Clown of Armageddon: The Novels of Kurt Vonnegut*, leads off this section with "Instructions for Use: The Opening Chapter of *Slaughterhouse-Five* and the Reader of Historiographical Metafiction." Freese argues that the widely neglected opening chapter of *Slaughterhouse-Five* is not the rambling mélange of odd bits and pieces often dismissed by critics, but is a masterly collage of literary quotations and autobiographical fragments that establishes the novel's tone, has subtle thematic relevance, and creates an adequate reader response. The four constitutive narrative strategies Vonnegut employs in this chapter are: the technique of the ingenious collage that establishes surprising connections, the postmodern play with competing realities that illustrate the subjectivity of all perception, the illusion-breaking interplay of fact and fiction that renders uncertain tradition representation, and the creation of cross-referenced repetitions in ever-changing configurations that reveal the imprisonment of humans in prevailing linguistic discourses. Freese's close reading of this chapter shows that it provides a kind of metafictional poetics that serve as a key to most of Vonnegut's novels.

Next, P. L. Thomas examines the "author/narrator" divide that typifies so many of Vonnegut's novels. This essay discusses the work of Vonnegut as a confrontation between assumptions about genre as well as about the roles of authorial and narrative voices in determining genre. In Thomas's reading, Vonnegut challenges students to reconsider their assumptions about genre, both as readers and as writers, and to imagine how the author's or narrator's voice contributes to those assumptions.

In "Vonnegut and Religion: Daydreaming about God," Susan Farrell examines Vonnegut's uneasiness with conventional Christianity, especially in its fundamentalist forms, and shows how his work frequently rewrites Gospel stories and biblical parables. While Vonnegut declares himself a religious freethinker—"I am of course a skeptic about the divinity of Christ and a scorner of the notion that there is a God who cares how we are or what we do"—Farrell points out that Vonnegut's relationship to Christianity and to organized religion in general is complex and nuanced. Calling himself a "Christ-worshipping agnostic," Vonnegut heartily admires the Sermon on the Mount and Christ's alliance with the poor, the meek, the hungry, and the peacemakers of the world. Farrell looks at the ways that Vonnegut depicts attempts to establish new religions or to create new moral and religious structures that give life meaning. In Vonnegut's novels, religious belief can shape our lives for the better, even if these beliefs finally prove futile or illusory.

Following up on this notion, Lara Narcisi examines Vonnegut's 1990 novel, *Hocus Pocus*, in which the narrator, Eugene Debs Hartke, refers humorously to *Bartlett's Quotations* as "the Atheist Bible." Narcisi argues that this novel itself, and by extension the entire body of Vonnegut's writings, might be said to form a sort of atheist Bible in offering us reasons to act sincerely and ethically in a world of futility and chaos. Hartke finds little hope in "dumb as heck" humans, but he himself has made an important transition from a soldier who follows orders to a "freethinker" like his namesake Eugene Debs. More importantly, he takes responsibility for his actions and believes that in "being a teacher . . . all I ever wanted to overthrow was ignorance" (88). *Hocus Pocus* inveighs against arrogance and dishonesty as well as racism, environmental devastation, and systems perpetuating poverty. Using *Hocus Pocus* as a touchstone, Narcisi demonstrates the value of a kind of atheist's Bible in Vonnegut's writings.

Although he never formally completed his degree there, a young Vonnegut studied anthropology at the University of Chicago in the 1940s. In "Anthropology across the Universe: Folk Societies in the Novels of Kurt Vonnegut," Shiela Pardee examines the influence of anthropology on Vonnegut's novels. Vonnegut was particularly interested in "folk societies," small interdependent communities that appear and reappear in Vonnegut's novels. Indeed, in recognition of its "halfway decent anthropology," *Cat's Cradle* was later accepted in lieu of an MA thesis when Vonnegut was awarded his degree. In this essay, Pardee shows how Vonnegut continued to look at human society with the eyes of an anthropologist throughout his career. Pardee reveals how conflicts within the discipline of anthropology itself—e.g., between emphasis on cultural uniqueness versus a view of universally shared cultural characteristics—are worked out in Vonnegut's novels partly by employing a science-fictional mode.

Drawing upon a difference branch of the natural sciences in "The Myth of the Two Monsters in *Breakfast of Champions*," Gilbert McInnis argues that Vonnegut's novels often illustrate the devastating consequences of a materialistic worldview on the human condition. In *Breakfast of Champions*, the character Kilgore Trout claims, "There

were two monsters sharing the planet with us when I was a boy, however, and I celebrate their extinction today. They were determined to
kill us, or at least to make our lives meaningless. . . . They were the arbitrary lusts for gold, and God help us, for a glimpse of a little girl's underpants" (25). In this essay, McInnis examines how the human mind
is transformed by this kind of materialism and explores how Vonnegut
parodies a fact-finding science (by way of measurements) in its pursuit
of happiness.

In "Time, Transformation, and the Reading Process in Vonnegut,"
Sharon Lynn Sieber addresses the reading experience itself in relation
theory of time in, especially, *Breakfast of Champions* and *Sirens of
Titan*. Time in these novels becomes the site of transformation, as the
reader enters a black hole of the text and comes out on the other side.
Sieber argues that Vonnegut accomplishes this by taking an ordinary
event, and turning it into an event of such significance and meaning
that the reader can no longer look at the commonplaces of his or her
own life in the same way again. Vonnegut inverts meaning and distances the reader from the cultural comfort zone, forcing the reader to
confront the alienation arising from the experience of time, a transformational process of shifting meanings, which can only be the reading
process itself. Time becomes a mode of transformation, and the experience of reading Vonnegut's transformational work ultimately transforms the reader as well.

Drawing upon the science-fictional elements of Vonnegut's work,
Ádám T. Bogár asks whether a machine can be a gentleman as a way to
approach the human-versus-machine dichotomy, which is explored in a
number of Vonnegut's writings. For instance, the eponymous "hero" of
the 1950 short story "EPICAC," one of Vonnegut's first publications,
is a fictional heavy-duty supercomputer whose "personality" calls the
classical hierarchy of human over machine into question. While machines with superhuman physical capabilities are pervasive in science-
fiction stories, computers morally superseding human are less easy
to find. In this essay, Bogár reviews the human/machine relationship

apparent in the short story, in *Player Piano* (which includes a computer named EPICAC XIV), and in other works. Drawing upon the ideas of British mathematician-cryptographer Alan Turing, Bogár considers how Turing's concerns about machine intelligence are embodied in Vonnegut's work, and discusses a possible world where these concerns have become reality.

Finally, Said Mentak examines the "humane Harmony" Vonnegut attempts to achieve between the natural environment and human culture in his novels. At the beginning of *Breakfast of Champions*, Vonnegut asserts that he is trying to make his head as empty as it was when he was born "onto this damaged planet fifty years ago." In the absence of harmony between what society has put into his head and the outside world, Vonnegut makes his famous confession: "I have no culture, no humane harmony in my brains. I can't live without a culture anymore." The "damaged planet," with its explicit ecological concerns, and the ideas put into his head, or the cultural malformation of the individual, will undoubtedly lead humanity to extinction, in Vonnegut's view. It is not surprising that Vonnegut's work is constantly tolling the bells of impending danger. Vonnegut may appear at times callously indifferent, but beneath the surface of his statements lies intense anxiety for humans, who have not yet managed to develop a permanent cure for their folly in spite of their "big brains." It follows then that humane harmony, a distant dream as it may seem to be, can be reached only if humans properly understand the mutual importance of both the cultural and natural. Proposing an ecocritical or "green" cultural studies as a means of approaching Vonnegut's work, Mentak shows how Vonnegut reconciles the perceived, but false, dichotomy of culture and nature.

The final section of this volume, "Resources," contains valuable information and materials to help with further study. First, a chronology of Vonnegut's life places his biography and works in their historical context. Second, a list of Vonnegut's books, including recently published posthumous work, offers the most complete list to date of the author's diverse writings. And, third, an extensive bibliography, featuring many critical resources for Vonnegut scholars, provides ample material for further reading and study.

This volume is dedicated to my mother, formerly a teacher, long an editor, and always a reader.

CAREER, LIFE, AND INFLUENCE

On Kurt Vonnegut

Robert T. Tally Jr.

Kurt Vonnegut is one of the most beloved American writers of the post–World War II era, but the trajectory of his life and career was anything but smooth. Although he found an audience for his early novels and magazine fiction and was able to eke out a living as a freelance writer for nearly two decades, it was not until his sixth novel, *Slaughterhouse-Five*, that Vonnegut became a household name. After its publication in 1969 at the height of the Vietnam War and the anti-war protests, Vonnegut never wanted for readers, and all of his subsequent books, as well as the earlier ones that immediately came back in print, sold quite well. Inevitably, perhaps, the story of Vonnegut's career appears as a steep climb to the top from his first short stories in 1950 to the publication of his best-known novel, then followed by a gradual descent towards mediocrity, as none of his post–*Slaughterhouse-Five* novels received the same sort of critical or popular acclaim. However, it is more appropriate to see Vonnegut's career as a series of "ups and downs, ups and downs," to quote a repeated phrase in *Slaughterhouse-Five*, which can perhaps be viewed as the normal, everyday conditions of life in the twentieth century.

A key to Vonnegut's tremendous popularity is just how very ordinary he really is. His works present stories of rather ordinary people going about their ordinary lives and facing often ordinary problems. The narrator, who frequently seems to be Kurt Vonnegut himself, always appears simple and direct, a familiar and reassuring presence that makes the reading deceptively easy and enjoyable. Part of the pleasure so many readers find in Vonnegut's novels derives from his compelling stories about normal, mostly middle-class people (engineers, journalists, insurance salesmen, optometrists, or pharmacists), who are sometimes faced with extraordinary circumstances (like the end of the world). The stories are almost always told by an avuncular, slightly curmudgeonly, but altogether human narrative voice. This voice is generally confused with Vonnegut's own personal voice, a confusion that Vonnegut himself actively promotes, sometimes deliberately, as he inserts himself—or, perhaps, a fictional character named "Kurt Vonnegut"—into his books. Famously, *Slaughterhouse-Five* not only includes an autobiographical and intimately personal introductory chapter written in Vonnegut's own voice, but it also features the author's interpolation at key moments in the story. For instance, when the fictional protagonist Billy Pilgrim overhears another soldier complaining, Vonnegut writes, "That was me. That was I. That was the author of his book" (125). *Breakfast of Champions* (1973) takes this strategy a step further when the author–character "Kurt Vonnegut" becomes an active participant in the events of the fictional narrative that he's creating, and this "Kurt Vonnegut" even introduces himself to characters he has created.

In fact, starting with *Slaughterhouse-Five*, all of Vonnegut's later novels are narrated either by a first-person Kurt Vonnegut or by a first-person narrator who could be viewed as a sort of alter ego for Vonnegut: Vonnegut himself (*Breakfast of Champions*), Wilbur Swain (*Slapstick*, 1976), Walter Starbuck (*Jailbird*, 1979), Rudy Waltz (*Deadeye Dick*, 1982), Leon Trout (*Galápagos*, 1985), Rabo Karabekian (*Bluebeard*), and Eugene Debs Hartke (*Hocus Pocus*, 1990). Moreover, all of these books, beginning with the 1966 reissue of *Mother Night* (1961), include some preface or introduction written in Vonnegut's own voice, regardless of who the narrator of the remainder of the book will be. Hence, readers feel a special bond with Vonnegut that they might not with another author since Vonnegut's books have the feel of a personal conversation. In addition to blending autobiography or nonfiction with his fictional narratives, Vonnegut also published several popular works of nonfiction, reprinting essays, speeches, or interviews often in what he called an "autobiographical collage." The reader of Vonnegut's complete works, then, will have a fairly strong idea, not just of Vonnegut's work, but of Vonnegut the person.

Or maybe not. The apparent intimacy or transparency suggested by his particular style and narrative voice is a ruse. Vonnegut is, after all, a practical joker, a funny writer who also delights in "putting one over" on others. In this, he is quite similar to his literary hero, Mark Twain. Careful readers may have already noticed that certain "nonfiction" elements of Vonnegut's stories were likely to have stretched the truth, which is certainly within the rights of an author who purports to write novels and short stories. With the publication of Charles J. Shields's authoritative biography, *And So It Goes: Kurt Vonnegut, A Life*, readers can now see that a great deal of Vonnegut's autobiographical material is as much shaped, constructed, and sometimes invented, as his more straightforwardly fictional work.

Of course, we cannot say we weren't warned. In his "Editor's Note" to his 1961 novel, *Mother Night*, Vonnegut cautions that the reader ought to be skeptical about a narrative written by a writer, especially a playwright. (*Mother Night* is presented as the memoirs of Howard W. Campbell Jr.; hence "Kurt Vonnegut" plays the role of a mere editor.):

> To say that he was a writer is to say that the demands of art alone were enough to make him lie, and to lie without seeing any harm in it. To say that he was a playwright is to offer an even harsher warning to the reader, for no one is a better liar than a man who has warped lives and passions onto something as grotesquely artificial as a stage. (x)

Vonnegut could also be warning about himself: he was a playwright (*Happy Birthday, Wanda June*, 1971) and his best-known writings incorporate a great deal of his own life's story, or, perhaps, his artfully crafted version of that story. If one were to take Vonnegut's fiction as a kind of autobiography, as Gregory Sumner does in *Unstuck in Time: A Journey through Kurt Vonnegut's Life and Novels*, then one could find the imaginary "Kurt Vonnegut" that fans (and, perhaps, Vonnegut himself) wanted to be real. But much like the fictional Campbell, Vonnegut's scattered autobiographical memories and reflections should be taken with a few grains of salt, and a more complete picture requires a scholarly biography like Shields's to flesh out the real person who achieved such a cult status in his own lifetime.

Yet it is Vonnegut's work, especially his novels, and not his life that provides the most interesting pictures of American civilization in the postwar, and postmodern, period. As I have argued in *Kurt Vonnegut and the American Novel: A Postmodern Iconography*, Vonnegut is a somewhat untimely figure. He is a writer consumed by nostalgia, not so much for the America of his own youth (although that sometimes appears in his work as well), but primarily for a time just before he was born, a *fin-de-siècle* age of the Progressive movement. Tellingly, his heroes include Eugene Debs, the socialist leader and perennial presidential candidate of this era. More disturbingly, perhaps, Vonnegut's embrace of this period of American history is obliquely connected to what he takes to be a simpler, more genial form of racism. For example, in *Jailbird*, the narrator celebrates the labor unions of the early twentieth century, while acknowledging that a "black or Hispanic" would not have been allowed to join the union in "the good old days" (203). And in *Slapstick*, the narrator depicts slaves, singing and smiling like caricatures from anti-abolitionist propaganda of the 1840s, as the happiest people on earth (204). In novel after novel, it seems, Vonnegut—whether through his narrative voice or in the voice of certain key characters—expresses a longing for a simpler modernity of extended communities and artificial families. (Interestingly, real or biological families are rarely desirable in Vonnegut's fiction.) In Vonnegut's bittersweet image of the American century, the best of times are inevitably just before our own times.

Vonnegut's nostalgia is not limited to the content of the historical epoch he longs to have been part of. In his style and narrative form, Vonnegut also strives for a modernism that seems to have been lost in the postmodern condition. Because of his use of metafiction, collage, genre-blending, and parody, Vonnegut has frequently been considered a "postmodernist" writer, as in Todd Davis's *Kurt Vonnegut's Crusade: Or, How a Postmodern Harlequin Preached a New Kind of Humanism*.

However, unlike other writers cast into the category, Vonnegut mourns the loss of some imagined organic whole, and he views the tasks of literature and of art more generally as fundamentally diagnostic and therapeutic. That is, rather than celebrating the fragmentary, vicissitudinous, unstable, and bewildering aspects of life in the postmodern condition, Vonnegut's fiction seeks to shore these fragments against his ruins, to borrow a phrase from T. S. Eliot's *The Waste Land*. Vonnegut sees the mission of art as the attempt to recover a lost wholeness or purity in our debased or fallen postmodern world. It is not surprising, for instance, that nearly all of Vonnegut's novels make direct reference to the Genesis myth and include characters longing to return to some lost Eden, as Leonard Mustazza has discussed in his excellent study, *Forever Pursuing Genesis: The Myth of Eden in the Novels of Kurt Vonnegut*. Even in his most experimental fictions, such as *Breakfast of Champions*, Vonnegut endeavors to show how the storyteller can overcome the most abstract forms of expression and alienation by paradoxically "bringing chaos to order" and thereby better representing the "real world" (215). Vonnegut's modernist techniques are thus used to represent the postmodern condition more realistically.

A brief survey of Vonnegut's career as a novelist can illustrate these themes and techniques. He published his first short stories in 1950, at which point he quit his job at General Electric, moved to Cape Cod, Massachusetts, and established himself as a full-time writer of fiction. In his early novels, starting with the dystopian *Player Piano* (1952), Vonnegut displayed his paradoxical blend of brutal cynicism and almost syrupy sentimentality, which so frequently appear in what I have called the "misanthropic humanism" of Vonnegut's worldview (*American Novel* 18–36). *Player Piano* is often lumped in with books like Aldous Huxley's *Brave New World* or George Orwell's *1984* as twentieth-century dystopian novels, but it shares at least as much with the 1950s-era suburban tale of quiet desperation, like *The Man in the Gray Flannel Suit*, inasmuch as it depicts a successful but discontented businessman in search of a more meaningful life. In this world, set in an imagined near-present, virtually all human needs are taken care of by a hybrid corporate-government, thanks in general to technology and especially to the supercomputer EPICAC XIV (named, perhaps, partly in homage to Vonnegut's love-poem-writing computer in his short story, "EPICAC"). No one is really poor or hungry, but because machines have replaced nearly all forms of meaningful labor, most people lack purpose. In the book's climactic moment, a revolution by man against machines appears to win a brief victory, but almost immediately the victorious rebels gleefully begin fixing the very machines they had smashed. The irony is summed up in the moment when the protagonist (Paul Proteus) recognizes a previously unemployed man engaged in repairing a soft-drink machine:

> The man had been desperately unhappy then. Now he was proud and smiling because his hands were busy doing what they liked to do best, Paul supposed—replacing men like himself with machines. (318)

The Sirens of Titan—published seven years later, during which time Vonnegut produced short stories and engaged in several unsuccessful business ventures—maintains the trappings of space-race-era science fiction, including time and space travel via a chrono-synclastic infundibulum, aliens and robots, interplanetary warfare, and "gimcrack religions." Yet, for all that, *Sirens* is among Vonnegut's most human offerings, and in recent years it has gained adherents who find its redemptive tale of Malachi Constant, the luckiest (then the unluckiest) man in the world, a fitting precursor to that of the unassuming optometrist Billy Pilgrim. Constant's odyssey from Earth to Mars, Mercury, and Titan, intermittently punctuated with Vonnegut's wry observations about life in "the Nightmare Ages, falling roughly, give or take a few years, between the Second World War and the Third Great Depression" (8), leads to a final, meaningful act, but one that seems ludicrously insignificant. Worse still, it is revealed that the entirety of human history has merely been in the service of this minor chore. However, the process reveals a conviction that Vonnegut clings to even in his later writings, that "a purpose of a human life . . . is to love whoever is around to be loved" (313).

Mother Night (first published in 1961 and rereleased with Vonnegut's Introduction in 1966), is rather different. Presented as the memoirs of a war criminal, an American Nazi on trial in Jerusalem, *Mother Night* contains no science fictional elements whatsoever. In its initial publication, the apparatus (including an "editor's note" signed by "Kurt Vonnegut, Jr.") made it appear that Howard W. Campbell, Jr. is the author of the memoirs. Campbell is, we are told, a double-agent who appeared to be an ardent Nazi propagandist but who was all along working secretly for the United States. After the war, living in New York while hiding from the Israeli Nazi hunters, he meets various characters who are also not what they seem, including his beloved wife who, he had thought, died during the war. The love between them, characterized by Campbell as a *Reich der Zwei* (or "Nation of Two"), presents that version of Eden that Vonnegut manages to smuggle into nearly all of his novels. Here Campbell, who like Eliot Rosewater will also appear in *Slaughterhouse-Five* in one memorable scene, eventually turns himself in and awaits trial in prison, where he hopes that the truth will come to light. However, as compelling as Campbell's tale of intrigue, betrayal, and patriotic duty is, Vonnegut's 1966 Introduction warns that the "moral" of *Mother Night* is "we are who we pretend to be, so we must be careful about what we pretend to be" (v). Hence, the oscillatory movement between fact and fiction, author and narrative voice, reality and fantasy in Vonnegut's novels finds its paradigmatic moment in this early novel.

In Cat's Cradle (1963), Vonnegut's satire and humor are at their sharpest, while the pathos that infuses his entire oeuvre provides its steady undercurrent. Vonnegut once claimed that he attempted to write this novel in such a way that each chapter is a joke with its own punchline, although it is clear that some jokes are funnier than others. The novel is most famous for its invention of Bokononism, a religion based on the concept of *foma*, or "harmless untruths," with its inventive vocabulary and its curious blend of nihilism and hopefulness. The story of ice-nine, a wampeter (to use Bokonon's term) that could figuratively stand in for nuclear weapons, unfolds as an absurd adventure through then present-day American civilization. The apocalypse, which also becomes a motif in Vonnegut's other works, is both horrific and somehow welcome, with a sort of "good riddance" added to the general terror. And, as usual in Vonnegut, the utter destruction of the world, itself clearly the fault of those flawed humans and their stupid ideas, yields an element of hope. Amid the mindless destruction and omnipresence of death and disease, Vonnegut provides a utopia of the small-scale community of survivors.

Vonnegut was belatedly awarded his master's degree in anthropology from the University of Chicago (which had rejected his thesis years earlier) for *Cat's Cradle* on the grounds that his invention and exploration of Bokononist beliefs demonstrated a knowledge of primitive societies and folk religion. Ironically, his original thesis was turned down for lack of academic rigor. But Vonnegut is at his best when telling the stories of everyday people in their everyday social conditions, as his next novel, *God Bless You, Mr. Rosewater* (1965) demonstrated. It is the story of "a sum of money," and it follows the fortunes of wealthy philanthropist Eliot Rosewater (who will also make memorable cameo appearances in *Slaughterhouse-Five* and *Breakfast of Champions*). Rosewater has caught a strange mental disease, the fetishization of Utopia. Indeed, utopianism is the real theme of *God Bless You, Mr. Rosewater*, as each character seeks his own version of an ideal state—whether that means wealth, status, love, or a sense of belonging. This novel also marks the first appearance of Vonnegut's greatest character, Kilgore Trout, who will reappear in a number of Vonnegut's works, with starring roles in *Breakfast of Champions* and *Timequake* (1997). A Trout-authored story cited in Rosewater asks the fundamental question of all of Vonnegut's fiction: "What in hell are people for?"

In *Slaughterhouse-Five*, Vonnegut offers no more celestial certainty as to the meaning of life or the purpose of human existence, but in working through Billy Pilgrim's traumas, as well as his own, Vonnegut comes to a peaceful understanding of the human condition. His misanthropic humanism is still very much present here, but it is leavened with a form of acceptance encapsulated in the "serenity prayer," which offers the only solace needed. The Tralfamadorian temporality, in which all moments coexist in an endless present tense, allows for fate or destiny to take away the burdens of free will. If something terrible happens, that's just because the moment was structured that way, and other moments are structured differently. Yet, for all of Billy Pilgrim's passive acceptance of fate, the popularity of *Slaughterhouse-Five* in the moment of its publication had far more to do with the active critique of the Vietnam War-era and the socioeconomic circumstances of the United States. The novel, for better or worse, made Vonnegut as spokesperson of the counterculture.

Vonnegut was not well-suited for such a role, and the pressure to meet expectations with a follow-up to *Slaughterhouse-Five* was tremendous. *Breakfast of Champions* bears the marks of this pressure. In an interview, Vonnegut noted that *Breakfast* was initially part of *Slaughterhouse-Five*, so it is formed from the detritus of the earlier novel, along with what Vonnegut refers to as the results of cleaning out his mind's attic. Yet the theme of the novel, which I take to be the inability of people to communicate effectively, is profound. The title itself is a fairly meaningless phrase bandied about in varying circumstances in the novel. Written as the writer approached his fiftieth birthday, *Breakfast of Champions* marks a turning point in Vonnegut's career.

Vonnegut's next two novels, *Slapstick* and *Jailbird* , are his most overtly political. The first is narrated by the "last" president of the United States, and it combines the tale of an eccentric family with the decline and fall of American civilization. *Slapstick* is most notable for Vonnegut's utopian vision of a government-sponsored program to create artificial families, such that every American is guaranteed a large number of siblings and cousins, making them "Lonesome No More!" (which is also the novel's subtitle). Notably, what *Cat's Cradle* had referred to as "harmless granfalloonery" here becomes the practical solution to modern anxieties. In *Jailbird*, the narrator is a minor figure in the Watergate scandal, now trying to make sense of his life and the world in the late 1970s. The novel also features a utopian scheme where a single, enormous corporation (secretly owned by a socialist) attempts to acquire nearly all of the businesses in the country, only to leave them to the American people as an ultimate form of "ownership of the means of production" by the workers. As with the idea of artificial families, the results are not ideal.

Vonnegut's next novel, *Deadeye Dick* (1982), is at once rather fanciful—with neutron bombs, ghosts, and a depiction of a young Adolf Hitler as a starving Vienna artist—and somewhat autobiographical with clear indications of Vonnegut's relationship with his own father. A tragic mistake alters the life of the narrator and his family, who then deal with the consequences for the remainder of the story. *Galápagos* (1985), possibly the best of Vonnegut's "later" novels, presents what I have called an "apocalypse in the optative mood," where humanity is saved by being nearly wiped out, and the small community of survivors evolves over a million years into happy, healthy, seal-like creatures. This novel is narrated by the ghost of Leon Trout, Kilgore's son, who can look back from the year 1,001,986 AD to see how the bewildering events of 1986 turned out to be blessings from a strictly Darwinian perspective.

Bluebeard (1987) purports to be the autobiography of Rabo Karabekian, an abstract expressionist artist who was a minor, but memorable, character in *Breakfast of Champions*. The novel contains many of Vonnegut's reflections on modernist art, and it chronicles the tumultuous twentieth century as seen through the eyes of a veteran. *Bluebeard* also includes Vonnegut's most positive and nuanced female character, Circe Berman (thought to be based on his own second wife), who challenges Karabekian's pessimism and helps him to rediscover joy in his own life. In *Hocus Pocus* (1990), Vonnegut returns to a somewhat dystopian United States of the near future. Narrated by a Vietnam War veteran who became a college president then a prison warden (when the college became a prison), *Hocus Pocus* dwells on personal responsibility in a country that has lost its way.

Finally, *Timequake* (1997) comes full circle from the place Vonnegut had established in *Slaughterhouse-Five* by once more blending autobiography with fiction. In this "failed" novel, Vonnegut tries to tell the story of Kilgore Trout who must help his fellow New Yorkers recover from the effects of a "timequake," which caused everyone to relive each moment of the last ten years, effectively suspending everyone's free will, only to have it start up again unexpectedly. In the second narrative, which Vonnegut calls "Timequake Two" and that intertwines with the first narrative throughout the book, Vonnegut merely gives his own personal opinions or reflections on life in the late twentieth century. Hence, *Timequake* is as much nonfiction as it is a novel, and it shares much in common with such other late nonfiction works as *Fates Worse Than Death* (1991), *God Bless You, Dr. Kevorkian* (1999), and *A Man Without a Country* (2005).

At the time of his death in 2007, all of Vonnegut's works were still in print, and he was as popular as ever. Although none of his post–1969 novels received as much acclaim as *Slaughterhouse-Five*, all of his novels sold well. Several posthumous books (mostly containing very early, unpublished stories, notes, and drafts) have appeared since 2008, and there has been an explosion of scholarly research and criticism devoted to Vonnegut's writings. The venerable Library of America has published two volumes of Vonnegut's work, effectively "canonizing" the author.

Perhaps owing to the difficulties experienced during the first twenty years as a writer, Vonnegut always felt underappreciated, notwithstanding his strong sales and ardent following in the latter half of his career. Shields notes that Vonnegut was really bothered that his dictionary contained no "Vonnegut, Kurt" entry, while Kerouac and others were in there. Vonnegut has inspired, and continues to inspire, generations of readers with his wry humor and bittersweet musings, but even at the pinnacle of his professional success, he felt that he was not getting his due. Vonnegut frequently discounted his manifest success and overreacted to even innocent slights. Mark Vonnegut, in the introduction to *Look at the Birdie* (2008), a collection of previously unpublished short stories, noted just how thin-skinned his father was—"Kurt could pitch better than he could catch"—and Mark explained that the elder Vonnegut often resented even mere jokes that might reflect poorly on him. But Vonnegut's defensiveness may have been a ruse. His deceptively simple syntax and diction, as well as his friendly and engaging narrative voice in both his fiction and nonfiction, make him all too affable in print. If "the demands of art alone were enough to make him lie, and to lie without seeing any harm in it" (*Mother Night* v), then perhaps the warning in *Mother Night* "can only be viewed as a caveat to his own readers, many of whom would embrace this artful artificer as the ultimate truth-teller. An extremely funny joke, when you think about it" (see Tally, "Kurt Vonnegut's Last Laugh").

From at least 1969 on, while Vonnegut never lacked for fans, he was not always taken seriously by scholars. That has clearly changed in recent years as seen in the establishment of the Kurt Vonnegut Society and the opening of the Kurt Vonnegut Memorial Library, not to mention the many new studies of Vonnegut's work in recent years, including this volume. In concluding this essay, it is worth mentioning the importance of Shields's biography, *And So It Goes*, in presenting Vonnegut's life without necessarily taking the fictional works as straightforward, autobiographical accounts. *And So It Goes* is a signal event in the history and the future of Vonnegut Studies. The biography demonstrates that Vonnegut is worthy of serious scholarly attention, rather than the largely uncritical adulation of mere fans. The time for scholars to say "Here's why Vonnegut is worth reading" has definitively ended, thank goodness. We know he's worth reading. Now tell us things we don't know.

Shields's biography, along with many recent studies, does just this. For one who had already read all of Vonnegut's published writings, Shields's version of Vonnegut's life dramatically enhanced the view of the humanity in the novelist's own work. And if this biography and other critical works were content to be occasions for a Vonnegut love-fest, a hagiographical appreciation for the "Great Man," they would have little to no scholarly or critical value whatsoever. Most serious critics could dismiss both the biography and its subject as being only good for hardcore fans, maybe, but useless to literary history and criticism. So I say, "God Bless You, Mr. Shields" for not writing that sort of book and, instead, for presenting a fully fleshed-out life of the author. Similarly, the critical work presented in this volume goes well beyond mere praise for Vonnegut, discovering in his work meaningful material for making sense of the world today.

And So It Goes does not really have much to say about Vonnegut's novels, short stories, or other writings. Shields mentions them, often just in passing, while focusing on letters and interviews. This produces an image of the man and his life, rather than of the writer and his work. I think that this is a great strength of the biography, since Shields never confuses the job of the literary critic with the main task of the biographer who must "write the life" of his subject. Shields's biography has all the scholarly rigor one could hope for, and nearly all of his 1,898 footnotes make reference to materials not widely available in print, if at all. Fans and scholars have read all they could by Vonnegut, but Shields—thanks in large part to information Vonnegut himself personally supplied—went out and discovered a wealth of new material. The more well-rounded man who emerges in *And So It Goes* is a writer worth researching. We are in the midst of a golden age of Vonnegut Studies with dozens of new scholarly and critical works published in just the last few years. Shields's biography stands as a powerful point of departure for future study, and it is itself a monument to the importance of studying, not just reading and enjoying, but actually studying, Kurt Vonnegut today.

Thus, the negative reaction of some Vonnegut scholars to Shields's biography is an absolute absurdity, one well-suited to Vonnegut's brand of humor. In the end, maybe the greatest gift Vonnegut gave to American literature was his uncanny ability to point absurdity of everyday life, noting how so many people needlessly made themselves unhappy through their own inane actions and desires. Whereas Hannah Arendt had marveled at "the banality of evil," Vonnegut duly recorded the banality of, well, everything. His novels poked fun at science and technology, commerce and warfare, patriotism and progress, sickness and health. Vonnegut had an especially sharp wit when it came to the American Dream, that much-admired and pursued hope that so often leads to disappointment and despair. As Vonnegut pointed out, behind this dream lies the haunting barb, "If you're so smart, how come you ain't rich?" Those who have not managed to achieve the dream must consider themselves failures, and those who have had even a great deal of success worry that they haven't done or received enough. Vonnegut's insights struck a nerve, not just with his fans who were weary of the empty triumphalism of American culture, but with the author himself. He has inspired, and continues to inspire, generations of readers with his wry humor and bittersweet musings, but even at the pinnacle of his professional success, he felt unappreciated. Vonnegut's persona as a straight-talking, down-to-earth, everyman social critic—as opposed to the skilled fabricator of nuanced *foma*, as "lies" or "harmless untruths" are called in *Cat's Cradle*—continues to form the image most beloved by readers. Yet Vonnegut proves to be a serious writer even in his apparent clowning. For students of modern American literature and culture, Vonnegut's work provides stories and pictures that are funny, sad, touching, and infuriating, but are also highly entertaining.

Works Cited

Davis, Todd F. *Kurt Vonnegut's Crusade: Or, How a Postmodern Harlequin Preached a New Kind of Humanism*. Albany: SUNY P, 2006. Print.

McHale, Brian. *Postmodernist Fiction*. New York: Routledge, 1987. Print.

Mustazza, Leonard. *Forever Pursuing Genesis: The Myth of Eden in the Novels of Kurt Vonnegut*. Lewisburg, PA: Bucknell UP, 1990. Print.

Shields, Charles J. *And So It Goes. Kurt Vonnegut: A Life*. New York: Holt, 2011. Print.

Sumner, Gregory D. *Unstuck in Time: A Journey through Kurt Vonnegut's Life and Novels*. New York: Seven Stories, 2011. Print.

Tally, Robert T., Jr. *Kurt Vonnegut and the American Novel: A Postmodern Iconography*. London: Continuum, 2011. Print.

___. "Kurt Vonnegut's Last Laugh." *Bloomsbury Literary Studies*. Bloomsbury Publishing plc., 15 Mar. 2012). Web. 28 Nov. 2012.

Vonnegut, Kurt, Jr. *Bluebeard*. New York: Dell, 1987. Print.

___. *Breakfast of Champions*. New York: Delacorte, 1973. Print.

___. *Cat's Cradle*. New York: Dell, 1963. Print.

___. *Deadeye Dick*. New York: Dell, 1982. Print.

___. *Fates Worse Than Death*. New York: Berkley, 1991. Print.

___. Galápagos. New York: Dell, 1985. Print.

___. *God Bless You, Mr. Rosewater*. New York: Dell, 1965. Print.

___. *Hocus Pocus*. New York: Berkley, 1990. Print.

___. *Jailbird*. New York: Dell, 1979. Print.

___. *Look at the Birdie: Unpublished Short Fiction*. New York: Delacorte, 2009. Print.

___. *A Man Without a Country*. New York: Seven Stories, 2005. Print.

___. *Mother Night* [1961] New York: Dell, 1966. Print.

___. *Palm Sunday*. New York: Delacorte, 1981. Print.

___. *Player Piano*. New York: Dell, 1952. Print.

___. *The Sirens of Titan*. New York: Dell, 1959. Print.

___. *Slapstick*. New York: Dell, 1976. Print.

___. *Slaughterhouse-Five*. New York: Dell, 1969. Print.

___. *Timequake*. New York: Berkley, 1997. Print.

___. *Wampeters, Foma, and Granfalloons*. New York: Delacorte, 1974. Print.

___. *Welcome to the Monkey House*. New York: Dell, 1968. Print.

Biography of Kurt Vonnegut

Charles J. Shields

Kurt Vonnegut, Jr. (no middle name) was a World War II combat solider who later championed pacifism, a public relations writer for General Electric who satirized technology, a family man who left his family, a self-styled literary outsider who was a member of the American Academy of Arts and Letters, a critic of capitalism and corporations who invested in stock and real estate companies, a college dropout who taught at Harvard, and, in his own words, "a Christ-worshipping agnostic." His only true allegiance was to ideas, which he treated in over twenty fiction and nonfiction books written and published over a fifty-year career, all of which were still in print at the time of his death in 2007.

John Updike praised him as a rare "imaginer, as distinguished from a reporter or a self-dramatizer"; Jay McInerney described him as "a satirist with a heart, a moralist with a whoopee cushion, a cynic who wants to believe. His fiercest social criticism is usually disguised in parable." Doris Lessing said, "because he is comic and sad at once, because his painful seriousness is never solemn, Vonnegut is unique among us." Harold Bloom argued that Vonnegut's 1963 novel *Cat's Cradle* belongs in the Western canon of literature, and in 2005, *Time* magazine chose his 1969 autobiographical, antiwar novel *Slaughterhouse-Five* as one of the Best 100 Novels from 1923 to the present. He was one of few American writers to have won and sustained a great popular acceptance while boldly introducing new themes and forms on the literary cutting edge.

Vonnegut was strongly influenced by his free-thinking, Unitarian-rationalist upbringing in Indianapolis, Indiana. He was born in 1922 and was the youngest of three children born to German-Americans—an upper-middle class architect and his socialite wife when there were seventeen Vonneguts in the city telephone directory, many of them cultural and civic leaders.

His paternal great-grandfather, Clemens Vonnegut, fled the Republican revolution in Germany as a political undesirable in 1848 and opened a hardware store in Indianapolis, which became one of the largest in the Midwest. He later introduced progressive ideas in secondary vocational education that eventually became part of a standard public school curriculum in United States. Clemens's son, Bernard—Vonnegut's grandfather—was a distinguished, German-trained architect, as was his son, Kurt's father. Vonnegut's maternal great-grandfather, also a German immigrant, was a Civil War veteran, the founder of what became one of the largest breweries in the United States, and later held an ambassadorial post in Düsseldorf. His daughter, Vonnegut's mother, Edith Leiber, was an heiress.

Nevertheless, German-Americans were generally held at arm's-length by American nativists who observed the arrival of the European with contempt and hostility through World War I. The *North American Review* warned of the "atheists or radicals" coming by the boatload and deplored the "irreligious influence of thousands of German infidels." The *Cleveland Plain Dealer* referred regularly to German immigrants as "hair-lipped, infidel red Republicans." The *New York Tribune* regarded "skepticism and materialism" as one of the "bad effects of the German immigration."

Consequently, Vonnegut grew up conscious that his intellectual heritage, which he summarized under the heading "humanism," had imbued him with ideals that were considered sacrilegious and, by extension, un-American.

"I am a humanist," Vonnegut wrote, "which means, in part, that I have tried to behave decently without any expectation of rewards or punishments after I'm dead. . . . My great-grandfather Clemens Vonnegut wrote, for example, 'If what Jesus said was good, what can it matter whether he was God or not?' I myself have written, 'If it weren't for the message of mercy and pity in Jesus' Sermon on the Mount, I wouldn't want to be a human being. I would just as soon be a rattlesnake.'"

In Vonnegut's novels, ethical behavior and intellectual honesty trump nationalism, tradition, custom, and conventional thinking. Success as a human being depends on the extent to which a person acts on his or her moral responsibilities. In his 1965 novel, *God Bless You, Mr. Rosewater*, a wealthy man, Eliot Rosewater, shocks his family by turning small-town philanthropist and answering his phone, "This is the Rosewater Foundation. How may I help you?" Throughout his fiction, Vonnegut's characters wonder what they should be doing with their lives, usually coming to the conclusion that they should try to be happy, be true to themselves, and help others who are less fortunate. In other words, be good human beings.

Vonnegut's interest in writing began in high school when he was editor of the Shortridge High School *Daily Echo*, the only daily high school newspaper in the country. Finding that he had a gift for humor in print, he was surprised that what came easily to him was difficult for most people. He wanted to stay in Indianapolis and become a journalist, but his family insisted he attend college and major in the sciences. At Cornell University he neglected his studies in favor of writing for the campus newspaper, and by the middle of his sophomore year, he was on academic probation. It was 1943, the United States was in the middle of World War II, and Vonnegut dropped out to join the army.

Although he was enrolled in an Army program that would have led to a commission, the program was cancelled and Vonnegut was shipped to Europe as a private in the 106th Infantry Division in the fall of 1944, which was also a few months after his mother committed suicide. His regiment was surrounded at the Battle of the Bulge in December, 1944. He was captured, transported by train to a POW camp, and then selected to join involuntarily a noncombat labor crew sent to Dresden, Germany. While there, the city was devastated by a massive Allied air attack that left an estimated sixty thousand people dead. Vonnegut was haunted by the memory and spent twenty-five years trying to explain the experience, which he was finally able to do in what became

Slaughterhouse-Five. For the rest of his life he was plagued by bouts of depression, anger, thoughts of suicide, and incipient alcoholism.

Just months after the war's end and his liberation, Vonnegut married his childhood sweetheart, the former Jane Cox of Indianapolis, who, despite her doubts about the marriage at times, became his advocate, first-reader, and creative adviser. The couple would have three children.

Vonnegut began his professional career moonlighting as a police reporter at *Chicago City News* while attending classes in anthropology at the University of Chicago on the G.I. Bill. His brother Bernard, an atmospheric physicist, landed him a fulltime job at General Electric in Schenectady, New York, in the public relations department. Vonnegut never completed his degree, despite repeated attempts, but years later he was granted an honorary master's degree from the University of Chicago with *Cat's Cradle* accepted in lieu of a thesis.

Vonnegut found his work at General Electric, which had a worldwide reputation in technological innovation, rewarding and stimulating. In fact, his first novel, *Player Piano*, published in 1952, was based loosely on what he saw at General Electric. It considered a dystopic scenario in which technicians and skilled workers have been replaced by the devices they invented. The novel did not sell well, but Vonnegut was convinced he could make a living as a freelance writer and novelist. He left General Electric and began pitching stories to popular magazines, many which were then running four or five short stories per issue.

He found, however, that his brand of science fiction, which was mainly about moral choices that the future might bring, wasn't wanted by coffee-table magazines such as *Collier's* and the *Saturday Evening Post*. Bowing to the market, he instead wrote stories for suburban readers who wanted optimism and memorable plot twists.

By the late 1950s, with the advent of television, the bottom fell out of the magazine market for short stories because advertisers were shifting their dollars to TV. Vonnegut scrambled for years to sell the occasional story; he also wrote novels such as the *Sirens of Titan* (1959) and *Mother Night* (1961) for paperback editor Knox Burger, a friend from Cornell days who paid him substantial advances because royalties on a thirty-five cent paperback were infinitesimal. In addition, he took short-term commuting jobs to Boston from his home on Cape Cod as an ad writer. He was desperate to support his family, which had doubled to six children—three of whom were nephews whose parents had suddenly died. At one time, Vonnegut owned a SAAB dealership on Cape Cod, mistakenly thinking that selling cars was a business that would help support his writing.

When Vonnegut was invited at the last-minute to teach at the Iowa Writers Workshop in 1965, he was out-of-print and practically broke. Reluctantly, he drove out to Iowa City alone. Compounding his unhappiness, he was the only person on the faculty without a college degree and his classes were too large because they were populated by students who hadn't gotten their first-choice instructor such as Nelson Algren, Donald Justice, or Vance Bourjaily.

But Vonnegut had come from the battlefield, so to speak, of writing and publishing, and slowly won over his students with practical advice, modesty, humor, and, during office appointments, friendly encouragement. He soon became one of the most popular instructors, and he befriended faculty members too because he was eager to learn from them. Vonnegut's introduction to many of his favorite metafictional and fabulist techniques came at the hands of fellow instructors such as Chilean-born José Donoso. Then, in December 1965, Vonnegut was invited by Sam Lawrence to bring out his backlist as a collection with uniform covers and editing and to sign a three-book contract, all for Delacorte Press. Suddenly, Vonnegut was well-off, highly regarded as a writing teacher, and looking forward to publishing work that was wanted by a major house. As one of his students, John Casey said, "He became famous before our eyes."

By the end of the sixties, the war in Vietnam had upstaged the civil rights movement and civil disobedience against the war had become widespread. Fighting between police and antiwar demonstrators in Chicago during the 1968 Democratic National Convention pitted demands to stop the war against appeals for law and order.

That year, Vonnegut was putting the finishing touches on a slim novel, *Slaughterhouse-Five, or, The Children's Crusade*. It is the story of Billy Pilgrim, a prisoner of war who takes shelter during an air raid on Dresden only to discover afterward that entire city has been destroyed. It evolves in a circular way, moving almost incoherently through the different time periods (pre- and post-Dresden bombing), and at one point leaving the solar system entirely for a safe planet where Billy finds love and acceptance. Seen in retrospect, *Slaughterhouse-Five* is a powerful, morbidly funny novel about what war-induced trauma feels like to a good soldier, a good citizen, who was just trying to do his duty.

Two weeks before *Slaughterhouse-Five* arrived in bookstores in early March 1969, the North Vietnamese attacked Saigon and more than 100 South Vietnamese towns and military targets, killing approximately 100 Americans in the first fifteen hours. During the first week of March, 453 Americans died, the highest losses in nearly a year. All ten thousand copies of the first edition of *Slaughterhouse-Five* sold out almost immediately, and the novel that Vonnegut had complained, "reads like a telegram" reached number one on the *New York Times Best Seller* list.

Vonnegut's marriage came to an end in the early 1970s, after which he left Cape Cod for New York City. There he met Jill Krementz, a photojournalist in Manhattan, whom he married in 1979; Jane Cox Vonnegut, who also remarried, died in 1986 from cancer.

The 1970s and 1980s were difficult decades for Vonnegut: He was famous and realized that his name was a brand that would guarantee good sales, but his fiction was giving way to more and more autobiography and essay-writing. His bleak, and darkly comic novels—*Breakfast of Champions* (1973), *Slapstick* (1976), *Jailbird* (1979), *Deadeye Dick* (1982), *Galápagos* (1985), and *Bluebeard* (1987)—continued to sell quite well, although his thematic treatments of dystopia, corrupt authority, and an indifferent universe tended to play less well with reviewers as time went on. He feared he was becoming less relevant and less creative; in 1984 he attempted suicide.

Vonnegut became an iconic figure to his readership and the post-war generation, and he continues to be read, almost as a rite of passage, by young people experiencing their first serious doubts about religion, the American way of life, the nature of good and evil, the use and misuse of science, and the purpose of life itself. He crafted his image carefully—the avuncular, curly-haired humorist, an anti-authoritarian, savage critic of the status quo, and a political pundit—although he was also the first to admit, "I myself am a work of fiction."

But he was not disingenuous; his values and ideals were shaped by his youth, which had been spent during an era of extended families, New Deal programs aimed at helping people hurt by the Great Depression, a small peacetime army, and general optimism about progress. His refrain was "decency," which he decried as missing in post-modern America. He was pleased that younger readers embraced him, saying his purpose was to "catch people before they become generals and senators and presidents, and you poison their minds with humanity. Encourage them to make a better world."

Following a serious fall outside his brownstone home in Manhattan in March 2007, he died a month later, age eighty-four.

CRITICAL
CONTEXT

Tralfamadore is America: Cultural History in *Slaughterhouse-Five*

Darryl Hattenhauer

Early scholars of *Slaughterhouse-Five* read it as Kurt Vonnegut's testament of acceptance. They see it as bleakly existentialist, as if Vonnegut believes and the novel implies that the world is without meaning or purpose. However, Vonnegut considered himself a socialist, which necessarily holds that there is meaning and purpose—not to mention cause and effect and chronology. It is not Vonnegut but Billy Pilgrim and the Tralfamadorians who believe life has no meaning or purpose. The narrator says, "There is nothing intelligent to say about a massacre" (19), but there are whole books written about them, for example the one written by Vonnegut. Todd F. Davis states, "The inhabitants of Tralfamadore make no attempt to fix meaning to any event" (76). By contrast, Vonnegut finds a lot of meaning. He finds that militarism is absurd. He finds that consumerism is absurd. He finds that misdistribution of income is absurd. This essay argues that Tralfamadore is a futuristic dystopia that parodies the United States. To that end, it begins by examining the cultural myths and ideologies implicit in *Slaughterhouse-Five*. Then it considers how the history of ideas about the US landscape inform this novel.

Peter Freese describes Billy as "a latter-day Christ crucified by a world of cruelty and lovelessness and a postlapsarian Adam pining for a return to paradise" (155). As an anti-hero, one of the "listless playthings of enormous forces" (164), he is, in the slang of his day, just a little pill. Moreover, he is a grim pill. Indeed, the name *Billy* suggests "goat." As in John Barth's *Giles Goat-Boy*, Billy is a new kind of scapegoat. Traditionally, the sins of the others wash away and attach to the scapegoat. Then the society gets rid of the sins by removing the scapegoat through either banishment or death. America's postmodern scapegoats, instead of suffering death or banishment, are usually just losers. They fit into the mainstream just enough to exhibit traces of it, and they suffer accordingly. Thus postmodern scapegoats bear the burden of their culture's contradictions and absurdities. They suffer not from exclusion but rather from inclusion. On his imaginary Tralfama-dore, Billy is with a movie star. The motif of an Everyman marooned with a beautiful woman is common in American narratives (e.g., think of *Gilligan's Island*, the popular 1960s television show).

Before he imagines his new world, Billy suffers mentally for de-cades under the burden of trying to fit into his old world. His baptism is not a traditionally religious one but rather a secular travesty of it. His father baptizes him by throwing him into the deep end of a swimming pool, and Billy is later baptized again by being thrown into the deep end of consumerism. The ritual incantation, "Sink or swim," exempli-fies social Darwinism, a myth that Vonnegut often reviled.

As innocent as a child, Billy is rather unaware of reality and often lives in a fantasy world. Also like a child, he falls asleep a lot. For example, he awakes in 1968 to hear his daughter tell him he acts like a child. As in Theodore Roethke's interpolated poem "The Waking," he wakes to sleep: his life is a dreamland. Sleepwalking through life, he dreams the American dream (on the problems with the American dream, see Gobat, Hurley, and Sieber). And when Billy enters adult-hood by proposing to Valencia, he does not believe the ritual phrases he hears himself recycling. He has a sense that he is taking on suffering. But not knowing why he is suffering, he does not realize that his cross to bear is to live a life consisting of beliefs and values that grow from the turbulent confluence of Puritanism, consumerism, and the frontier (see, e.g., Bercovitch and Howe). Mistaking the cause of the disease for the cure, he makes his malady worse by redoubling his pursuit of happiness. More specifically, he makes the acquisition of luxuries a necessity. From his humble origins as a barber's son, he begins his rise into the upper-middle-class by marrying the boss's daughter. He buys her a Cadillac, unaware that it will be the death of her. Like almost all of his compatriots, this representative American buys his wife dia-monds, unaware that there is death and destruction in Africa's diamond mines just as there was in Dresden's corpse mines. He buys the big house and everything in it. A shopper in the American dream, he buys the story of the consumer paradise, the big lie that Eliot Rosewater refers to when he says we need "a lot of wonderful new lies" (101).

Like Rip Van Winkle, he is a perpetual child who is asleep—literally and figuratively. After the Revolutionary War, in Washington Irving's tale, Rip does not comprehend the changes in himself, his family, or his society. Likewise, after World War II, Billy does not understand the changes in himself, his family, or the world. Leslie Fiedler's influential argument is that the perpetual adolescent, "Rip Van Winkle presides over the birth of the American imagination" (26). It is axiomatic that Americans of the dominant culture are childish. Never maturing, Billy tries to stay in never-never land of Tralfamadore. As if he is living in timelessness, he imagines that there is no past, present, or future. David W. Noble argues, "We have had a constant self-definition as a nation from the 1830s to the present" (*Historians* 16). Similarly, Leonard Mustazza shows that Vonnegut's novels grapple with that myth of timelessness. Note the first word in the title of Mustazza's book: *Forever Pursuing Genesis: The Myth of Eden in the Novels of Kurt Vonnegut*. Wai-Chee Dimock has noted that "America marked not only the beginning of a 'New Heaven and a New Earth' but also an absolute, atemporal order of truth and justice. It stood at once as the culmination of progress and end to progress, fulfillment of history and emancipation from history. Unfolding in time, America remained ultimately timeless" (14).

As a representative American and as a scapegoat of American history, Billy Pilgrim makes his fatal sacrifice exactly two hundred years after the American Revolution begins—the birth of America. He contains multitudes of American artifacts, which are the raw materials that go into the construction of hegemonic myths. As an Everyman, he is a mosaic of what he has experienced in a society that is itself a mosaic. His mind consists of traces of events, rather like Tralfamadore's spaghetti mass of happy trails that earthlings do not see. All of his experiences are still happening, but they are happening as memories. Like everyone, he is always a history book; all of the events in the history book of Billy Pilgrim always exist, although some are just in his mind. However, he cannot read all of those events at the same time any more than he could read a stack of stained-glass windows, or a stack of photographic slides, or a stack of transparencies. Like everyone, he cannot look at each moment at the same time, even though bits of each of them are meeting his mind's eye.

As a result, Billy cannot truly reinvent himself. He can rearrange himself by shrinking some elements, expanding others, and putting different elements in the forefront. That is exactly the technique of Marsden Hartley's famous painting, *Portrait of a German Officer* (1914). However, such rearranging invents not a new self but rather a new costume. In Hartley's painting, there is only a rearrangement of the officer's uniform. The clothes make the man. Billy's new costume of intergalactic traveler does not illustrate re-invention. It reveals a representative American's rearrangement of ideas and values implicit in American movies, pulp fiction, romantic songs, and so on.

Read as a satiric parody, Billy Pilgrim is not unstuck in time. He is trapped in it. He never leaves it any more than he ever leaves Earth. More specifically, he is trapped in American history. The values and beliefs that furnish his mind do not change; they just get re-arranged. As a representative American, he imagines a Tralfamadore that is a projection of America. Everything there, from artifact to idea, derives from everyday American objects and beliefs. As Loree Rackstraw notes, one of the bitter ironies of *Slaughterhouse-Five* is that Billy escapes a cataclysm like Dresden but then helps renew the same myths that enable such horrors (58).

Fiction has often used space travel as a voyage analogous to time travel. In particular, traveling to a primitive place has been viewed as a kind of travel into the past. This combination of time and space travel is most famous in Daniel Defoe's *Robinson Crusoe*. In *A Connecticut Yankee in King Arthur's Court*, Mark Twain sends his protagonist back to the Dark Ages as a kind of American missionary. (According to Ronald Reagan, America's mission depends on restoring "material affluence on a scale unequalled in history." Otherwise, we "will put an end to everything we believe in and to our dreams for the future" ["Creative" 267]. Garry Wills has made a counter-argument: "Since we had a special mission, we could assume special powers. . . . The virtue of our aims sanctified the means—so we could indulge in a righteous Hiroshima or two, in napalm and saturation bombing, in a Diem coup, or a Chile putsch" [*Inventing* ix–xx]. On the myth of America's "mission," see Tony Smith.) Twain's missionary of secular progress, , tries to bring Yankee ingenuity to the benighted, but the end is an apocalyptic shoot-out with Hank manning the weapon of mass destruction (WMD) of his time, a Gatling gun. As with Vonnegut, much of Twain's work exposes America's myth of itself as a redeemer nation bringing democracy to the world (see Harris on the theme of timelessness in Twain's work).

Similar to those stories, a narrative of America that historians study is the European myth about returning to Eden, regaining paradise, starting anew, and reinventing the world to make the future consistent with God's plan. Thus the myth of America is to go back to the future—into the past and future simultaneously. The early European immigrants would reestablish the innocence and purity of Eden by going forward into what they regarded as a new world, even though the natives had been there for ages. In that story, the new world was a magic and sacred place that would transfigure newcomers by purifying them, cleansing them of the old world, making them new by baptizing them into democracy. Unlike other nations, the myth goes, American history became a function of nature. For example, Perry Miller called it "nature's nation."

Vonnegut also uses spatial images to indicate temporal ideas. For example, the bug trapped in amber recalls a novel popular during World War II, Kathleen Winsor's *Forever Amber*. It also recalls another perpetual adolescent's anxiety, Holden Caulfield's apprehensiveness about where the ducks and fish go in the winter when the water freezes. Ducks can travel with the seasons, but fish cannot survive in ice, and humans cannot survive in amber. Tralfamadorians use the Rocky Mountains, a seemingly endless stretch of space that might as well be infinite, as a metaphor for timelessness. Myra Jehlen refers to this as "America's translation of time into space" (18). Indeed, at the beginning of America as a nation, a dominant myth was that it would take a thousand years to populate the West. A millennium might as well be infinite. But that myth was exploded when historian Frederick Jackson Turner pointed out in 1893 that the "errand into the wilderness" filled the open land after only a century (see Simonson).

Slaughterhouse-Five features two characters whose names are themselves reminders of the Rocky Mountains: Montana Wildhack and Wild Bob from Wyoming. Both characters have difficulty cutting through the amber and avoiding death. Wildhack has been reported as possibly dead, while all of Wild Bob's soldiers die, and then he himself dies. The image of "the West" is itself part of the national mythology. For instance, Reagan often expressed the myth of the West: "Ideals of courageous and self-reliant heroes, both men and women, are the stuff of western lore. . . . Integrity, morality and democratic values are the resounding themes" (Murdoch 1); and "They built the west without federal planners" ("Additional" 6; see also Findlay, Limerick, Murdoch, and Nordholt). Wild Bob identifies with the mythic westerner Wild Bill Cody, who, with his typical immodesty, barbecued entire buffalo and had a town named in his honor: Cody, Wyoming. Wild Bob is from Sheridan, Wyoming, named after the Civil War general Philip Sheridan, who supposedly said, "The only good Indian is a dead Indian." Sheridan is about twenty-five miles south of the Wyoming–Montana border. About fifty miles north is the Little Bighorn Battlefield, made famous by another Civil War general. Thus Wild Bob exemplifies those who still believe in the American myths of the frontier and its corollaries: manifest destiny and Social Darwinism. He wants the present and future to repeat a past that existed only in the imagination.

In F. Scott Fitzgerald's *The Great Gatsby*, Jay Gatsby says, "Can't repeat the past? . . . Why of course you can" (84). His mission is to recapture the time before World War I when he held fresh green nature in the person of pure white Daisy in a pure white dress. He thinks of her as an expression of pure nature at the same time that he thinks of her as a wealthy urbanite who is "above the hot struggles of the poor" (114). For Gatsby, this denial of time includes the denial of birth. The fact that Daisy has married and borne a child is insignificant compared to his quest to regain his ostensibly innocent past. He says of Daisy's new life, "It was just personal" (116). By contrast, he regards his personal pilgrimage through life as metaphysical, transcendent, even sacred, and therefore timeless. Daisy's marriage was physical, mundane, even profane, and therefore time-bound. Scholars have long adhered to the view of David W. Noble and Leslie Fiedler that Gatsby reflects America's anxiety about generativity. They show that birth is a reminder of death and time because one generation replaces the other.

Billy, too, associates reproduction with death. It is on his wedding night that he imagines his tombstone's epitaph: "Everything was beautiful and nothing hurt" (122). His wife Valencia—a name of an orange, the Halloween color that is also one of the colors on the prisoners' boxcar, the maps of bombing targets, and the tent at Billy's party—asks her conquering hero, her Wild Bob, for some war stories. One of Billy's stories derives from a narrative that is very popular in America, Alexander Dumas's novel *The Three Musketeers*. It goes through countless permutations, such as Roland Weary's projection of the story onto his parasitic relationship with the two scouts, to the television show aimed at Billy's children called *The Mouseketeers*, to the movie aimed at his grandchildren called *The Three Amigos*, and so on, like the song of Yon Yonson. For a long stretch of American history, the notion has metaphorically nourished American culture the way it literally nourishes Valencia: too much sweetness and not enough substance.

If neither war, nor imprisonment, nor forced labor, nor a plane crash can kill him, then to become dead to the world without being dead, he has to imagine he is not there. He has to deny, ignore, and forget. He is like Harrison Bergeron's father when he is faced with his son's death, who says, "Forget sad things" (10). Forgetting life so he can forget death approximates timelessness because it makes time go faster; Billy can be as mystified by time as his mother, who wonders, "How did I get so old?" (44). Forgetting life, he imagines that his pilgrimage to Tralfamadore and his childish crusade to spread the gospel of Tralfamadore transcend the limits of time and place. However, he has only reinscribed the children's crusade of World War II into a new children's crusade. America's crusading spirit is not only tragic but also comic. There was another youthful crusader named Billy at the time, Billy Graham, who headed up what he called a "Christian crusade"; and, in his first inaugural address, Reagan said, "Can we begin our crusade joined together in a moment of silent prayer?" (260). Indeed, "Crusader Rabbit" was television's first serialized cartoon. Billy's son, who did not get squared away until given the opportunity to crusade in Vietnam, might well have watched those cartoons, one of many children's programs promoting truth, justice, and the American way. The episodes featured motifs of nature ("Crusader and the Schmohawk Indians"), science fiction ("Crusader and the Mad Hollywood Scientist"), and time travel ("Crusader in the Tenth Century").

Billy's crusade is to go where no man has gone before. Like Vonnegut's Cape Cod neighbors the Kennedys, who affirmed a new frontier, and like Billy's apparent pick for President, Ronald Reagan, who believed in the "high frontier" (the name for his star wars space initiative), Billy does not reinvent himself and his universe. Rather, he rearranges elements of America's values and beliefs. Like a child with Lincoln logs, he can build different homes, but always out of the same materials.

So it is that Tralfamadore parodies America in the 1960s. More specifically, Tralfamadore is a fantasy built on rearrangements of American myth. According to William Boelhower, "The American Dream is to this day an unchanged narrative segment lifted from sixteenth-century cartographic logic" (46). If America continues its history of going into the future by rearranging the mythic materials of the past, it will resemble Tralfamadore. Billy Pilgrim's regress does not solve his problems; it exemplifies them. Like many other people, he thinks he is pushing towards a utopia when he is really slouching towards a dystopia.

Tralfamadorians have evolved (but not progressed) until they have no head, which suggests they are not only brainless but also faceless. Likewise, they are so flexible that they might as well be spineless. Tralfamadorians evolved in an atmosphere of increasing entropy. After the holocaust victims die from poison gas, and after Valencia dies from poison gas, it is perhaps notable that the Tralfamadorians live in an environment that is all poison gas. Their one foot is adapted for the management of waste. They have only one eye because they are as single-sighted as Billy, whose primary function is to consume and fantasize and, as an optometrist, to make people see life the way he does. They have only one hand because they are inactive. They overlook the part of the Serenity Prayer that says we should accept what we cannot change. Rather than change what they can, they look on the bright side. However, their version of optimism is to ignore reality rather to be hopeful about improving it. (Therefore, they are actually pessimists.) They live as if difficulty is something they should ignore, like treating people in a ghetto with benign neglect. In their single-minded passivity, they have impaired depth perception. In addition, Billy's talk of a is the kind of adolescent metaphysics that he would have heard about in Boy Scouts and Little League and on the radio, that he would have seen in movies and on television, or that he would have read about in pulp science fiction.

The Tralfamadorians often contradict themselves. They claim there is no future even as they pursue an improved future by experimenting with new rocket fuels. Their anti-intellectualism is so evolved that they deny causality even as they say that one of their rocket ships causes the end of the universe. Employing causality, Vonnegut's narrator notes that every action has a reaction: "This can be useful in rocketry" (80); Werner von Braun would have agreed.

Their contradictions have a consistent premise. They are true believers in the pursuit of what they think is their self-interest. As Wills says of Americans, "Selfishness is a duty with us" (*Nixon Agonistes* 230). Like people who say, "the poor will always be with you," they ignore causality when they prefer to do nothing. Yet like people who say "you can't stop progress," they assert causality as inevitable. Like Billy, they believe that they cannot change the future. Like current Americans who want change but have been unable to produce it, Billy cannot change the future because he is so burdened with the sins of the fathers (in the form of the absurdities of his culture) that he cannot change much of anything. Tralfamadorians cannot touch the future because they believe it is impossible. They claim the cause of that impossibility is that events are pre-determined, since the moments are "structured that way" (117). Thus they raise the question: What structures can we change? The Tralfamadorians say none, and that this inability is eternal. But only eternal adolescents live in never-never land.

Yet with the Tralfamadorian version of the novel, they have accomplished the impossible, though only in Billy's imagination. As Klinkowitz points out, their novels cannot exist because it is impossible to read hundreds of scenes simultaneously (*Vonnegut Effect* 83). A story might be timeless, but a plot is necessarily timeful. They believe that they have achieved timelessness, so they believe that their novels have too. In a future made from what Christopher Lasch calls "the culture of narcissism," they confuse their response to a stimulus with the nature of the stimulus. Their myth is that they live in a pure timeless place where nothing comes between them and reality. They are literal minded, so they do not have to think; they can take for granted what meets the eye. Without knowing it, the Tralfamadorians see through history-colored monocles. They live in the illusion of direct contact with the world when in truth they see not reality but only their myths about it.

Like Americans who claim they are the world's exemplar at promoting philanthropy, democracy, and peace, they project their myth of America as a redeemer nation and then applaud themselves for something that does not exist outside themselves. Moreover, they do so even when their effect is the opposite of their intentions, such as in *Slaughterhouse-Five* when the marine addresses the Lyons Club on the subject of the Vietnam War and states that Americans have to stop the communists' plan to "force their way of life on weak countries" (59). So it is fitting for Wills to say, "It is when America is in her most altruistic mood that other nations better get behind their bunkers" because we might have arrived "at that fatal recurring moment in our country's diplomatic benefactions, the moment when it makes sense to start shooting people philanthropically, for their own good" (*Nixon Agonistes* 396, 397).

Psychologists tell us the recurring moments that are the most significant to us form the basis of the unconscious mind, and Alan McGlashan describes the unconscious as a "savage and beautiful country." The analogy between a journey into a landscape and a journey into the self is an old one. It has informed myths for ages. In *Slaughterhouse-Five*, the landscape of Billy's unconscious consists of the wide-open spaces of the mythic American Wild West. By imagining that the name of his love interest is "Montana," he associates himself with the image of a mountain man. Yet he can have it both ways, because she also suggests Dresden; both she and the city are baroque. Historians and literary critics have long noted the irony that American culture proceeds as if urbanization has not eroded the naturalness of nature's nation.

Like his fellow suburbanites in housing developments with names like "River Park" in towns with names like "Eden Prairie," who believe in nature and consumerism at the same time and place, Billy imagines that his modern home on Tralfamadore is paradise. Thus he imagines himself as a space-age pioneer, living off the land, subsisting on what nature gives him, a stoic surviving on bare necessities, like a television, a recliner, and a movie star. Such is the new world he imagines through his rearrangement of the American dream.

In truth, he is more like a fossil, a bug trapped in amber, existing in a transparent museum amidst. an atmosphere that is virtually a cosmic gas chamber. Quite literally, this place is a zoo. That is how he forgets about such things as fire-bombings and concentration camps. He is as unconcerned about Tralfamadore's atmosphere as he is when he drives away from the African American in the ghetto, leaving him in a cloud of poison gas, the same gas that kills his wife. However, he gets over it by replacing her with a trophy wife. In Billy's vision of a new world, government does not exist. Taxation does not exist. He does not have to work, so somebody else has to work for him, like the laborers at his Tastee Freeze junk food stand.

So it is that in 1968, Vonnegut anticipated the future of American thought. He saw that the not-so-brave new world would be much like the old one, that the central myth would still be the defeat of time.

Works Cited

Bercovitch, Sacvan. *The Puritan Origins of the American Self.* New Haven: Yale UP, 1975. Print.

Berryman, Charles. "Vonnegut's Comic Persona in Breakfast of Champions." *Critical Essays on Kurt Vonnegut.* Ed. Robert Merrill. Boston: Hall, 1990. 162–69. Print.

Boelhower, William. *Through a Glass Darkly: Ethnic Semiosis in American Literature.* New York: Oxford UP, 1987. Print.

Boon, Kevin Alexander, ed. *At Millenium's End. New Essays on the Work of Kurt Vonnegut.* Albany: SUNY P, 2001. Print.

Davis, Todd F. *Kurt Vonnegut's Crusade: Or, How a Postmodern Harlequin Preached a New Kind of Humanism.* Albany: SUNY P, 2006. Print.

Dimock, Wai-Chee. *Empire for Liberty: Melville and the Poetics of Individualism.* New Jersey: Princeton UP, 1991. Print.

Dunnigan, Brian Leigh. *Frontier Metropolis: Picturing Early Detroit, 1701–1838.* Detroit: Wayne State UP, 2001. Print.

Ehrlich, Susan. *Point of View: A Linguistic Analysis of Literary Style.* London: Routledge, 1990. Print.

Fiedler, Leslie. *Love and Death in the American Novel.* New York: Criterion, 1960. Print.

Findlay, John M. *Magic Lands: Western Cityscapes and American Culture After 1940.* Berkeley: U of California P, 1993. Print.

Fitts, Robert K. *Inventing New England's Slave Paradise: Master/Slave Relations in Eighteenth-Century Narragansett, Rhode Island.* New York: Routledge, 1998. Print.

Fitzgerald, F. Scott. *The Great Gatsby.* New York: Scribner, 1925. Print.

Freese, Peter. "Vonnegut's Invented Religions as Sense-Making Systems." *The Vonnegut Chronicles: Interviews and Essays.* Eds. Peter Reed and Marc Leeds. Westport, CT: Greenwood, 1996. 145–64. Print.

Gayle, Addison. *The Way of the New World: The Black Novel in America.* New York: Anchor, 1976. Print.

Gobat, Michel. *Confronting the American Dream: Nicaragua under U.S. Imperial Rule.* Durham: Duke UP, 2005. Print.

Greenblatt, Stephen. *Marvellous Possession: The Wonder of the New World.* Chicago: U of Chicago P, 1992. Print.

Guelzo, Allen C. *Abraham Lincoln: Redeemer President.* Grand Rapids, MI: Eerdmans, 2003. Print.

Harris, Susan K. *Mark Twain's Escape from Time: A Study of Patterns and Images.* Columbia: U of Missouri P, 1982. Print.

Hofstadter, Richard. *Anti-Intellectualism in American Life.* New York: Random, 1962. Print.

Howe, Daniel W. *Making the American Self: Jonathan Edwards to Abraham Lincoln.* Cambridge, MA: Harvard UP, 1997. Print.

Hume, Kathryn. "Vonnegut's Self-Projections: Symbolic Characters and Symbolic Fiction." *The Critical Response to Kurt Vonnegut.* Ed. Leonard Mustazza. Westport, CT: Greenwood, 1994. 231–44. Print.

Hurley, Andrew. *Diners, Bowling Alleys, and Trailer Parks: Chasing the American Dream in Postwar Consumer Culture.* New York: Basic, 2002. Print.

Jackson, Kenneth T. *Crabgrass Frontier: The Suburbanization of the United States.* New York: Oxford UP, 1985. Print.

Jacoby, Susan. *The Age of Unreason.* New York: Pantheon, 2008. Print.

Jehlen, Myra. *American Incarnation: The Individual, the Nation, and the Continent.* Cambridge, MA: Harvard UP, 1986. Print.

Kowinski, William Severini. *The Malling of America: An Inside Look at the Great Consumer Paradise.* New York: Morrow, 1985. Print.

Klinkowitz, Jerome. *The Vonnegut Effect.* Columbia: U of South Carolina P, 2004. Print.

___. *Vonnegut in Fact.* Columbia: U of South Carolina P, 2004. Print.

Lasch, Christopher. *The Culture of Narcissism: American Life in an Age of Diminishing Expectations.* New York: Norton, 1978. Print.

Lewis, R. W. B. *The American Adam: Innocence, Tragedy and Tradition in the Nineteenth Century.* Chicago: of U Chicago P, 1955.

Limerick, Patricia Nelson. *The Legacy of Conquest: The Unbroken Past of the American West.* New York: Norton, 1987. Print.

Madden, Etta M., and Martha L. Finch, eds. *Eating in Eden: Food and American Utopias.* Lincoln: U of Nebraska P, 2006. Print.

McGlashan, Alan. *The Savage and Beautiful Country: The Secret Life of the Mind.* Einsiedeln, Switz.: Daimon, 1988. Print.

Merrill, Robert, ed. *Critical Essays on Kurt Vonnegut.* Boston: Hall, 1990. Print.

___. "Vonnegut's Breakfast of Champions: The Conversion of Heliogabalus." In Merrill 153–161.

Miller, Perry. Errand into the Wilderness. Cambridge: Harvard UP, 1956.

___. *Nature's Nation.* Cambridge, MA: Harvard UP, 1967. Print.

Murdoch, David H. *The American West: The Invention of a Myth.* Cardiff: Welsh Academic P, 1996. Print.

Mustazza, Leonard, ed. *The Critical Response to Kurt Vonnegut.* Westport, CT: Greenwood, 1994. Print.

___. *Forever Pursuing Genesis: The Myth of Eden in the Novels of Kurt Vonnegut.* Lewisburg, PA: Bucknell UP, 1990. Print.

Noble, David W. *The Eternal Adam and the New World Garden: The Central Myth in the American Novel Since 1830.* New York: Braziller, 1968. Print.

___. *Historians against History: The Frontier Thesis and the National Covenant in American Historical Writing Since 1830.* Minneapolis, MN: U of Minnesota P, 1965. Print.

Nordholt, Jan Willem Schulte. *The Myth of the West: America as the Last Empire.* Herbert H. Rowen trans. Grand Rapids, MI: Eerdmans, 1995. Print.

O'Gorman, Edmundo. *The Invention of America: An Inquiry into the Historical Nature of the New World and the Meaning of Its History.* Bloomington: Indiana UP, 1961. Print.

Rackstraw, Loree. "Quantum Leaps in the Vonnegut Minefield." *At Millenium's End. New Essays on the Work of Kurt Vonnegut.* Ed. Kevin Alexande Boon. Albany: SUNY P, 2001. 49–64. Print.

Reagan, Ronald Wilson. "Additional Reductions in Federal Spending: Our Plan for Recovery Is Sound." The White House, Washington, D.C. 24 Sep 1981. *Vital Speeches of the Day* 48 (15 Oct. 1981): 6. Print.

___. "The Creative Society: California and the U.S. Economy." The Economic Club of New York. New York City. 17 Jan 1968. *Vital Speeches of the Day* 34 (15 Feb. 1968): 267. Print.

___. "Inaugural Address: Putting America Back to Work." Washington, D.C. 20 Jan 1981. *Vital Speeches of the Day* 47 (15 Feb. 1981): 260. Print.

Reed, Peter J., and Marc Leeds, eds. *The Vonnegut Chronicles: Interviews and Essays.* Westport, CT: Greenwood, 1996. Print.

Sanford, Charles L. *The Quest for Paradise: Europe and the American Moral Imagination.* Urbana: U of Illinois P, 1961. Print.

Schrag, Peter. *Paradise Lost: California's Experience, America's Future.* Berkeley: U of California P, 2004. Print.

Schriber, Mary Sue. "Bringing Chaos to Order: The Novel Tradition and Kurt Vonnegut, Jr." *The Critical Response to Kurt Vonnegut.* Ed. Leonard Mustazza. Westport, CT: Greenwood, 1994. 175–86. Print.

Sieber, Sam D. *Second-Rate Nation: From the American Dream to the American Myth*. Taos, NM: Paradigm, 2005. Print.

Simmons, James C. *Star-Spangled Eden: An Exploration of the American Character in the 19th Century*. New York: Basic, 2001. Print.

Simonson, Harold P. *The Closed Frontier: Studies in American Literary Tragedy*. New York: Holt, 1970. Print.

Simpson, John W. *Visions of Paradise: Glimpses of Our Landscape's Legacy*. Berkeley: U of California P, 1999. Print.

Slotkin, Peter. *The Fatal Environment: The Myth of the Frontier in the Age of Industrialism, 1880–1890*. New York: Atheneum, 1985. Print.

___. *Gunfighter Nation: The Myth of the Frontier in 20th-Century America*. New York: Atheneum, 1992. Print.

___. *Regeneration through Violence: The Mythology of the American Frontier*. Middletown: Wesleyan UP, 1973. Print.

Smith, Henry Nash. *Virgin Land: The American West as Symbol and Myth*. Cambridge, MA: Harvard UP, 1950. Print.

Smith, Tony. *America's Mission: The United States and the Worldwide Struggle for Democracy in the Twentieth Century*. Richard C. Leone Foreword. Princeton: Princeton UP, 1995. Print.

Stephenson, R. Bruce. *Visions of Eden: Environmentalism, Urban Planning, and City Building in St. Petersburg, Florida, 1900-1995*. Columbus: Ohio State UP, 1997. Print.

Tuveson, Ernest Lee. *Redeemer Nation: The Idea of America's Millennial Role*. Chicago: U of Chicago P, 1968. Print.

Twain, Mark. *Adventures of Huckleberry Finn*. New York: Harper, 1912. Print.

Wade, Richard C. *The Urban Frontier: The Rise of Western Cities, 1790–1850*. Cambridge, MA: Harvard UP, 1967. Print.

Wertheimer, Eric. *Imagined Empires: Incas, Aztecs, and the New World of American Literature, 1771–1786*. New York: Cambridge UP, 1999. Print.

Westling, Louise Hutchings. *The Green Breast of the New World: Landscape, Gender, and American Fiction*. Atlanta: U of Georgia P, 1996. Print.

Whitman, Walt. "Manifest Destiny and Westward Expansionism." *Everything2*. Everything2 Media, LLC, 4 Mar. 2002. Web. 6 Jan. 2008.

Vonnegut, Kurt. "Harrison Bergeron." *Magazine of Fantasy and Science Fiction* Oct. 1961: 5–10. Print.

___. *Slaughterhouse-Five*. New York: Delacorte, 1969. Print.

Wills, Garry. *Inventing America: Jefferson's Declaration of Independence*. New York: Houghton: 1978. Print.

___. *Nixon Agonistes: The Crisis of the Self-Made Man*. Boston: Houghton, 1970. Print.

Wrobel, David M. *The End of American Exceptionalism: Frontier Anxiety from the Old West to the New Deal*. Lawrence: UP of Kansas, 1996. Print.

Wyatt, David. *The Fall into Eden: Landscape and Imagination in California*. New York: Cambridge UP, 1990. Print.

The Curious Reception of Kurt Vonnegut

Donald E. Morse

Rarely, if ever, in the history of American literature has an author gone so quickly from obscurity to celebrity as happened in the case of Kurt Vonnegut. Beginning in 1950 as a short story writer, Vonnegut found a ready market in the family "slick" magazines that paid exceptionally well. Had television not come along to kill such magazines, he might have labored on, relatively unknown but comfortably well-off as a professional writer of conventional fiction. With the demise of the slicks and with a growing family to support, Vonnegut switched from writing short stories for magazines to writing paperbacks for drugstores and airports. But such works went unreviewed on the assumption that they had to be hackwork. A "check [of] the *Book Review Index* [shows that] from 1952 to 1963 no book of Vonnegut's is recorded as having appeared or been reviewed" (Fiedler 197). The exception had been his first novel, *Player Piano* (1952) that received "rather friendly" but very few reviews (see Freese, Clown 36).[1] There was, however, a small group of fellow writers along with a few academics who saw his fiction as highly innovative and possibly important. Terry Southern, for instance, in a short favorable review of *Cat's Cradle* buried on page 288 of the *New York Times Book Review*, called it "an irreverent and often highly entertaining fantasy concerning the playful irresponsibility of nuclear scientists." But even such brief reviews were sparse indeed.

Vonnegut's fifth novel, *God Bless You, Mr. Rosewater* (1965), attracted more attention but reviews were decidedly mixed, with both the *New York Times* and its *Book Review* panning it, and even today opinions continue to be divided on its literary worth and proper place in the Vonnegut canon. Given the mixed and missing reviews, it becomes all the more surprising that Vonnegut's sixth novel, *Slaughterhouse-Five* (1969), would merit a review on the front page of the *New York Times Book Review* by Robert Scholes. Scholes's praise was both lavish and specific: Slaughterhouse-Five was, he proclaimed "a book we need to read, and . . . reread" (1). He also defended Vonnegut's humor as necessary given the horror of the Dresden massacre and his use of science-fiction motifs and techniques as terribly appropriate "to the comic absurdity of life" (1) as mirrored in the book. He concluded by magisterially announcing that "the truth of Vonnegut's vision requires his fiction" (23).

A second important review of *Slaughterhouse-Five* by the then-dean of reviewers, Granville Hicks, placed Vonnegut with the satirists Jonathan Swift and Mark Twain, a comparison that later became standard in Vonnegut criticism—so much so that when Vonnegut died, Norman Mailer hailed him as "a marvelous writer with a style that remained undeniably and imperturbably his own" calling him "our own Mark Twain" (Pilkinton). There were the begrudgers, perhaps best represented by Charles Thomas Samuels who, in a highly negative assessment, argued forcefully that Vonnegut "can tell us nothing worth knowing" (30), but such assertions were drowned out in the chorus of praise for the novel that became both a critical and popular success leading to the reprinting of all of Vonnegut's previous novels. He could then boast that all his novels were in print, a rare phenomenon in an age when booksellers began keeping zero inventories.

While there were scattered reviews and the occasional scholarly essay on Vonnegut's novels, extensive academic criticism begins a few years after the appearance of *Slaughterhouse-Five* with Peter J. Reed's excellent study *Kurt Vonnegut, Jr.* (1972), which remains essential reading. In assessing all the novels through *Slaughterhouse-Five*, Reed sees them as attempting to come to grips with an intractable dilemma that might be summarized as the perennial American moral issue of using questionable or evil means to achieve a good end. In addition, he also discusses aesthetic matters, concluding that Vonnegut has put "the traditional American novel in contemporary dress" (217), thus accounting for Vonnegut's extensive use of popular forms of fantasy, the spy novel, and science fiction—the problem of genre that continues to plague Vonnegut criticism. Reed's study was followed by several others, including introductions to Vonnegut by Stanley Schatt (1976), James Lundquist (1977), Richard Giannone (1977), Clark Mayo (1977), Jerome Klinkowitz (1982), and Donald E. Morse (1992). The series culminated with the challenging *The World According to Kurt Vonnegut: Moral Paradox and Narrative Form* by Bo Pettersson (1994), but since Pettersson published it in Finland, there was no real acknowledgment of this work in the United States.

A year after Reed's book, the first in a long continuing line of collections of original essays on Vonnegut appeared, *The Vonnegut Statement* (1973), edited by Jerome Klinkowitz and John Somer and featuring what many critics assess as the most important early essay on *Player Piano* and *The Sirens of Titan* by James M. Mellard (178–203). These early essays remain a good starting point for any examination of Vonnegut's work when supplemented with later collections, especially those edited by Leonard Mustazza and Robert Merrill. Merrill's introduction to *Critical Essays on Kurt Vonnegut* (1990) neatly summarizes the ups and downs of Vonnegut's reception over three decades. He reprinted two major essays apiece by Kathryn Hume and Charles Berryman along with an original essay on *Cat's Cradle* by John L. Simon. Mustazza's collection *The Critical Response to Kurt Vonnegut* (1994) superseded Merrill's by covering an additional two novels (*Bluebeard* and *Hocus Pocus*) and by reprinting almost twice as many reviews and essays as Merrill. *The Vonnegut Chronicles* (1996), edited by Reed and Marc Leeds, included three important interviews with the author along with essays on topics that have remained constant in Vonnegut criticism, such as the need for love in a world of loneliness in an essay by Reed (113) and the necessity and impossibility of finding or inventing a meaningful religion in a piece by Peter J. Freese (145). Similarly, Leeds and Reed's edited collection *Kurt Vonnegut: Images and Representations* (2000) featured Sharon Sieber's discussion of Vonnegut's explorations of time, while Kevin A. Boon's *At Millennium's End* (2001) included David Andrews in-depth discussion of Vonnegut's aesthetic humanism (17), Donald Morse's view of

Vonnegut and the notion of progress (91), and Bill Gholson's lucid examination of the moral center in Vonnegut's fiction (133)—all themes that have often been at the center of discussions about Vonnegut. Boon also included an exacting discussion of the various films made from Vonnegut's fiction (Boon and David Pringle 167). The Harold Bloom critical anthology factory has also been busy producing volumes on Vonnegut, perhaps the best of which is the newest edition of *Kurt Vonnegut* (2009) with notable essays by Kathryn Hume, Donald Morse, Tamás Bényei, and Gilbert McInnis.

Barriers to Acceptance: Science Fiction, the Youth Cult, a Simple Style

Through the 1970s and 1980s, three provocative topics kept recurring in negative reviews and essays: Vonnegut's unfortunate use of popular literary forms, especially science fiction and fantasy; his extensive appeal to the young, often described as the youth cult or the Vonnegut youth cult, and the seeming simplicity of his ideas and language. Ironically, these perceived weaknesses or flaws in Vonnegut's work were among his greatest strengths.

Reed argued that science fiction (SF) gave Vonnegut's fiction "an outside perspective on human affairs" (Vonnegut, Jr. 195) and, rather than being an evasion or an avenue of escape, his use of SF allowed him to dramatize "the general condition of man in an absurd universe" (196, 198); or, as he put it in his concluding chapter, SF enabled "a hyperbolic description of the present" (205). Lundquist also mounted a spirited defense of Vonnegut's use of SF as a vehicle for irony and wit, while wisely cautioning readers that "science fiction is as much a publisher's marketing category as it is a literary genre" (87). When Vonnegut wrote for that market, as he did with his early stories in science-fiction magazines, he worked to meet but not to exceed the genre's expectations; but, when he wrote his highly original novels that combined "the special effects of science fiction with extended cosmic irony" then, as Lundquist rightly claims, "he transforms one of the most important forms of pop culture into his own distinctive form of astral jokebook" (100).

Unfortunately, in their attempts to rescue Vonnegut from any science-fiction taint, in the process some critics often reveal their own lack of knowledge about SF in the late twentieth century when Vonnegut wrote. One asserts, for example, that Vonnegut's innovation in *Slaughterhouse-Five* lies in providing readers with a new notion of time, unlike other time-travel novels (Klinkowitz, *Vonnegut's America* 60). Yet, one could argue that any time-travel novel worth reading will provide just such a "new notion" beginning with H. G. Wells's use of Professor Simon Newcomb's theory of "a Four-Dimensional geometry" in *The Time Machine* and continuing with George Gaylord Simpson's use of time-slip theory in The *Dechronization of Sam Magruder* to Joe Haldeman's use of time dilation in *The Forever War*, and Michael Flynn's configuration of multiple universes branching off from any given moment in "The Forest of Time." Moreover, like most serious writers, Vonnegut continually tests the limits of the genre, innovating within it in novel after novel.

The same critic consistently maligns Vonnegut's science fiction, going so far as to claim that in the pre-*Slaughterhouse-Five* novels the "few science-fiction elements existed only as devastating satires of the sub-genre" (Klinkowitz, *Vonnegut in Fact* 3), but such a statement is almost impossible to reconcile with *Player Piano*, *Cat's Cradle*, or even *The Sirens of Titan*. While this trio of novels may be classified as satire, the satire is directed not at science fiction but at the corporate world and meaningless work in *Player Piano*, the amoral scientist and human irresponsibility in *Cat's Cradle*, and megalomania and the search for purpose in *The Sirens of Titan* (see Morse, "Once and Future"). Nor does the late novel, *Galápagos* fare much better, although elsewhere almost uniformly and often extravagantly praised as excellent science fiction. In *The Vonnegut Effect*, Klinkowitz—himself a superb critic—unaccountably relies on one of the weakest introductions to Vonnegut (Allen's *Understanding Kurt Vonnegut*) to conclude that

Galápagos "employs a serious use of hard science that has nothing in common with the fantasies of sci-fi writing" (128). The term *sci-fi* gives the game away since it is not a term used by science-fiction writers, critics, scholars, or even fans but is one employed by the media. "[O]ften pronounce[d] 'skiffy,' [the term refers to] what comes out of Hollywood" and conveys "the non-SF–reading public's impression of what the field is all about," writes Brian Attebery, a well-respected science-fiction scholar (71) here drawing on Gary Wolfe's *Critical Terms for Science Fiction and Fantasy* (114–15; see also Simmons xiii). SF, on the other hand, refers to "written science fiction . . . a coinage that has been used to stand not only for science fiction but also for speculative fiction and even structural fabulation" (Attebery 70; again drawing on Wolfe 117). Both Klinkowitz and Gregory D. Sumner (in *Unstuck in Time*) use *sci-fi*, *sci fi*, and *SF* interchangeably and neither appears to know much about science fiction.

As for the claim that Vonnegut's "serious use of hard science has nothing" to do with SF, the recognized sub-division of SF known as "Hard Science Fiction" is distinguished by "getting the science right" (Samuelson 494)—which is exactly what Vonnegut prided himself on doing in *Galápagos* (see interview with Hank Nuwer in Allen, *Conversations* 259). Moreover, critics need to get the text right before leaping to conclusions. Klinkowitz, for example, erroneously attributes the demise of most of humanity in Galápagos to "the nuclear war that ends human life everywhere" (*Vonnegut Effect* 129), which he modifies later in *Kurt Vonnegut's America* to an "apocalyptically destructive world war" (128). Both assertions miss Vonnegut's point that the demise of humanity, except for those in the Noah's Ark of the *Bahía de Darwin*, occurred not through an act of war but from an act of nature when an in utero virus that eats human eggs appeared first at the Frankfurt Book Fair and spread rapidly through the world, thus ending human reproduction (162). "Nature . . . kill[ed] them all" (*Galápagos* 25). This virus is Vonnegut's prescient, powerful metaphor for a pandemic that many scientists believe lies just over our horizon.[2] A similar misreading occurs with *Jailbird* where Klinkowitz claims that O'Looney's legacy "helped the broad masses" (*Vonnegut Effect* 118), which the novel contradicts (*Jailbird* 280). If readers need to read with careful attention to such details, how much more so scholars, critics, and biographers.[3]

Today, Vonnegut may be considered one of the premiere science-fiction writers of our time, one who extended the genre. While Vonnegut did object very strongly to being labeled as only a science-fiction writer, as have most SF writers, in fact, he never denied that he wrote SF and, indeed, his four greatest novels are pure SF: *Slaughterhouse-Five* (time travel), *Galápagos* (far future), *Cat's Cradle* (apocalypse), and *The Sirens of Titan* (space opera). Plus, both his last and first novels are clearly informed by SF themes: *Player Piano* (dystopia) and *Timequake* (time-lips). Nevertheless, the perceived (and undeserved) stigma of the SF genre undoubtedly contributed to the early critical dismissal or ignorance of his work.

Similarly, Vonnegut was often ignored because he really did appeal to the young, especially those disaffected by the Vietnam War and "business as usual." Sometimes this identification became far too limiting, as some reviewers and critics suggested that only the young would read him.[4] Even Vonnegut himself was heard to lament, "I wish grown-ups would read me" (Thompson). And they did. Rudy M. Baum, for example, the grown-up editor of *Chemical Engineering News* testified in an editorial that "Kurt Vonnegut is one of the reasons I am a writer" (3). All writers and all artists call into being their own audience—one uniquely suited to their art. So Vonnegut's appeal to the young was genuine but so was his appeal to "grown-ups," including mature engineers, such as Baum, teachers of literature, those stuck in airports, and occupants of a hundred other categories. Vonnegut has proven to be that most rare of all writers: one whose appeal cuts across many categories of readers from young to old, from engineers to the technologically challenged, and from the academic to the general reader. When Vonnegut appeared at Barnes

& Noble's flagship store in Manhattan for the launch of *Timequake*, "it was the biggest such event Barnes & Noble ever had anywhere" attracting hundreds of readers (Rackstraw 197).

Vonnegut's style has also been criticized. He once compared himself to Henry David Thoreau when he admitted that like Thoreau, he wrote in the voice of a child" (Allen, *Conversations* 301). It was a child who asked why the emperor wore no clothes and, using that voice, Vonnegut also asks the naïve questions that adults find impossible to answer: Why do good people suffer? What are people for? Does a good end ever justify using an evil means? John Irving, his fellow writer and former student, argues that "Vonnegut's lucidity is hard and brave work in a literary world where pure messiness is frequently thought to be a sign of some essential wrestling with 'hard questions'" (114). His direct style coupled with his humor and personal warmth helped propel Vonnegut onto the national stage as a speaker in demand on college campuses and at national meetings where he often responded to national issues from a clear moral stance based on the values enunciated in the Sermon on the Mount. (For a detailed examination of Vonnegut as a public spokesperson, see Klinkowitz, *Vonnegut in Fact*.)

Literary Critical and Theoretical Approaches to Vonnegut's Novels

Vonnegut has been approached from a host of literary critical or literary theoretical viewpoints, including myth, psychology, chaos theory, American traditions and culture, and postmodernism. Mustazza, in *Forever Pursuing Genesis: The Myth of Eden in the Novels of Kurt Vonnegut* (1990), assesses the novels through *Bluebeard* using the myth of the Fall, the loss of innocence, and Vonnegut's wish to go back to a better time that never was: "The typical Vonnegut protagonist has had a troubled childhood in the company of irresponsible parents," Mustazza observes (157). And more surprisingly, he documents that often "the cause of human suffering turns out to be, paradoxically . . . our own inventiveness" (169). Decades later, Gilbert McInnis argued in *Evolutionary Mythology in the Writings of Kurt Vonnegut* (2011) that Vonnegut was preoccupied not so much with the myth of Eden and the Fall as with Darwin's theory of evolution as it has permeated American culture and science. Clearly Vonnegut and myth remains a fruitful topic.

Lawrence R. Broer's *Sanity Plea: Schizophrenia in the Novels of Kurt Vonnegut* (1989) explored the thesis that each Vonnegut novel deals with schizophrenia in characters, plot, or theme—a thesis that admirably suits *Mother Night* but that offers many other Vonnegut novels a Procrustian bed on which they must be cut or stretched to fit the theory. For instance, Broer fails to mention entirely the end of the world in *Cat's Cradle*, arguably the novel's central event and one that might have challenged his thesis. (Moreover, the first edition of Broer's book had prominent errors of quotation, fact, and interpretation that went uncorrected in the second; see Morse, "Bringing Chaos to Order" for a partial list.)

Kevin Alexander Boon's *Chaos Theory and the Interpretation of Literary Texts* (1997) skillfully employs chaos theory to illuminate Vonnegut's work. "Man created the checkerboard; God created the karass," Bokonon observed in *Cat's Cradle* (12). Boon identifies a karass as a fractal that reflects natural chaos, which is what Vonnegut attempts to present in his novels. "Others may bring order to chaos, I am bringing chaos to order," announces the narrator of *Breakfast of Champions*—a choice that Boon claims may help account for "marginal characters [being] the focus of Vonnegut's fiction" (Boon, *Chaos* 97). "Vonnegut has always been suspicious of all systems of whatever kind preferring natural chaos to human creations of order" (Morse, "Bringing Chaos" 398).

In *The Novels of Kurt Vonnegut: Imagining Being an American* (2003) I made the case for Vonnegut as "the representative American writer"; that is, Vonnegut is an ethical writer who focuses on representative post–World War II social and national problems while attempting to define what it means to be an American in the second half of the twentieth century. Like Ralph Waldo Emerson, Vonnegut assures us that we are not alone in thinking and feeling as we do about America and our own lives (178). Like Thoreau, he sees himself as a sojourner driving life into a corner and publishing "what he found there" (173). Like Twain, he satirizes his country's and society's shortcomings, failures, and pretensions, but at the same time, also like Twain he "engages and absorbs the common and the vulgar" (107).

Todd Davis's *Kurt Vonnegut's Crusade* (2006) provides a good introduction to Vonnegut and his novels that might have been even stronger had he engaged more widely and deeply with previous criticism. Davis is at his best in discussing ethical issues in Vonnegut and weakest in recalling exact details, such as the shape of Salo in *Sirens*. His labeling Vonnegut's later novels as "postmodern social realism" warrants amplification as their "realism" becomes constrained by two of them taking place in the near future (*Hocus Pocus*, *Bluebeard*), one featuring the successful test of a neutron bomb (*Deadeye Dick*), and another investing a bag lady with incredible corporate wealth (*Jailbird*). Davis lucidly discusses *Timequake* as a "postmodern pastiche" and Vonnegut's "fabulous metaphor" of the timequake.

Postmodernism is also the focus of Robert Tally's *Kurt Vonnegut and the American Novel: A Postmodern Iconography* (2011) where he draws a subtle distinction in arguing that Vonnegut's novels are "his typical modernist rendering of the postmodern condition" (17). Tally brings into the discussion a considerable number of theorists from Gilles Deleuze and Félix Guattari to Michel Foucault, Friedrich Nietzsche, Theodor Adorno, and, more surprisingly, Sacvan Bercovitch, as well as Garrett Hardin and Jean-Paul Sartre. He argues that Vonnegut is a modernist novelist who attempts to represent a postmodern United States. Tally discusses each of the novels under topics such as "Misanthropic Humanism," "The Dialectic of American Enlightenment,"

"Imaginary Communities," and "Apocalypse in the Optative Mood" as he explores his thesis in great detail.

Biography and Biographical Criticism

With Vonnegut's death in 2007, an assessment of both his life and his work became fully realizable, as may be seen in three recent studies: Freese's *The Clown of Armageddon* (2009), Klinkowitz's *Kurt Vonnegut's America* (2009), and Sumner's *Unstuck in Time* (2011). While each of the three discusses systematically all fourteen Vonnegut novels, each does so from a distinct point of view, and each chooses quite different qualities and/or facets to emphasize. Freese, for example, attempts nothing less than total coverage of all of the novels in a very large book that describes everything from their inception to publication to reviews and to later, more considered scholarship. His goal is to account for the reception of every novel, to reach a considered evaluation of each, and to accord Vonnegut his overall place in post–World War II American fiction, while engaging with much of the previous scholarship. The result is an essential resource for Vonnegut studies— one that, alas, would be far more useful had it arrived with an index.

Klinkowitz's *Kurt Vonnegut's America*, while repeating material from his previous books, looks at the totality of Vonnegut's life and then views the fiction in light of that story. Klinkowitz ties both together in a knowledgeable, attractive package chattily told but, unlike Freese, makes no acknowledgement of any Vonnegut scholar's work other than his own with a brief nod to Peter Reed's *The Short Fiction of Kurt Vonnegut* (1997), as if no one else had thought or written about Vonnegut. The result is readable, informative, but for anyone even somewhat acquainted with Vonnegut scholarship, sometimes profoundly irritating. Moreover, questionable assertions from earlier books are repeated in slightly different form here (as discussed earlier).

Sumner's *Unstuck in Time* is not a scholarly book but an "appreciation" in that his emphasis falls on what he finds personally valuable in Vonnegut's fiction. His method is to draw on an outline of

Vonnegut's life to illuminate the various novels while using the novels in turn to illuminate the events in Vonnegut's life as in his discussion of *Bluebeard*'s plot and characters (276). His discussions of *Jailbird* and *Slaughterhouse-Five* are particularly convincing, especially his analysis of the character and function of Edgar Derby (158) and his discussion of Vonnegut and free enterprise (*Jailbird* 223–24). Because he spends most of his time recapitulating the novels' plots in considerable detail, his reading, although thorough and reliable, leaves little room for any extended commentary of his own.[5] His idyllic view of the Vonnegut family (95) contrasts sharply with other biographers (see Shields). A significant stumbling block for experienced Vonnegut readers, critics, or scholars is Sumner's failure to consult much of the critical literature relying instead on a few very early essays: Freese's *The Clown of Armageddon*, Rackstraw's *Love as Always, Kurt*, and various newspaper reviews and comments. The result is a congenial, well-written, but thin, study.

Over time Vonnegut evolved a highly personal style of fiction by injecting himself directly into his work, beginning with the new preface to *Mother Night* written in 1966 and becoming prominent in *Slaughterhouse-Five*'s well-known opening chapter and continuing on into the later novels. In addition, his collections of essays, speeches, and miscellaneous autobiographical fragments *Wampeters, Foma & Granfaloons* (1974), *Palm Sunday* (1981), *Fates Worse than Death* (1991), and *A Man Without a Country* (2005) communicate a core set of humane values rooted deeply in humanism that espouse common decency and courtesy. The nature of Vonnegut's fiction gave rise naturally to a demand for autobiography which, while he was alive, he mostly satisfied through an extensive series of interviews. Readers have a sense that a real person writes these books—a person we'd like to know. Vonnegut himself suggested that as a writer his duty was to try and speak for all people, to "utter [their] . . . painful secret," as Emerson put it (448). "America has proven to be 'an impossibly tough-minded experiment in loneliness,'" he once observed (quoted in Sumner 17).

And, as Sumner rightly suggests, "Vonnegut's art is a record of the ways in which the experiment has gone terribly wrong" (16). Vonnegut believed that "many people need desperately to receive this message: 'I feel and think much as you do, care about many of the things you care about, although most people don't care about them. You are not alone'" (*Timequake* 193; compare Emerson 448).

Charles J. Shields set out to satisfy this interest in Vonnegut and in 2011 published his marvelously full biography, *And So It Goes*, chronicling Vonnegut from before birth to after death discussing much of the fiction along the way. Readers need to be aware, however, that Shields, unlike Sumner, gives a particularly bleak view of much of Vonnegut's life, especially his last years and should, therefore, be read in tandem with Rackstraw's warm and exceptionally well informed *Love as Always, Kurt* (2009) and Jane Yarmolinsky's *Angels without Wings* (1987). The latter is Vonnegut's first wife's view of their life together and particularly the difficulties and opportunities arising from their adopting Vonnegut's sister Alice's children when both she and her husband died.

Rackstraw has a proven track record as a particularly astute reviewer of Vonnegut's novels as well as a perceptive essayist. In describing her relationship with Vonnegut, she includes a good deal of important literary criticism and biographical data. (Both Shields and Sumner— but not Klinkowitz—draw on her observations.) One reviewer praised her as an "epistolary confidante" of Vonnegut's and "[i]n this capacity she does a fine job of suggesting Vonnegut's intellectual vitality, the breadth of his moral concerns, and the insecurities that plagued him" (Almond).

Other research tools for both the novice and experienced Vonnegut reader include the compilation of interviews, *Conversations with Kurt Vonnegut* edited by William Rodney Allen (1988), Marc Leeds's exhaustive *Vonnegut Encyclopedia: An Authorized Compendium* (1995), and Susan Farrell's equally exhaustive *Critical Companion to Kurt Vonnegut* (2008). Vonnegut was never shy about granting interviews and in them often reflected on his fiction as well as whatever else was going on in his life. In Allen's collection, especially perceptive interviews were conducted by Charles Reilly (196), David Standish for *Playboy* (76), David Hayman et al. for the *Paris Review* (168), and Hank Nuwer (240). Another important interview done by Zoltán Abádi-Nagy appeared originally in Hungarian Studies in English (1991) then reprinted later, with unfortunate and crucial omissions by the editors, in Reed and Leeds.

Vonnegut's Reception Today

More than sixty years after the first Vonnegut stories and initial novel appeared, all his novels remain in print and his world-wide reputation as a major American writer appears secure and increases with each passing year. The Library of America honored him with a projected multivolume edition of his works, two of which have been published: *Novels and Stories, 1950–1962* and *Novels and Stories, 1963–1973*. Both *Time* and The Modern Library selected *Slaughterhouse-Five* as one of the one hundred best novels of the twentieth-century. His works have been translated into dozens of languages and outstanding Vonnegut scholars may be found not only in North America, but also in Europe, Asia, and elsewhere. The University of Debrecen (Hungary) library, for instance, has eighty-seven different Vonnegut items in its collection, while its Institute of English and American Studies has a shelf of Vonnegut criticism. The establishment of the Kurt Vonnegut Memorial Library in Indianapolis—with its growing resources for the study of Vonnegut's works, its bringing together Vonnegut enthusiasts through its new journal launched in 2012, *"So It Goes": The Literary Journal of the Kurt Vonnegut Memorial Library*, and its exhibitions and lecture series—is a fitting memorial to the city's most famous citizen. Academic journals world-wide often feature special issues and sections devoted to his work (for example, *Hungarian Journal of English and American Studies* 2011.2 and *Studies in American Humor* 2012). For a writer who had to labor in obscurity without benefit of any reviews for years, then within a year became a celebrity with a devoted following, Vonnegut now retains that devoted following while being the subject of numerous collections of academic essays and full-length books.

Yet Vonnegut still has detractors that scorn his work as too facile, too simple, too popular. Janet Maslin, in her *New York Times* review of Shields's biography, asserted that this "is not a book to rekindle the popularity of its subject's work." She describes the novels after *Slaughterhouse-Five* as becoming "increasingly unreadable," but this statement would be almost impossible to substantiate given the acknowledged clarity of novels such as *Jailbird*, *Galápagos*, and *Bluebeard*. Everyone is entitled to their own opinion, but no one is entitled to their own facts. Vonnegut remains one of the most readable of twentieth-century writers. Moreover, his work attracts wide and deep academic scholarship where he is often acknowledged as a major American writer. As such, his life has been documented and chronicled by an excellent biographer and fine biographical critics, and his work has been analyzed by eminent academic and general literary critics and theorists. In many ways this compendium of essays edited by Robert Tally testifies to the substantial claims now made for his work, whether for his technical and stylistic innovations or his thematic sweep, and for the fact that he is now firmly, if sometimes controversially, ensconced in the American and world literary canon as well as in high school, college, and graduate curricula.

Notes

1. In *The Clown of Armageddon*, Peter Freese gives a quick summary of most of the reviews for each novel beginning with *Player Piano*, while Leonard Mustazza in *Critical Response* gives the full text of some of the more important reviews through *Hocus Pocus*, published in 1990.

2. See, for example, Mirsky 78.

3. Seven years later, Shields repeats that nuclear war caused the demise of humans in *Galápagos* despite published evidence to the contrary (369).

4. Perhaps the most blatant example remains Samuels (30–32).

5. Thus, for example, after a two-page introduction to *Mother Night*, plot outline occupies the next seventeen pages with barely a single page left for a conclusion. *Galápagos* has a two-page introduction, eighteen pages of plot outline, and a final page of conclusion.

Works Cited

Abádi-Nagy, Zoltán. "'Serenity,' 'Courage,' 'Wisdom': A Talk with Kurt Vonnegut." *Hungarian Studies in English* 22 (1991): 23–37. Print.

Allen, William Rodney, ed. *Conversations with Kurt Vonnegut*. Jackson: UP of Mississippi, 1988. Print.

___. *Understanding Kurt Vonnegut*. Columbia: U of South Carolina P, 1991. Print.

Almond, Steve. "God Bless You, Mr. Vonnegut: A Former Lover Renders a Riveting, if Too Reverent, Portrait." Rev of. *Love as Always, Kurt: Vonnegut as I Knew Him*, by Loree Rackstraw. *Boston Globe* 17 May 2009: C.5. Print.

Attebery, Brian. "Cultural Negotiations in Science-Fiction Literature and Film." *Anatomy of Science Fiction*. Ed. Donald E. Morse. Newcastle: Cambridge Scholars P. 2006. 70–82. Print.

Baum, Rudy M. "Editorial." *Chemical and Engineering News*. 85.17 (Apr. 2007): 3. Print.

Bloom, Harold, ed. *Kurt Vonnegut*. New York: Infobase, 2009. Print.

Boon, Kevin A. *At Millennium's End: New Essays on the Work of Kurt Vonnegut*. Albany: SUNY P, 2001. Print.

___. *Chaos Theory and the Interpretation of Literary Texts: The Case of Kurt Vonnegut*. Lewiston, NY: Mellen, 1997. Print.

Broer, Lawrence R. *Sanity Plea: Schizophrenia in the Novels of Kurt Vonnegut*. 1989 Tuscaloosa: U of Alabama P, 1994. Print.

Davis, Todd F. *Kurt Vonnegut's Crusade: Or, How a Postmodern Harlequin Preached a New Kind of Humanism*. Albany: SUNY P, 2006. Print.

Emerson, Ralph Waldo. "The Poet." *Ralph Waldo Emerson: Essays and Lectures*. Ed. Joel Porte. New York: Library of America, 1983. 445–68. Print.

Farrell, Susan. *Critical Companion to Kurt Vonnegut: A Literary Reference to His Life and Work*. New York: Facts on File, 2008. Print.

Fiedler, Leslie. "The Divine Stupidity of Kurt Vonnegut." *Esquire* (September 1970): 195–204. Print.

Flynn, Michael. "The Forest of Time." *The Forest of Time and Other Stories*. New York: TOR, 1997. 19–68. Print.

Freese, Peter. *The Clown of Armageddon: The Novels of Kurt Vonnegut*. Heidelberg, Ger.: Winter, 2009. Print.

Geller, Andy. "Literary 'Titan' Voice of an Era: Pals." *New York Post* 13 Apr. 2007: 25. Print.

Giannone, Richard. *Vonnegut: A Preface to His Novels*. Port Washington, NY: Kennikat, 1977. Print.

Haldeman, Joe. *The Forever War*. 1974. Expanded ed. New York: Avon, 1991. Print.

Hicks, Granville. "Literary Horizons." *Saturday Review* 52.13 (29 Mar. 1969): 25. Print.

Irving, John. "Kurt Vonnegut and His Critics: The Aesthetics of Accessibility." *New Republic* 22 Sep. 1979: 41–49. Print.

Klinkowitz, Jerome. *Kurt Vonnegut*. London: Methuen, 1982. Print. Contemporary Writers Ser.

___. *Kurt Vonnegut's America*. Columbia: U of South Carolina P, 2009. Print.

___. *The Vonnegut Effect*. Columbia: U of South Carolina P, 2004. Print.

___. *Vonnegut in Fact: The Public Spokesmanship of Personal Fiction*. Columbia: U of South Carolina P, 1998. Print.

Klinkowitz, Jerome, and John L. Somer. *The Vonnegut Statement: Original Essays on the Life and Work of Kurt Vonnegut, Jr.* New York: Dell, 1973. Print.

Leeds, Marc. *The Vonnegut Encyclopedia: An Authorized Compendium*. Westport, CT: Greenwood, 1995. Print.

Leeds, Marc, and Peter J. Reed. *Kurt Vonnegut: Images and Representations*. Westport, CT: Greenwood, 2000. Print.

Lundquist, James. *Kurt Vonnegut*. New York: Ungar, 1977. Print.

Maslin, Janet. "Vonnegut in all His Complexity." *New York Times* 3 Nov. 2011: C1. Print.

Mayo, Clark. *Kurt Vonnegut: The Gospel from Outer Space*. San Bernardino, CA: Borgo, 1977. Print.

McInnis, Gilbert. *Evolutionary Mythology in the Writings of Kurt Vonnegut: Darwin, Vonnegut and the Construction of an American Culture*. Palo Alto: Academica P, 2011. Print.

Merrill, Robert. *Critical Essays on Kurt Vonnegut*. Boston: Hall, 1990. Print.

Mirsky, Steve. "Bring Out Your Dead: A Member of the Species Describes How Homo Sapiens Could Go Out." *Scientific American*. Sep. 2012: 78. Print.

Morse, Donald E. "Bringing Chaos to Order: Vonnegut Criticism at Century's End." *Journal of the Fantastic in the Arts* 10.4 (2000): 395–408. Print.

___. *Kurt Vonnegut*. 1992. Mercer Island, WA: Starmont, 1992. Print. Rpt. Rockville, MD: Wildside, 2007. Print.

___. *The Novels of Kurt Vonnegut: Imagining Being an American*. Westport, CT: Preager, 2003. Print.

___. "Kurt Vonnegut: The Once and Future Satirist." *The Dark Fantastic: Selected Essays from the Ninth International Conference on the Fantastic in the Arts*. Ed. Charles. W. Sullivan. Westport, CT: Greenwood, 1997. 161–69. Print.

Mustazza, Leonard, ed. *Forever Pursuing Genesis: The Myth of Eden in the Novels of Kurt Vonnegut*. Lewisburg, PA: Bucknell UP, 1990. Print.

___. *The Critical Response to Kurt Vonnegut*. Westport, CT: Greenwood, 1994. Print.

Pettersson, Bo. *The World According to Kurt Vonnegut. Moral Paradox and Narrative Form*. Abo, Fin.: Abo Akademi UP, 1994. Print.

Pilkington, Ed. "Writers Praise Work of Kurt Vonnegut Who Has Died Age 84." *Guardian Books*. Guardian News and Media Limited, 12 Apr. 2007. Web. 29 Nov. 2012.

Rackstraw, Loree. *Love as Always, Kurt: Vonnegut as I Knew Him*. Cambridge, MA: Da Capo, 2009. Print.

Reed, Peter J. *Kurt Vonnegut, Jr.* New York: Warner, 1972. Print.

___. *The Short Fiction of Kurt Vonnegut*. Westport, CT: Greenwood, 1997. Print.

Reed, Peter J., and Marc Leeds, eds. *The Vonnegut Chronicles: Interviews and Essays*. Westport, CT: Greenwood, 1996. Print.

Samuels, Charles Thomas. "Age of Vonnegut." *New Republic* 164.24 (12 June 1971): 30–32. Print.

Samuelson, David N. "Hard sf." The Routledge Companion to Science Fiction. Eds. Mark Bould, Andrew M. Butler, Adam Roberts, and Sherryl Vint. New York: Routledge, 2009. 494–99. Print.

Schatt, Stanley. *Kurt Vonnegut, Jr.* Boston: Hall, 1976. Print.

Scholes, Robert. "Slaughterhouse-Five." *New York Times Book Review* 6 Apr. 1969: 1, 23. Print.

Shields, Charles J. *And So It Goes. Kurt Vonnegut: A Life*. New York: Holt, 2011. Print.

Simmons, David, ed. Introduction. *New Critical Essays on Kurt Vonnegut*. New York: Palgrave, 2009. xi–xv. Print.

Simpson, George Gaylord. *The Dechronization of Sam Magruder: A Novel*. New York: St. Martin's, 1996. Print.

Southern, Terry. "After the Bomb, Dad Came Up with Ice." *New York Times Book Review* 2 June 1963: 288. Print.

Sumner, Gregory D. *Unstuck in Time: A Journey through Kurt Vonnegut's Life and Novels*. New York: Seven Stories, 2011. Print.

Tally, Robert T., Jr. *Kurt Vonnegut and the American Novel: A Postmodern Iconography*. London: Continuum, 2011. Print.

Thompson, Bob. "So He Goes, Not Quietly: Kurt Vonnegut Helped Us Find Joy in Outrage." *Washington Post*. Washington Post Company, 13 Apr. 2007. Web. 30 Nov. 2012.

Wells, H. G. *The Time Machine*. Ed. Nicholas Ruddick. Peterborough, ON: Broadview, 2001. Print.

Wolfe, Gary K. *Critical Terms for Science Fiction and Fantasy: A Glossary and Guide to Scholarship*. New York: Greenwood, 1986. Print.

Yarmolinsky, Jane Vonnegut. *Angels without Wings: A Courageous Family's Triumph over Tragedy*. Boston: Houghton, 1987. Print.

Worlds of Wordcraft: The Metafiction of Kurt Vonnegut

Ralph Clare

This Unreal American Life

Kurt Vonnegut and many writers at the end of the 1950s and the beginning of the 1960s felt as if literature had reached a dead end, as if everything that could be said had been said before. Modernism, the era of great artistic innovation that had occurred earlier in the century (running from roughly 1910 to 1940), had been a time of explosive formal and stylistic experimentation amid great cultural, social, and political upheaval by writers and poets such as James Joyce, Ernest Hemingway, Virginia Woolf, and T. S. Eliot. The generation of American writers who rose to prominence following World War II, however, was faced not only with this daunting literary legacy to overcome, but also with a host of new and pressing *post*modern concerns, including the legacy of the Holocaust, the advent of the Cold War and McCarthyism, the civil rights movement, and the Korean and Vietnam Wars. Television also began to broadcast important events on a daily basis, bringing them straight into American living rooms; for the first time in history, people could watch everything from sitcoms to the House Un-American Committee trials, from coverage of the Vietnam War to the moon landing. Indeed, television made reality seem stranger than fiction.

In response, some writers wondered whether literature was relevant anymore. How could fiction keep up, let alone compete, with such a world? In 1967, the American writer John Barth famously attested to a sense of "exhaustion" that was linked to the "felt ultimacies of our time" by himself and many other writers who were seeking to reinvent the dead-end literary techniques of the past to suit a confusing present (71). Critics and writers began to discuss what they called "the death of the novel." Vonnegut humorously incorporated this debate into *Slaughterhouse-Five*, when Billy Pilgrim stumbles into a live radio broadcast in which critics are debating "whether the novel was dead or not" (263). Vonnegut's masterpiece proved that the history of literature was still twisting and turning, more suggestive of growth than grave. Nevertheless, the sense was that the novel, seemingly an eighteenth-century invention, was outdated and outmoded.

In keeping with the revolutionary spirit of the 1960s, which encouraged the questioning of authority and the official narratives regarding the Cold War and Vietnam, many writers felt that literature should question its own fundamental assumptions in order to respond radically to this new chaotic and seemingly unreal world (McCaffery 19–22). Many authors began questioning the idea that fiction should inspire what the poet Samuel Taylor Coleridge called a "willing suspension of disbelief" in the reader, who tacitly accepts a fiction on faith and suppresses, to some degree, the knowledge that the narrative is not real. But what happens when a writer breaks this unspoken rule? What happens if a writer deliberately reminds the reader that the story or novel is not real, that it is, in fact, fiction?

Provoking the reader's awareness in such a fashion is a primary aim of metafictional texts, which seek, in one way or another, to expose their own fictional foundations. Metafiction is a literary technique that establishes a special kind of relationship between the reader and the text by calling attention to itself as fiction. As Patricia Waugh writes in *Metafiction: The Theory and Practice of Self-Conscious Fiction*

> *Metafiction* is a term given to fictional writing which self-consciously and systematically draws attention to its status as an artifact in order to pose questions about the relationship between fiction and reality. In providing a critique of their own methods of construction, such writings not only examine the fundamental structures of narrative fiction, they also explore the possible fictionality of the world outside the literary fictional text. (2)

Metafiction, then, is fiction about fiction. It is fiction that self-consciously lets the reader know that what they are reading is fiction, sometimes for playful reasons and sometimes for profound ones.

Many of the major American writers of the 1960s—particularly John Barth, Robert Coover, Thomas Pynchon, and Donald Barthelme—employed metafictional techniques in some fashion. These authors did not invent metafiction (it could be argued that the development of metafiction began with Laurence Sterne's eighteenth-century novel *Tristram Shandy*), but they did develop metafiction to such an extent that they prompted critical responses attempting to understand metafiction. By 1975, metafictional narrative techniques had become so popular that the writer and literary critic Raymond Federman could argue, thenceforth, that "the primary purpose of fiction will be to unmask its own fictionality" (8–9).

Although Vonnegut did not deliberately set out to write experimental novels, his work nonetheless responded uniquely to the challenges of developing new metafictional forms that could represent *and* critique a political and social reality that seemed increasingly unreal to him. Vonnegut's use of metafiction is evidenced in the creation of a self-aware fictional universe populated by recurring characters who are occasionally visited by the character "Kurt Vonnegut," by the fact that so much of "reality" in Vonnegut's stories turns out to be a lie or a script that people have been living by, and through the suggestion that even history itself is textual and that competing historical narratives are constructed with the help of fictional devices.

The Universe According to Vonnegut

Metafictional qualities are inherent in Vonnegut's fictional world, or, to be more accurate, his fictional universe and the characters who populate it. Self-contained fictional worlds have been created by writers before, such as J. R. R. Tolkien's Middle-earth or James Joyce's re-creation of Dublin. In his works, William Faulkner created Yoknapatawpha County, a mythic region of the American South, for which he traced certain fictional families' histories from generation to generation and novel to novel. Literary critic Jerome Klinkowitz writes that Vonnegut "teases" his readers with a "Mod Yoknapatawpha County" (*"Mother Night"* 83).

Vonnegut's universe, spanning the humdrum streets of Midland City to the planet Tralfamadore, appears stranger than these other authors' fictional worlds because of its metafictional aspects. Vonnegut, for instance, seemingly creates continuity in his universe by recasting certain characters in different works. To name a few: Rabo Karabekian has a cameo role in *Breakfast of Champions* and narrates *Bluebeard*; Eliot Rosewater appears in *Slaughterhouse-Five* and *Breakfast*, and he is the subject of *God Bless You, Mr. Rosewater*; Bernard V. O'Hare, Vonnegut's real-life friend introduced *Slaughterhouse-Five*, becomes Bernard B. O'Hare in *Mother Night*; Howard W. Campbell Jr. narrates *Mother Night* and appears in *Slaughterhouse-Five*; and different versions of the Tralfamadorians exist in *The Sirens of Titan* and *Slaughterhouse-Five*, and their planet is mentioned in *Hocus Pocus* and *God Bless You, Mr. Rosewater*. Yet while many of these characters seem familiar, they are not necessarily the "same" incarnation from one novel to the next. They appear almost as reincarnations. Vonnegut deliberately upsets any firm sense of ontological stability in his metafictional universe by self-consciously calling attention to the fact that his characters *are* characters. This also explains why Vonnegut's characters can be two-dimensional and sometimes feel as if they are puppets controlled solely by external forces. At times, Vonnegut expressed a dislike of "realistic novels and their accumulations of nit-picking details" (*Breakfast* 278). Creating characters that feel like caricatures, as critic Charles B. Harris notes, "serves as a conscious burlesque of the whole concept of realism in the novel" (140). This move against realism results in a metafictional universe in which characters will always bear the stamp of their characterization.

Vonnegut's most enduring character, the science-fiction writer Kilgore Trout, is also his most metafictional. Trout himself is a writer, and his stories give Vonnegut an "imaginary library to quote from, a universe of volumes he could have written but need not thanks to Trout's presence as their 'author,'" as Klinkowitz argues (*Vonnegut in Fact* 127). Trout's stories are peppered throughout *God Bless You, Mr. Rosewater*, *Slaughterhouse-Five*, *Breakfast of Champions*, *Jailbird*, and *Timequake* (in *Jailbird* "Kilgore Trout" is merely a pseudonym for another science-fiction writer), and his stories often trigger decisive turns in the novel's plot. Trout's son, Leon, even becomes the ghostly narrator of *Galápagos*. Moreover, Trout embodies Vonnegut's personality to such a degree that Vonnegut calls Trout his "alter ego" (*Timequake* xiii). Trout truly is the portrait of the artist as an aging and cranky man.

The most obvious metafictional elements in Vonnegut's work, however, arrive when Vonnegut enters the story as "himself." Vonnegut's prefaces and prologues do this to a certain degree by directly addressing the reader and disclosing autobiographical details, thereby "violating the aesthetic distance that critics assume must exist between reality and the fictive," according to Klinkowitz (*Vonnegut in Fact* 111). But readers should remember that the prefaces actually *create* the literary persona "Vonnegut," however sincere these characterizations may seem. Even Walt Whitman was careful to depict himself as a rugged "everyman" in the engraving inside the first printing of *Leaves of Grass*. Furthermore, critic Charles Berryman argues that while writing *Breakfast of Champions*, Vonnegut began developing new ways of representing himself fictionally and that the Vonnegut presented in the novel "is an obtuse, comic self-parody" (166).

Vonnegut first radically breaks the boundary between author and text in *Slaughterhouse-Five* (1969), in which the autobiographical "preface" actually appears as the novel's opening chapter, thus problematizing the division between authorial introduction and the story itself. Things get a little weirder, though, when Billy and his comrades arrive at the German prisoner-of-war camp. "I was there," Vonnegut tells his readers (86). This intrusion is disruptive to the narrative's flow and takes the reader briefly out of the story to recall the first words of the novel—"all this happened, more or less" (1)—but this could be construed as simply the author justifying his authority by citing experience. However, when Billy later receives a phone call, a wrong number from a "drunk" whose breath he imagines is "mustard gas and roses" (92), the implication is that the caller is Vonnegut himself, who has earlier confessed to the habit of drunk-dialing (5). This communication with Billy is topped by Vonnegut's final narrative intrusion. This time Vonnegut is clearly in the narrative, and in embarrassing fashion, appearing as the incontinent prisoner caught on the latrine in the German prison camp (160).

In *Breakfast of Champions*, Vonnegut completely collapses the boundary between author and text, and this time not just as a mere character. After Vonnegut beams down into the cocktail lounge of a Holiday Inn to spy on his characters, he announces, "I was on par with the Creator of the Universe" (200). Here, Vonnegut draws the analogy between an author and a god, since both can create worlds in which they are all powerful. Vonnegut flexes his authorial muscles on occasion, destroying and recreating his universe and foretelling the future, but he also admits to the limitations of his power to control his characters: "I could only guide their movements approximately" (202). In fact, the emotionally and spiritually depressed Vonnegut is renewed by the speech of a character he dislikes, the painter Rabo Karabekian, whose words come not from Vonnegut but from "chaos" (218). Later, Vonnegut is even attacked by a fictional Doberman pinscher, Kazak (288–89). While Vonnegut may hold the power to create or destroy characters and his fictional world, there are still certain constraints that the author must abide by, and his fictional characters humorously take on a reality of their own.

The metafictional crux occurs when Vonnegut decides to meet his alter ego Kilgore Trout. As the two writers are similarly distrustful of stable notions of reality, Trout holds a special place in Vonnegut's esteem. During their encounter, Trout senses who the disguised Vonnegut really is since Trout "was the only character I ever created who had enough imagination to suspect that he might be the creation of another human being" (240). During their meeting, Vonnegut informs Trout of his fictional status and tells him that, just as Thomas Jefferson freed his slaves, and Russian writer Leo Tolstoy his serfs, Vonnegut intends "to set at liberty all the literary characters who have served me so loyally" (293). The result is a doubly metafictional moment. Not only has Vonnegut broken the narrative frame and entered as a godlike character, so too has a character, Trout, become aware of this fictional frame and that he is a character in a fictional work.

But this is not mere empty metafictional game-playing, as amusing a scene as it is. While Jefferson can tangibly free his slaves, and Tolstoy his serfs, Tolstoy cannot "free" his literary characters in the same way. Tolstoy's Ivan Ilyich and Anna Karenina are forever trapped in their fictional worlds. The meeting between Vonnegut and Trout is important because it ties the metafictional author/god analogy to the novel's meditation on free will versus determinism (that human beings may be machines). A metaphysical conundrum arises, then, at the level of the text *and* the real world: how can an author truly grant his characters freedom? Similarly, how can a god be omnipotent in a world where beings supposedly have free will? After all, once an author has created a character with a certain history, set of tendencies, and motivations, even the author must adhere to these parameters or risk "breaking" character, just as an all-powerful god cannot control the choices of a being whose will is truly its own, without negating the concept of free will. This theme intersects with the biblical story of Job (which Vonnegut quotes in the epigraph), wherein God decides to test Job's faith by destroying his life. When Job finally curses the day he was born, God confronts Job with a show of his power, telling Job that there are things beyond his comprehension and that he must accept that. Job does so, and God rewards him with a new life. It is an unsettling tale. In his postmodern, metafictional retelling of the Book of Job, however, Vonnegut as author/god admits to his mistakes and powerlessness (he cannot fulfill Trout's wish to be young again), and apologizes to Trout.

In his final novel, *Timequake*, Vonnegut completely deconstructs the wall between author and text. The action of the novel is nearly non-existent (Trout tries to wake the world up after a "timequake" makes everyone repeat the last ten years of their lives), because the novel is really about Vonnegut's failure to write *Timequake One*, *Timequake*'s unpublished predecessor. A collage of autobiographical pieces, political commentary, jokes, and Kilgore Trout stories, the published novel is Vonnegut's goodbye to his characters and readers, and a self-conscious reflection on art and artifice. *Timequake* is thus Vonnegut's most literarily aware novel and even includes a reference to David Markson's metafictional novel *Reader's Block,* which is composed solely of fragments and reflects on the reader's ability to make sense of it all. This is Vonnegut's gambit in *Timequake*, which, in the words of Klinkowitz, is similarly about "the making of the book, a process the reader replicates in reading it" (*Vonnegut's America* 108).

Vonnegut's final appearance—at "a clambake on the beach at Xanadu" with his fictional characters and real-life friends ("if not in person, then represented by look-alikes")—is aptly compared to the final scene of Federico Fellini's film *8 1/2* (1963). Like *8 1/2*, Fellini's metafilm about a creatively blocked, famous filmmaker struggling with his personal life and unable to finish his ninth film, *Timequake* blurs the boundaries between art and life in order to dwell on the connections between them and to emphasize the power of creative fictions to create real and lasting meanings.

Chaos and (Fictional) Order

Because so many of his novel's worlds are based on a lie or fiction that are pulled out from under the characters' feet (and the reader's, for that matter), Vonnegut continually calls his readers' attention to the fictional or textual foundations of the real world. This distrust of "reality" recalls Brian McHale's argument in *Postmodern Fiction* that postmodern (metafictional) writing is primarily concerned with questions of ontology; that is, what is a world, and what is reality? (10, 26–40). Vonnegut believes that "there is no order in the world around us, that we must adapt ourselves to the requirements of chaos instead" (*Breakfast* 210). It is fiction and narrative that weave one's sense of reality, just as the understanding of reality is reproduced in language and narrative as well. Vonnegut's diagnosis of Americans' ills in *Breakfast of Champions*, for instance, is that "they were doing their best to live like people in invented story books" (210). So where does the "story" begin, and where does it end? The chaotic plot twists in Vonnegut's most reality-bending novels raise such metafictional questions about the complex relationship between reality and textuality.

The Sirens of Titan (1959) seems, at first, to be a straightforward science-fiction novel, but is actually a metafictional parody of one. The novel signals its playfulness in the dedication, wherein Vonnegut claims that "all persons, places, and events in this book are real." Another self-conscious wink to readers occurs when Vonnegut offers the notion of "chrono-synclastic infundibula" to explain how Winston Niles Rumfoord is able to move throughout space and time. The explanation comes from a fictional children's encyclopedia (13–14). Not interested in scientific verisimilitude, Vonnegut relishes the ridiculousness of the concept, and lampoons those who feel the need to legitimate their fictions. Even the cliché of the Martian invasion is as humorous as it is horrifying and does not consist of any actual Martians.

The novel is also highly aware of texts and textuality. Letters, songs, and excerpts from various fictional books are sprinkled throughout, including Rumfoord's *Pocket History of Mars* and his *Authorized Revised Bible*, which themselves lead to scholarly debate by other quoted authors. The novel even quotes itself and its fictional sources in the epigraphs to each chapter. This textuality extends to the world of the novel itself. Rumfoord believes he is rewriting human history (and even invents a new religion) by scripting a number of important events, from the Martian invasion to the return and exile of the novel's protagonist, Malachi Constant. His world is based explicitly on the texts that he writes, which because of his time traveling, are curiously already "written" in the future. Vonnegut also shows, through Rumfoord's authorial success, that people actually desire fictions and rituals to live by.

Rumfoord the author-savior, however, eventually learns that even his part has been scripted by the Tralfamadorians. Just as Rumfoord used Malachi Constant (whose name means "faithful messenger," another allusion to text), so too does the Tralfamadorian robot Salo use Rumfoord. Somewhat like in *Breakfast of Champions*, the "author" realizes he is a character after another character reveals that *he* is the author. In fact, Salo admits that all of human history has been manipulated by the Tralfamadorians in order to send messages to Salo while he awaits a replacement part for his ship. All of human history, it turns out, is a text. But Salo, like Constant, is also just a messenger, and it is no surprise that such a metafictional novel actually has a punch line. Salo's long-awaited message to the galaxy, which translates simply to "greetings," mocks those who think they can (re)write history so easily as Rumfoord, and Rumfoord's great epic becomes a simple joke. In short, *The Sirens of Titan* marks its metafictional status in parodying science fiction, foregrounding its textuality, and revealing that "reality" consists of a number of texts or scripts that are forever being written, edited, and emended.

Mother Night also foregrounds its textuality by claiming to be the "confession" of an American playwright-turned-spy, Howard Campbell Jr., who "plays" a Nazi radio propagandist during the war. Vonnegut also self-consciously reveals the novel's moral in the Introduction (added in 1966 to the 1961 novel), and poses as the book's editor in the Editor's Note, warning us to be wary of Campbell's "lies." Readers of the novel's first edition, which did not contain the Introduction, would have had a difficult time establishing whether Campbell *was* real, especially since *Mother Night* metafictionally includes infamous real-life Nazis like Rudolf Hoess, Joseph Goebbels, and Adolf Eichmann as characters. Yet Vonnegut's metafiction here is not simply a resurrection of modernism's unreliable narrator trope. By conflating the confessional genre with a light parody of the spy genre, Vonnegut blends epistemological with ontological concerns, creating an unstable world of disguises, trap doors, and role-playing. Metafictional concerns ultimately mingle with metaphysical ones because people *actually are* "what they pretend to be" (v). As befits a novel about a playwright, identities in *Mother Night* are based on performance.

Fictions are, once again, shown to be powerful forces. As a romantic artist who idealizes reality, Campbell ignores the rise of fascism in the prewar Germany where he lives because he believes art and truth transcend the world. But he is dragged back to reality and recruited as an American spy by Major Frank Wirtanen. Campbell complains but accepts the task, partly because he is "a ham" who enjoys acting (39). He soon fills the role of propagandist, even creating a ridiculous costume/ uniform (97–98). The fiction works so well it fools his wife, Helga, and even Wirtanen despises him after the war (187–88). He fools the Nazis and the German people too, since "so many people *wanted* to believe me" (160). Unfortunately, Campbell persists in believing, idealistically, that a higher truth exists somewhere else, just like "the honest me I hid so deep inside" (39). Campbell does not see that in a world where performativity *is* reality, one cannot perform a role and then argue that it is a pretense.

Campbell is so accustomed to performing that when he has no role to play later in life, he freezes: "I had absolutely no reason to move in any direction. What had made me move through so many dead and pointless years was curiosity" (232). This metafictional pause comically reveals Campbell's failure to act on his own account, which leads to his manipulation by others. Those who follow any script mindlessly— as the Nazis who were "just following orders"—are dangerous because they believe their actions, no matter how abominable, are justified by "higher" truths or a divine authority that exist outside of the world.

Mother Night thus inverts the warning against the hubris of "scripting" history in *The Sirens of Titan* by cautioning against accepting someone else's casting decision. The "truth" lies somewhere in-between: while overwhelming forces may be shaping, or writing, history, individuals still have choices to make, however limited, in terms of how they will perform the role in the "script" in which they find themselves. Campbell's unacknowledged guilt is essentially due to his non-choices to fight against fascism and to become a spy. He submits to "performing a part" and does not truly embrace his role as a spy as he does his role as a Nazi propagandist. As Robert T. Tally Jr. writes, "even if that were simply a part he played, he played it authentically" (51). Campbell is more an "accidental" spy than an "accidental" Nazi, following whatever script is placed in front of him and never taking personal responsibility for his actions. Arpad Kovacs, a Hungarian Jew who joined the *Schutzstaffel* (SS) and played "a pure and terrifying Aryan," is a case in point (12–13). Kovacs's anger at the Jews who "passively" went to their deaths in the camps is clearly a psychological response born of his own unfortunate form of resistance. He looks "bitter and affronted" recalling those days and lambastes Campbell's propaganda as "weak," but he proudly admits to killing fourteen SS soldiers and regrets not killing Eichmann. Kovacs was truly "working undercover," while Campbell was just performing under one.

Kovacs, as well as the guilt-wracked Andor Gutman, an Estonian Jew who volunteered for the *Sonderkommando* (who led fellow prisoners into the gas chambers and carried out their corpses), bear the terrible scars of history but do not offer excuses for their actions. They live having learnt, as Todd F. Davis writes about *Mother Night*, that "the fictions we construct, even if their constructedness is exposed, still do as much harm as those that are hidden" (60). Whether Campbell's suicide for "crimes against himself" at the novel's end symbolizes a true understanding of his culpability or merely marks another escape through melodramatic performance—"Goodbye, cruel world!" (268)—remains a troubling question.

Cat's Cradle is the most metatextual of all Vonnegut's novels. While researching a book about the inventor of the atomic bomb, the novel's narrator, Jonah, travels to the politically faltering Republic of San Lorenzo. There he learns about the state's most-wanted man, the elusive religious mystic Bokonon, author of *The Books of Bokonon*. Yet Jonah confesses at the beginning of the novel that he, as a result of his journey, has converted to Bokononism. In fact, the novel's epigraph comes from *The Books of Bokonon*, thus immediately confusing the true boundaries between the novel and the real world. Indeed, *The Books* take up a life of their own, as Jonah quotes from them numerous times throughout the story. Jonah even interprets all his experiences through the tenets of Bokononism. As such, *Cat's Cradle* is a book about a book, and a fiction about the power of fictions.

The Books function as a metafictional device because they comment on the fictional or textual nature of all belief systems. As Jonah says, "anyone unable to understand how a useful religion can be founded on lies will not understand this book" (6). To this end, Vonnegut creates his own religion out of several delightful concepts, such as the *karass*, "teams that do God's Will without ever discovering what they are doing" (2); *foma*, or harmless lies (191); *granfalloons*, or false *karasses* (91); and *sinookas*, the tendrils of a person's life (6). In short, an entire belief system with its own rituals and language grows with every turn of the page. Note that Vonnegut could have merely mentioned the ideas of Bokononism, but actually quoting from *The Books* makes the religion seem more "real" to the reader while simultaneously calling attention to how fictions and texts similarly work in real life. The fiction that challenges reality exposed the fictionality of reality itself.

Moreover, *The Books* have a metafictional side to them as well. "Nothing in this book is true," *The Books* quotation in the novel's epigraph declares, and the first sentence of *The Books* is, "all of the true things I am about to tell you are shameless lies" (5). Such self-conscious and contradictory statements force the reader to reflect not only on the claims to knowledge and truth that one may hope to find in *The Books* (Bokonon warns the reader to accept the limits of knowledge), but also to question the possibility of extracting the one "true" meaning from any text at the exclusion of other readings. Vonnegut is warning against the fetishization of texts and meaning here. A final, authoritative copy of *The Books*, for instance, does not even exist, since Bokonon is continually rewriting it (183). What *The Books* do, and surely what Vonnegut's metafiction intends to do, is to encourage the reader/believer's willing suspension of belief, rather than the usual willing suspension of disbelief.

Textuality, as in *Sirens*, does not reside only in *The Books* either. When we learn that the entire political reality of San Lorenzo is based on a fiction imagined by the shipwrecked Lionel Boyd Johnson (who later changes his name to Bokonon) and Corporal Earl McCabe (who assumes the role of dictator) in order to save the hopelessly depressed island, Vonnegut again underscores the textual and fictional foundations of reality. The islanders could escape from "the awful truth." But, "as the living legend of the cruel tyrant in the city and the gentle holy man in the jungle grew, so, too, did the happiness of the people grow. They were all employed full time as actors in a play" (174–75). As in *Mother Night* and *Breakfast*, characters become "actors" who merely follow a script and operate within the limited roles that they haven't chosen. Reality, and a dismal one at that, turns out to have a fictional basis—a fiction that eventually becomes the reality. Yet the desire to follow a single, stable script even leads Bokonon's followers astray. Their mass suicide in the face of a world apocalypse would appear to show that they did not quite understand Bokonon's "bittersweet lies" (2) and that *foma* or fictions can still have real and negative consequences if taken seriously. Vonnegut's metafictional reflection on fiction, belief, and truth allows us, however, to learn the crucial lessons that Bokonon's followers do not.

(Re)writing History

Vonnegut's metafiction also challenges the idea of history as a stable and unified narrative, especially in *Slaughterhouse-Five*. Literary critic

Linda Hutcheon calls the kind of writing that problematizes the relationship between history and narrative "historiographic metafiction," which refutes the natural or common-sense methods of distinguishing between historical fact and fiction. It refuses the view that only history has a truth claim, both by questioning the ground of that claim in historiography and by asserting that history and fiction are discourses, human constructs, signifying systems, and both derive their major claim to truth from that identity. (93) Through its suspicion and revision of the commonly accepted notion of history, *Slaughterhouse-Five* proves to be a fine example of historiographic metafiction.

Slaughterhouse-Five offers a meta-moment in the questioning of official historical narratives when Billy Pilgrim shares a hospital room with Bertram Copeland Rumfoord, a history professor at Harvard. Rumfoord, "the official Air Force historian" (236), is rewriting a history of the Allied bombing of Dresden in World War II, which Vonnegut himself experienced. Rumfoord is emending his own earlier account because there "was almost nothing in the twenty-seven volumes [on the Air Force in World War II] about the Dresden raid" (244). Once happy to have erased the gritty details of the raid from the record, Rumfoord now laments that "Americans have finally heard about Dresden." Adding that, "A lot of them know now how much worse it was than Hiroshima" (245). He defends his veritable silence on the bombing because "a lot of bleeding hearts . . . might not think it was such a wonderful thing to do," and claims, ironically, that his new account will be "from the official Air Force standpoint, it'll all be new" (245), which it already supposedly was. Vonnegut thus calls our attention to the fact that the victors and those in power write histories that reflect their points of view, often through the total exclusion of other voices, viewpoints, and inconvenient facts.

Rumfoord's aggressive assertion that the bombing "had to be done" (253) is never directly challenged by Billy (or Vonnegut), who simply claims, as does Vonnegut in the novel's opening chapter, "I was there" (245, 247). This reminder of a first-person account from the ground deflates any narrative that comes from on high, like the Air Force's story. Even Rumfoord belies that his narrative is incomplete, telling Billy, "you must have had mixed feelings, there on the ground" (254). Vonnegut, therefore, is fairer than Rumfoord in his historical portrayal of Dresden since his novel is able to criticize the initial silence about the raid while offering arguments for and against it. The novel's context creates a strong condemnation of war, but the debate is nevertheless given space to play out. Vonnegut's self-reflective metahistorical "fiction" is, then, more historically complete and accurate than some of the "official" narratives of the time.

To this end, Vonnegut brings actual historical documents into the novel. Rumfoord works with President Harry S. Truman's atomic bomb speech (237–38), as well as three of the forwards (written by his friends) to David Irving's *The Destruction of Dresden* (239). This underscores the textuality of history—that it is a written narrative assembled from various and varying accounts. *Slaughterhouse-Five*, therefore, is doing "real" historical work, which is why Vonnegut ponders what good his history-as-fiction can do to stop wars after a friend suggests that he "write an anti-*glacier* book instead" (4). Moreover, Vonnegut is metafictionally aware of the historical representations of war and the history of these representations. He discusses several history books with the O'Hares (19–23), and carefully notes the fears of Mary O'Hare, the wife of his war buddy Bernard, who is concerned that Vonnegut's novel will glorify war: "You'll pretend you were men instead of babies, and you'll be played in the movies by Frank Sinatra and John Wayne or some of those other glamorous, war-loving, dirty old men" (18). Instead of contributing to the dubious depictions of war, as do many Hollywood films, Vonnegut heeds Mary's advice and shows the novel's only "hero," who is tragically shot for stealing a teapot after the bombing of Dresden, reading Stephen Crane's *The Red Badge of Courage* (122–23), a novel that refuses to idealize war. In short, Vonnegut writes a powerful metafictional antiwar book that allows readers to understand how history is written and constructed, and what is at stake in its various revisions and representations.

Conclusion

While metafiction's heyday in the 1960s and 1970s has passed, some younger writers have continued to expand on its possibilities in their work, such as David Foster Wallace, Mark Z. Danielewski, and Jonathan Lethem. Today, metafiction has permeated all aspects of popular culture, from television shows such as *Seinfeld* and *The Simpsons* to such films as *Inception* and *Black Swan*. Even some advertising employs metafictional strategies, airing purposefully cheesy commercials that "wink" at the viewer by playing on the cliché conventions of advertising. Not all metafiction, then, has a true cutting edge to it. Vonnegut's use of metafiction, however, goes far beyond the window dressing of advertisements or the playfulness of television. Vonnegut's deft use of metafiction throughout his work reminds us of the power and potential of language to construct reality, to affect one's behaviors and beliefs, and to define history itself.

Works Cited

Barth, John. "The Literature of Exhaustion." *The Friday Book: Essays and Other Nonfiction*. New York: Putnam, 1984. 62–76. Print.

Berryman, Charles. "Vonnegut's Comic Persona in *Breakfast of Champions*." *Critical Essays on Kurt Vonnegut*. Ed. Robert Merrill. Boston: Hall, 1990. Print.

Davis, Todd F. *Kurt Vonnegut's Crusade: Or, How a Postmodern Harlequin Preached a New Kind of Humanism*. Albany: SUNY P, 2006. Print.

Federman, Raymond. "Surfiction—Four Propositions in Form of an Introduction." *Surfiction: Fiction Now and Tomorrow*. Ed. Raymond Federman. Chicago: Swallow, 1975. Print.

Harris, Chales B. "Illusion and Absurdity: The Novels of Kurt Vonnegut." *Critical Essays on Kurt Vonnegut*. Ed. Robert Merrill. Boston: Hall, 1990. Print.

Hutcheon, Linda. *A Poetics of Postmodernism: History, Theory, Fiction*. New York: Routledge, 1988. Print.

Klinkowitz, Jerome. *Kurt Vonnegut's America*. Columbia: U of South Carolina P, 2007. Print.

___. "*Mother Night, Cat's Cradle*, and the Crimes of Our Time." Merrill 82–93. Print.

___. *Vonnegut in Fact: The Public Spokesmanship of Personal Fiction*. Columbia: U of South Carolina P, 1998. Print.

McCaffery, Larry. *The Metafictional Muse: The Works of Robert Coover, Donald Barthelme, and William H. Gass*. Pittsburgh: U of Pittsburgh P, 1982. Print.

McHale, Brian. *Postmodernist Fiction*. New York: Routledge, 1987. Print.

Merrill, Robert, ed. *Critical Essays on Kurt Vonnegut*. Boston: Hall, 1990. Print.

Tally, Robert T., Jr. *Kurt Vonnegut and the American Novel: A Postmodern Iconography*. London: Continuum, 2011. Print.

Vonnegut, Kurt. *Breakfast of Champions*. New York: Dell, 1973. Print.

___. *Cat's Cradle*. 1963. New York: Dial Press, 2010. Print.

___. *Mother Night*. 1961. New York: Dial Press, 2009. Print.

___. *The Sirens of Titan*. New York: Dell, 1959. Print.

___. *Slaughterhouse 5*. 1969. New York: Dial Press, 2009. Print.

___. *Timequake*. New York: Putnam's, 1997. Print.

Waugh, Patricia. *Metafiction: The Theory and Practice of Self-Conscious Fiction*. New York: Methuen, 1984. Print.

Walker Percy: Kurt Vonnegut for Adults_____

Henry L. Carrigan, Jr.

In the late 1950s and into the 1960s, Kurt Vonnegut's novels, especially *Cat's Cradle* and *Slaughterhouse-Five*, dotted college campuses and high-school classrooms as eager youth found in Vonnegut a voice who spoke for them and with which they could identify. Here were novels that with irony and morose humor pointed to the terrible ravages of war and its enduring impact both on those who fought in the conflicts and those who did not, that cautioned against blindly embracing scientific achievements that were contributing to the destruction of humankind, and that questioned the wisdom of various authority figures. In a society where the gap between age and youth grew wider every day, and the disagreements about politics, culture, and morality evolved into full-scale violent confrontations, Vonnegut's novels at once named these struggles but also offered a way beyond them. In addition to these two major novels of the time, Vonnegut also wrote science fiction, such as *The Sirens of Titan* (1959) and some of the stories in *Welcome to the Monkey House* (1968) as well as one of the plots in *Slaughterhouse-Five*, in which he asked questions about the nature of humanity and explored the ways that humankind would measure up against if and when it met up with life that resembled it but differed dramatically from it. Yet, Vonnegut was no existentialist—a philosophy popular in the 1960s through the early 1970s among college students and their professors that encouraged individuals the embrace the courage to exist as an authentic person by throwing off an identity not of their own making in the midst of the despair and anxiety around them—and his novels depict characters who, in spite of the ravages that humanity often wreaks on itself, find some hope even in the midst of hopelessness without giving up and giving into a constant malaise caused by their surroundings. These characters reject institutions that offer false hopes and lies about the human situation—religion, science—recognizing that they themselves must gather the will to carry on with dignity and authenticity in the face of a world falling apart. Vonnegut's novels spoke to a generation ready and willing to embrace such a quest for human dignity during the years when the Vietnam War and duplicitous politicians trampled over respect for such dignity.

When Walker Percy's last novel, *The Thanatos Syndrome* (1987), was published, critic Robert Trower commented in the *New York Review of Books* that Percy was "the adult's Kurt Vonnegut" (qtd. in Samway 392). Indeed, the two writers resemble each other in many ways. Each writer used satire to reveal the gaping holes between reality and illusion in the worlds of their characters, and by extension, of course, our own world. Percy and Vonnegut each explore themes of alienation, loss, and despair through characters attempting to make some sense of life in a world gone somehow awry and to restore some dignity, wholeness, and hope to this world. In his own way, Percy had been popular among college students just as Vonnegut had, but students weren't often as likely to have a copy of Percy's *The Moviegoer* in their backpacks as much as they were likely to have *Slaughterhouse-Five*. While Vonnegut's novels were entertaining, with relatively simple plots and characters with whom readers could identify quickly, Percy's novels were more philosophical, requiring some effort on the part of the reader to understand and identify with the characters, and they pushed readers to untangle complex themes of alienation, despair, repetition, and wandering. Percy's characters sometimes wander aimlessly in search of a purpose in life, and in this wandering they confront difficult choices about the way to live their lives: Should they live the "normal" life of a responsible businessman or doctor supporting a family in a comfortable middle-class neighborhood, or is such a way of life false, never allowing the character to confront the issues of what it means to be human in a world falling apart? While Vonnegut's readers picked up his books after reading Joseph Heller and Norman Mailer, Percy's readers often came to his novels after reading Albert Camus's novels and essays or Jean Paul Sartre's novel, *Nausea*, or the writings of the Danish philosopher Søren Kierkegaard. Percy's first novel, *The Moviegoer*

(1961), for example, portrays a young man, Binx Bolling, whose very life is defined by wayfaring and looking at life from the outside: He watches movies and loses himself in them as a way of coping with and making sense of his everyday life. *The Moviegoer* captures the heavy burden of the malaise of everydayness through which all individuals move on their quest for a life of authentic meaning; the novel also illustrates that this quest is never complete, that every person is a pilgrim and a wayfarer on this never-ending search. Being human, for Percy, means being plunged into this everydayness and being confronted with the constant "either-or" of existence: either fall into the malaise and live an inauthentic life or continue on the search for a way beyond the malaise and embrace honesty and authenticity.

Yet, there are some major differences between the two writers and nowhere more evident than in Percy's Catholicism—though he considered himself a lapsed Catholic and thus not a practicing one, the major elements of the Catholic faith are essential components of his novels—his Southern heritage and his medical training. A great reader of the Catholic medieval theologian, Percy portrayed all of his characters struggling with the tension between faith and doubt. Can faith and knowledge go hand-in-hand? Can they complement each other, or are they completely incompatible? Percy places all of his main characters in situations where they must ask such questions, where at the same time they ask existential questions about the meaning of life. Moreover, the Catholic Church provides much of the backdrop against which many of his novels are set in and around New Orleans, a city that embraces a carnivalesque version of the Catholic observance of Lent each year in Mardi Gras celebrations. In addition, in at least two of his novels, *Love in the Ruins* (1971) and *The Second Coming* (1980), Percy places his main characters in a post-apocalyptic world where the protagonist struggles to distinguish the heroes from the villains. Percy takes this end-time scenario straight out of the biblical book of Revelation that depicts the devastation of this present world in a battle between forces of light (good) and forces of darkness (evil) out of which emerges a new ideal world where order and justice is restored.

Percy's Southern roots also run deep. After his father died, Percy and his family went to live with Percy's uncle, William Alexander Percy, in Greenville, Mississippi; his uncle was a poet and a well-known man of letters whose book, *Lanterns on the Levee* (1941), provided important insights into pre-World War II southern culture, and the younger Percy soaked up his uncle's Southernness, recognizing the deep code of honor and shame that characterized Southern culture as well as the emphasis on the separation of whites and blacks that existed as part of the fabric of the culture well into Percy's own life. In *The Last Gentleman* (1966) and *Love in the Ruins*, Percy's protagonists struggle with issues of racial equalityWalker Percy and" and codes of honor, themes that are absent from Vonnegut's novels.

Percy's medical training also influences his writing, and two of his novels—*Love in the Ruins* and *The Second Coming*—feature Dr. Thomas More as their main character. While More struggles with philosophical and religious questions regarding the nature of humankind, his understanding of what constitutes human identity derives from neurology, and he believes that many of the tensions facing humanity can be resolved by diagnosing a medical condition and then treating it with the best scientific instruments. While Vonnegut and Percy deal with similar themes regarding the human condition, Percy's Catholicism, his Southern heritage, and his medical training lead him to ask significantly questions about these themes that Vonnegut often asks.

Roughly contemporaries—Walker Percy was born in 1916 and died in 1990 and Kurt Vonnegut was born in 1922 and died in 2007—Percy and Vonnegut witnessed some of the most devastating events of the twentieth century—the Great Depression, World War II, the Holocaust, the Vietnam War, among others—and these experiences shaped the visions that produced their novels. Born in Indianapolis, Indiana, Vonnegut was the youngest of three children. His father was an architect; his older brother was a scientist, and when Vonnegut entered Cornell

University in 1940, he followed in his brother's footsteps, majoring in chemistry, even though he had little interest in science; he was more engaged in his editorial work on the college newspaper, *The Cornell Daily Sun*, for which he not only wrote columns but also contributed comics. Vonnegut would follow this aptitude for drawing by illustrating many of his later novels with line drawings to illustrate particular scenes in the fiction. In 1944, his mother committed suicide, an event that he never overcame and with which he dealt the rest of his life. Ironically, Walker Percy's mother died in a car crash that he believed was a suicide. Vonnegut enlisted in the Army while at Cornell, and his experience in the war profoundly influenced his fiction. Captured as a prisoner of war by the Germans, Vonnegut witnessed the firebombing of Dresden by the Allies, which he and other POWs survived by being sequestered in an underground slaughterhouse to which the Germans referred to as "slaughterhouse-five." Vonnegut captured his experience most forcefully in the novel of the same name, but the firebombing and its display of man's inhumanity to man finds its way thematically into most of Vonnegut's fiction. After the war, he lived in Chicago, where he worked as a newspaper reporter and took coursework for a Master's degree in anthropology at the University of Chicago. He soon left Chicago for Schenectady, New York, where he worked as a technical writer for General Electric and started writing short stories that he would soon begin submitting to a number of magazines in hopes of publication. Initially unsuccessful in these attempts, he was on the verge of giving up when he was offered a writing job at the University of Iowa Writers' Workshop; during this time, his novel, *Cat's Cradle*, became a best-seller, and his writing life, never easy, took off. Many of Vonnegut's autobiographical collages and essay collections, especially *Palm Sunday* (1981) and *Wampeters, Foma, & Grandfalloons* (1974) contain the outline of his life, and he laid his life bare in his novels, starting with *Slaughterhouse-Five* (and in some ways even before then). Throughout his novels and stories, Vonnegut draws on these experiences to focus on themes of anti-authoritarianism, the perils and promises of science, pessimism about the future of humanity, resignation in the face of this pessimism, and the will to go on with the belief that humanity will triumph over its shortcomings.

Born in Birmingham, Alabama, Walker Percy lived all his life in the South. By the time he was fifteen, both of his parents had died, and he lived with his uncle, William Alexander Percy, until he entered the University of North Carolina at Chapel Hill, where he studied chemistry; four years later, Percy began medical school at Columbia University where he entered into psychotherapy in order to try to come to terms with his family legacy of suicide. While he was an intern at Bellevue Hospital in New York City, he contracted tuberculosis and during his treatment period he embarked on a program of reading that included Kierkegaard, Camus, Thomas Mann, and Dostoevsky, among others. Such reading, along with his conversion to Catholicism a few years later, deeply influenced his own writing. After he recuperated, he realized that few patients would consult a physician with tuberculosis, so he moved to New Orleans and then to Covington, Louisiana, where he would live for the rest of his life. Not long after his return to the South, he began working out his ideas about language, philosophy, and religion in essays; in 1961, after two years of writing and rewriting, he published his first novel, *The Moviegoer* to great acclaim, winning the National Book Award in 1962. In the succeeding years, he wrote five novels—*The Last Gentleman, Love in the Ruins, Lancelot, The Second Coming,* and *The Thanatos Syndrome*—as well as two collections of essays—*The Message in the Bottle* and *Lost in the Cosmos.* In his fiction and nonfiction, Percy explores humans as wayfarers in this world, searching to make sense of the culture and nature around them by symbolizing the world in language and signs, but discovering that science alone cannot offer humans a full view of our human nature or the nature of the world.

Vonnegut's fourth novel, *Cat's Cradle,* introduces themes and ideas that dominate the rest of Vonnegut's fiction and nonfiction. The novel's epigraph offers in a nutshell the manner in which Vonnegut's protagonists, and especially the characters in this particular novel, hope to live and illustrates the manner in which these characters hope the world goes: "'Nothing in this book is true. 'Live by the foma [harmless untruths] that make you brave and kind and healthy and happy.'" The novel takes its name from the children's game of string that one of the main characters, the absent-minded scientist Dr. Felix Hoenikker, is always playing as he is working on the substance that has the power to alter the physical structure of the universe. Hoenikker's son, Newt, after years of having his father encourage him to see the cat and see the cradle in the game, gives up with exasperation, seeing through the lie and the joke by declaring that there's "no damn cat, and no damn cradle" (114). The plot of the novel revolves around the Hoenikker family and its various members' reaction to their father and to his invention of ice-nine. John, aka Jonah, the narrator of the novel, insinuates himself into the family, recording for posterity the divisions in the family as well as the disastrous results that occur when Dr. Hoenikker's invention gets into the wrong hands. In a subplot, John learns about Bokononism, a religion that is on the one hand is cynical about the nature of the world and on the other is very loving and peaceful, promoting rituals such as communicating love and joy through touching the bare souls of each other's feet. In the end, disaster cannot be averted, and ice-nine falls into hands that misuse it, destroying the world by freezing it. Bokonon, the founder of Bokononism, has the last laugh: "If I were a younger man, I would write the history of human stupidity . . . and I would make a giant statue of myself, lying my back, grinning horribly, and thumbing my nose at You Know Who" (191).

In an allusion to the opening words of another great American novel, *Moby-Dick* ("Call me Ishmael"), the narrator of *Cat's Cradle* declares in the novel's opening sentence: "Call me Jonah" (11). Although the narrator quickly tells the reader that his real name is John, he has nevertheless offered a compelling clue about the nature of the story that the narrator is about to tell. The first three sentences alone offer a number of clues about the themes of the novel. First, the narrator's very name alludes to the great—or not so great, depending on one's point of view—biblical prophet, Jonah. In the biblical book of Jonah, the teller of that tale follows the exploits of a reluctant prophet who receives a word from God to perform his prophetic duty but who seeks every way he can to run from that duty. In a kind of ironic turn of events, Jonah buys a ticket on a ship that will take him away from his task, and in so doing invokes God's wrath; God sends a violent storm to force Jonah to turn back, and when he refuses, God sends a fish to swallow him. Jonah eventually repents and accepts God's call. The story remains one of the Bible's most humorous and ironic tales, and though Vonnegut is no believer, the use of the name Jonah in the opening sentence signals that the novel will be a tale told by an outsider who seeks to understand the terrifying judgment—religious, political, cultural, scientific—that humans often invoke against each other. This theme becomes very clear in the novel's opening pages. Second, the narrator reveals that his name is John—even after encouraging readers to call him Jonah—and this name operates on two thematic levels. On one level, and following the biblical structure invoked by the name Jonah, John recalls two biblical characters whose activity provides a parallel for this narrator's activity. The John of the Gospels in the New Testament is the prophet who announces the coming of a new figure, Jesus of Nazareth, who will change the world; in the same way, this John announces the coming of a figure to the reader, Newt Hoenikker, whose work will change the world, and much in the same way that Jesus changes the world, for Newt and his siblings introduce a new world order through their use of ice-nine. On another lever, John of Patmos is the biblical figure who is exiled to an island, much as this novel's John is exiled to San Lorenzo, where he records his dreams and visions of the end. John of Patmos's visions are recorded in the biblical book of Revelation, while this novel's John's visions and tales are recorded in this book that he was going to call *The Day the World Ended*, but now called *Cat's Cradle*. Finally, the novel's opening sentences contain an allusion to yet another important work of literature, the nineteenth-century poet Samuel Taylor Coleridge's "The Rime of the Ancient Mariner." Not long after he introduces himself, John aka Jonah forcefully utters the word: *Listen* (11). In Coleridge's poem, the Ancient Mariner meets the Wedding Guest and compels him—simply by commanding the guest to "listen"—to hear his tale of woe. Like the Mariner, John is one of the few to have survived to tell the tale, and he tells his tale so that readers must listen to him if they are to avoid the same mistake and if they are to learn the greatest lessons about the nature of humanity that John has learned on his own journey.

Vonnegut's little apocalypse warns clearly of the arrogance of a humanity that sees reality in the fabric of a game—cat's cradle—that is only a lie conceived by a liar and passed along, like many other lies that humans formulate, as the truth. The bumbling Felix Hoenikker might be forgiven for his inability to see the truth, or to believe that science contains the ultimate truth about the world and humanity, but there are plenty of other like him whose passionate embrace of science interferes with their ability to see the truth clearly. For Vonnegut, Bokonon (and religion) and not Hoenikker (and science) have the last word. In spite of the tendency of humans to operate on their own with no thought for others—and sometimes intentionally to work for the harm of others—individuals can gather the will and the strength to overcome such attitudes. On the one hand, one of the novel's characters, Fred Castle, expresses the persistent pessimism that characterizes a world in which each person lives for himself or herself with no thought of others: "Man is vile, and man makes nothing worth making, know nothing worth knowing" (116). Yet, on the other hand, individuals are not alone in this world, and participation in community fosters solidarity and love and can overcome the selfish tendency of individual humans. In the opening pages of the novel, John, the narrator, reveals that "we Bokononists believe that humanity is organized into teams, teams that do God's Will without ever discovering what they are doing" (11). This tension between individual and community, love and justice, pessimism and hope so dramatically portrayed in *Cat's Cradle* underlies all of Vonnegut's novels.

In his essay, "Notes for a Novel about the End of the World," collected in *The Message in the Bottle*, Walker Percy ruminates on the nature and effect of a novel that depicts the end of the world: "A serious novel about the destruction of the United States and the end of the world should perform the function of prophecy in reverse. The novelist writes about the coming end in order to warn about present ills and so avert the end" (*Message* 101). Taking seriously his role as a prescient prognosticator, Percy attempts in all of his novels to warn about the ills of his society and the ways that such ills might be cured so as to avert disaster. He observes that most people are simply fascinated with catastrophe and the results of destruction. Most people, he points out in another essay, will willingly slow down on a Sunday afternoon drive to gaze at a terrible car wreck because of their fascination with such disaster and loss. This is part of the nature of humanity, and given such human nature, how can humans avert the self-fulfilling activities that turn all the world into one large car wreck? "The present-day novelist is more interested in catastrophe than he is in life among the flower people. Uncertain himself about what has gone wrong, he feels in his bones that the happy exurb stands both in danger of catastrophe and in need of it" (109). The central question for Percy is "how do we come to ourselves" in order to avoid catastrophe. In all of his novels, Percy explores this idea to some extent or another. In *The Moviegoer*, for example, the main character, Binx Bolling, wanders aimlessly, always in search of himself. He is a dreamer, a wayfarer, a pilgrim, but he undertakes this wandering as an effort to get out of his everydayness and come to himself. He eventually discovers meaning beyond his everydayness in the movies that he wanders into daily.

Yet, in *Love in the Ruins* Percy writes a novel about the end of the world—or at least the end of the main character's world as that character knows it—in which the protagonist, Dr. Thomas More, lives through catastrophe in order to learn more about himself and others and to fashion a new relationship to the community around him. The full title of the novel reveals the plot and the themes around which the novel revolves: *Love in the Ruins: The Adventures of a Bad Catholic at a Time Near the End of the World*. Unlike Vonnegut's *Cat's Cradle*, Percy's novel edges close to the end times without ever sinking into the oblivion of the apocalyptic abyss; there is the promise that living near the end of the world will shake this "bad Catholic" out of his torpor, causing him to come to himself before his own selfishness helps to destroy the world fully. In true existentialist fashion, Percy has his protagonist peer over the edge into nothingness so that he, the main character, can affirm his own existence in this world. In addition, the subtitle reveals that, unlike Vonnegut, Percy is exploring what the role of religion might be in understanding and comprehending the actions that move a society to the edge of the end of the world.

The plot of the novel is fairly simple. Dr. Thomas More is a psychiatrist in a small Louisiana town called Paradise. In the novel, there is trouble in Paradise, which is a microcosm for the entire nation. More suffers from "More's syndrome, or: chronic angelism-bestialism" (*Love* 383), which also characterizes, he believes, the "beloved old U.S.A" (17). Just as he is the victim of an ailment that emphasizes a mind-body disorder, so his society is divided by forces that are entirely opposite to one another. In a landscape where vines sprout in Manhattan and wolves roam in downtown Cleveland, races and political parties are divided dramatically and often dangerously: "race against race, right against left, believer against heathen" (17). Moreover, "conservatives have begun to fall victim to unseasonable rages, delusions of conspiracies, high blood pressure, and large bowel complaints. Liberals are more apt to contract sexual impotence, morning terror, and a feeling of abstraction of the self from itself" (20). Most of society doesn't seem to care that this rapid destruction is tearing apart the fabric of America, and everyone is out for themselves. More, a lapsed Catholic and alcoholic, invents a device that he calls the More Quantitative-Qualitative Ontological Lapsometer, which he calls the "first caliper of the soul" and with which he can measure "the length and breadth and motions of the very self" (106–07). More spends the novel trying to protect his invention from being stolen and falling into the wrong hands, just as he spends his time shuffling from one woman to another, each representing aspects of the world around him: from the staid, conservative Presbyterian religion (Ellen) to the erotic and fertile hope for the future (Lola).

Percy's novel operates on several levels as it reveals the nature of humankind and its efforts to define itself. First, the protagonist's name, Thomas More, clearly echoes the name of the author of sixteenth-century treatise, *Utopia*, that lays out the structure and possibilities of a new world order. Second, More's invention provides an important clue into the human condition as he understands it. On the one hand, More arrogates himself to a position just below God—the angelic part of More's soul—by believing that his scientific instrument can diagnose the disorders of the soul. On the other hand, in his very attempt to play God, More demonstrates his bestial—close to the animals—personality, a side of his identity that he also reveals in his animality with relation to his women. Moreover, the name of his instrument reveals the very difficulty with humans depending solely on science to determine matters of the soul. More's is a lapsed soul; that is, his soul is fallen and already corrupt, and by using a machine to determine the corruption of others, he's contributing to an already fallen world. Percy points in this novel that science alone cannot resolve the distortions and divisions within the human mind and body and within the social body; humans must first come to themselves through a process of search and discovery that involves, and requires, dependence on forces outside of themselves. In the end, More learns this lesson as he "goes to bed for a long winter's nap" (379) with Ellen, the good religious woman who has brought him back to himself.

Although significant differences exist between Vonnegut's *Cat's Cradle* and Walker Percy's *Love in the Ruins*, each novel nevertheless explores the tale of humankind searching to find itself in the midst of a world that is broken by catastrophes of humankind's own making. Both novels offer instructive parables of the ways that humanity can come to itself before it destroys itself: Vonnegut achieves this with his raucous humor and irony; Percy achieves this with his central emphasis on our philosophical and religious character. Vonnegut's novel tells a grand joke, while Percy—as a Vonnegut for adults—creates a kind of existential dilemma and dialogue that takes individuals out of themselves in order to explore the world around them. Both novelists, however, provide compelling stories about the enduring nature of the human spirit as it seeks to understand itself and its world more fully.

Works Cited

Allen, William Rodney, ed. *Conversations with Kurt Vonnegut*. Jackson: UP of Mississippi, 1988. Print.

___. *Understanding Kurt Vonnegut*. Columbia: U of South Carolina P, 1991. Print.

___. *Walker Percy: A Southern Wayfarer*. Jackson: UPress of Mississippi, 1986. Print.

Boon, Kevin A., ed. *At Millennium's End: New Essays on the Work of Kurt Vonnegut*. Albany: SUNY P, 2001. Print.

Brinkmeyer, Robert H., Jr. *Three Catholic Writers of the Modern South: Allen Tate, Caroline Gordon, Walker Percy*. Jackson: U P of Mississippi, 1985. Print.

Broughton, Panthea Reid, ed. *The Art of Walker Percy: Stratagems for Being*. Baton Rouge: Louisiana State UP, 1979. Print.

Ciuba, Gary M. *Walker Percy: Books of Revelations*. Athens: U of Georgia P, 1991. Print.

Coles, Robert. *Walker Percy: An American Search*. Boston: Little, Brown, 1978. Print.

Hobson, Fred. *Tell about the South: The Southern Rage to Explain*. Baton Rouge: Louisiana State UP, 1983. Print.

Hobson, Linda Whitney. *Understanding Walker Percy*. Columbia: U of South Carolina P, 1988. Print.

Klinkowitz, Jerome. *Kurt Vonnegut's America*. Columbia: U of South Carolina P, 2009. Print.

___. *The Vonnegut Effect*. Columbia: U of South Carolina P, 2004. Print.

Luschei, Martin. *The Sovereign Wayfarer: Walker Percy's Diagnosis of the Malaise*. Baton Rouge: Louisiana State UP, 1972. Print.

O'Gorman, Farrell. *Peculiar Crossroads: Flannery O'Connor, Walker Percy, and Catholic Vision in Postwar Southern Fiction*. Baton Rouge: Louisiana State UP, 2004. Print.

Percy, Walker. *Lancelot*. New York: Farrar, 1977. Print.

___. *The Last Gentleman*. New York: Farrar, 1966. Print.

___. *Lost in the Cosmos*. New York: Farrar, 1983. Print.

___. *Love in the Ruins*. New York: Farrar, 1971. Print.

___. *The Message in the Bottle*. New York: Farrar, 1975. Print.

___. *The Moviegoer*. New York: Knopf, 1961. Print.

___. *The Second Coming*. New York: Farrar, 1980. Print.

___. *The Thanatos Syndrome*. New York: Farrar, 1987. Print.

Samway, Patrick, S. J. *Walker Percy: A Life*. New York: Farrar, 1997. Print.

Shields, Charles J. *And So It Goes. Kurt Vonnegut: A Life*. New York: Holt, 2011. Print.

Sumner, Gregory D. *Unstuck in Time: A Journey through Kurt Vonnegut's Life and Novels*. New York: Seven Stories, 2011. Print.

Tally, Robert T., Jr. *Kurt Vonnegut and the American Novel: A Postmodern Iconography*. London: Continuum, 2011. Print.

Tolson, Jay. *Pilgrim in the Ruins: A Life of Walker Percy*. New York: Simon & Schuster, 1992. Print.

Vonnuegut, Kurt, Jr. *Breakfast of Champions*. New York: Delacorte, 1973. Print.

___. *Cat's Cradle*. New York: Dell, 1963. Print.

___. *God Bless You, Mr. Rosewater*. New York: Dell, 1965. Print.

___. *Palm Sunday*. New York: Delacorte, 1981. Print.

___. *Slaughterhouse-Five*. New York: Dell, 1969. Print.

___. *Wampeters, Foma, & Granfalloons*. New York: Delacorte, 1974. Print.

Wyatt-Brown, Bertram. *The House of Percy: Honor, Melancholy, and Imagination in a Southern Family*. New York: Oxford, 1994. Print.

CRITICAL
READINGS

"Instructions for Use": The Opening Chapter of *Slaughterhouse-Five* and the Reader of Historiographical Metafictions_____

Peter Freese

I.

In December of 1944, twenty-one-year-old Kurt Vonnegut Jr., a fourth-generation German American from Indianapolis who served as a private in the 423rd Infantry Regiment, was taken prisoner during the Battle of the Bulge. He was transported to Dresden, Germany, where he was interned in Schlachthof Fünf, one of the buildings of the city's stockyards that had been converted into a prison camp. There, he miraculously survived the February 1945 bombing of Dresden in what he described as "a meat locker three stories beneath the surface, the only decent shelter in the city," in a 1974 interview with Joe David Bellamy and John Casey (202). The apocalyptic fire storm wiped out the city known as Florence on the Elbe and, according to *Slaughterhouse-Five*, "ate everything organic, everything that would burn" (qtd. in Harris 232), resulting in "the largest massacre in European history" (Scholes 117). Afterward, young Vonnegut and his fellow prisoners were made to dig out the charred corpses from bomb shelters and basements and stack them in piles, where they were cremated with flamethrowers to prevent the spread of epidemics. In a recently released letter, which he wrote home on May 29, 1945, from a repatriation camp in Le Havre, France (*Armageddon* 11–13), he described his experiences in a general way meant to spare his family, but in his 1977 *Paris Review* interview, he recalled the gruesome details and revealed how traumatic the events in Dresden had been. Thus, it is no small wonder that they haunted him for twenty-three years and that, as he explained in both his July 1973 *Playboy* interview with David Standish and his talk with Bellamy and Casey, it took him numerous abortive attempts before he could exorcise his tormenting memories. He eventually managed to do so in his sixth novel, the antiwar book *Slaughterhouse-Five; or, The Children's Crusade* (1969), and only then could he say to Richard Todd: "It was a therapeutic thing. . . . I'm a different sort of person now. I got rid of a lot of crap" (32).

This short novel marked Vonnegut's sudden breakthrough as a major writer, it was successfully filmed in 1972 by George Roy Hill, and it has meanwhile gained the status of a modern classic (see Fairfield; Mustazza). Although it deals with a historical event as recalled by an eyewitness, it is anything but a traditional "historical novel," and its baroque subtitle, which on the title page describes it as "a novel somewhat in the telegraphic schizophrenic manner of tales of the planet Tralfamadore, where the flying saucers come from," announces its daringly experimental nature. *Slaughterhouse-Five* is what critics have come to call a "historiographical metafiction," a self-reflexive and transgeneric narrative that openly asserts its status as an artifact and not only calls into question the traditional distinction between fact and fiction, history and story, but also plays with established genre conventions and the standard rules of narration. Moreover, it dares to combine a mass destruction that really happened with what Vonnegut called "science fiction of an obviously kidding sort" (qtd. in Standish 94), and it makes its painfully drawn-out genesis a part of the text. In Vonnegut's own words, it is a book "about what it's like to write a book about a thing like that [the firebombing of Dresden]" (qtd. in Bellamy and Casey 203).

Kurt Vonnegut is one of the rare writers who managed, after a long and arduous apprenticeship and years of unwarranted critical neglect, to gain both the love of common readers who enjoy his zany and easily accessible tales and the respect of academic critics who admire his experimental and innovative narrative strategies. That he could simultaneously fulfill the widely different expectations of these two audiences and prevent his rather demanding strategies from estranging his lay readers is due to his keen awareness that a literary text must not overtax its readers and cannot succeed without their willing cooperation.

Thus, in 1974, he stated that "the limiting factor is the reader. No other art requires the audience to be a performer. You have to count on the reader's being a good performer, and you may write music which he absolutely can't perform—in which case it's a bust" (qtd. in Bellamy and Casey 203). And in 1997, more than two decades later, he observed in *Timequake* that "any work of art is half of a conversation between two human beings, and it helps a lot to know who is talking at you" (168). In his conversation with Robert Scholes, Vonnegut made it clear that he not only wanted to entertain but also to instruct his readers when he observed that he had been worrying about why people are taught "to write books when presidents and senators do not read them, and generals do not read them" (123) and continued that he had come up with "a very good reason, that you catch people before they become generals and presidents and so forth and you poison their minds with . . . humanity, and however you want to poison their minds, it's presumably to encourage them to make a better world" (123; ellipses in orig.). It is due to this strong didactic impetus that his narrators take great care to establish rapport with readers and frequently explain statements that might not be understood. In *Slaughterhouse-Five*, a typical example occurs when a character counters the narrator's announcement that he wants to write "an anti-war book" by saying, "Why don't you write an anti-*glacier* book instead?" and the narrator finds it appropriate to explain: "What he meant, of course, was that there would always be wars, that they were as easy to stop as glaciers" (3).

II.

Slaughterhouse-Five plays with almost every constitutive element of narration. With regard to its narrative perspective—the choice of which is the most momentous decision a storyteller has to make—the novel alternates between three overlapping points of view, which must be carefully distinguished in order to avoid such frequent misreadings as the unwarranted identification of Vonnegut's humanistic position with Billy Pilgrim's fatalistic acceptance of whatever happens. The opening chapter of the book is told by a narrator who seems to be Vonnegut himself, but it is definitely not, as Donald J. Greiner asserts, "written in Vonnegut's own voice" (42). Since the book is a novel and not an autobiography, its narrator is not the historical Kurt Vonnegut but a fictional projection of him. The "Vonnegut" of the first chapter, then, "is, indeed, a *character* in *Slaughterhouse-Five*" (Harris 230; italics in orig.), but he nevertheless claims a pseudoautobiographical reality for his narrative. When "Vonnegut's" eyewitness perspective is abandoned in the story proper, Billy Pilgrim provides the central focus of narration. But when the readers are informed about the past of Roland Weary (34ff.), Edgar Derby (83), and Paul Lazzaro (84) or about the former lives of Howard W. Campbell Jr. (128ff., 162ff.), Kilgore Trout (166f.), and Professor Rumfoord (183ff.), this information can neither be provided by "Vonnegut" nor can it be told from Billy Pilgrim's perspective; therefore, a third and seemingly omniscient voice comes into play. Thus, for example, Valencia Pilgrim's death by carbon monoxide poisoning cannot be related through Billy's focus, as he is in the hospital and "knew nothing about it" (183), nor can it be reported by "Vonnegut," who was not present on that occasion.

With regard to its plot, *Slaughterhouse-Five* is a frame narrative, but here again the conventional structure is playfully violated. The first and the last of the novel's ten rather arbitrarily divided chapters function as a frame that surrounds an inset tale. The opening chapter presents the ramblingly digressive monologue of "Vonnegut," but the last chapter mixes semiautobiographical fragments from "Vonnegut's" life with Billy Pilgrim's listless journey through the remnants of burnt-out Dresden. This construction has the inset tale stick out beyond a frame that is not fully closed, and thus the book begins in the quasifactual and ends in a fictional world, and the narrative process and the narrated action intermingle in an unusual way. Such a structure results in the puzzling interplay of two realms of "reality" that are located on opposite sides of "the ontological divide" (Waugh 131), and in a mixture of two time levels that in mimetic fiction are clearly separated. This playful violation of narrative conventions is continued in the inset tale in which the narrator, "Vonnegut," unexpectedly intrudes as an actor and eyewitness and thus again blends two strands that tradition demands to be carefully distinguished. When Colonel Wild Bob is dying of double pneumonia, the dramatic action is abruptly interrupted by a voice that says: "I was there. So was my old war buddy, Bernard V. O'Hare" (67). When, on his wedding night, Billy Pilgrim ponders what would make an appropriate inscription for his gravestone, the text reads: "It would make a good epitaph for Billy Pilgrim—and for me, too" (121). When an overwhelmed American POW exclaims "Oz" upon seeing the beautiful city of Dresden for the first time, his utterance is followed by a surprising "That was I" (148). When a sick POW wails that he has excreted everything but his brain, the text reads, "That was I. That was me. That was the author of this book" (125). And when the shocked prisoners are marched through the ruins of smoldering Dresden, it is said that "I was there. O'Hare was there" (212).

These sudden intrusions, however, are not the only signs of the ir-ritating interference of an openly manipulative narrator who reveals his central dilemma when he self-ironically introduces himself as "a trafficker in climaxes and thrills and characterization and wonderful dialogue and suspense and confrontations" (5), but admits only a little later that "there is nothing intelligent to say about a massacre" (19). This worried narrator keeps his readers constantly aware that they are confronted with the idiosyncratic and painfully self-reflexive tale of a man who is obsessed with his memories and wrestles with his difficul-ties in storifying what turns out to be an intractable subject. This is why he not only intrudes into his story but also has no scruples explaining his narrative procedures, as when he observes that Billy finds himself once more engaged "in the argument with his daughter, with which this tale began" (165) or when he states that "there are almost no characters in this story, and almost no dramatic confrontations, because most of the people in it are so sick" (164). And he also takes the liberty of deliv-ering harsh value judgments—for example, "like so many Americans, she [Billy's mother] was trying to construct a life that made sense from things she found in gift shops" (39)—and irreverent, illusion-breaking comments, as when the coughing prisoners' diarrhea is "in accordance with the Third Law of Motion according to Sir Isaac Newton" (80). Both the alternating points of view and the periodical interference of "Vonnegut's" mediating voice prevent the novel's readers from a pragmatic reception, interrupt their empathy with Billy Pilgrim, and repeatedly remind them that what they learn about Billy Pilgrim's adventures is filtered through "Vonnegut's" carefully arranged memories.

Its frequently shifting perspectives and its unusual plot construction make *Slaughterhouse-Five* a highly unconventional novel that expects its readers to perform a demanding task, and therefore Vonnegut must familiarize them with both his major thematic concerns and his innovative narrative strategies in order to enable them to develop the appropriate mode of reception. Although he can take it for granted that his contemporary readers, who are moviegoers and thus know about cuts and fades, will be able to coauthor erratic narratives into sense-making wholes, his knowledge that a writer has "to count on the reader's being a good performer" causes him to put his readers in the appropriate mood by familiarizing them with his major themes and narrative strategies. And this is what he does brilliantly in his opening chapter, which is not what some critics have dismissed as the dysfunctional prattle of a garrulous writer. It is not only "of great importance in providing us with a means of tracing the author's evolving attitude both to the horrors of war and to the composition of his book as well" (Matheson 229), but it also offers built-in directions for use in the form of an artfully crafted collage of semiautobiographical facts, seemingly irrelevant observations, and literary references and quotations that will turn out to have important thematic relevance, set the tone of the narrative, anticipate things to come, and create the "attitudinal norms by which we are to judge Billy's experience" (Edelstein 137).

Behind its surface action, *Slaughterhouse-Five* is concerned with three central issues: the treacherous opposition between seeming and being, a wholesome appearance and a faulty reality; the all-encompassing power of time that conditions man's fickle memory, makes human life a transitory affair and leads to death as its ineluctable end; and the central concern of Vonnegut, the self-professed "Christ-worshiping agnostic" (*Palm Sunday* 327)—namely, the decisive choice between the fatalistic acceptance of the inherent meaninglessness of human existence in a contingent universe on the one hand and the daring attempt to discover or, should it become necessary, even to invent a meaning and a purpose for life on the other.

Appearance versus Reality

In the opening chapter, "Vonnegut" deprives the destruction of Dresden of its singularity by placing it in a long sequence of manmade atrocities that range from the biblical Sodom and Gomorrah (21) to the medieval Children's Crusade (15ff.) and that will later be extended to the Vietnam War, which was a major public concern at the time of publication and contributed to the novel's unexpected success. The novel, then, toward the end of which "Vonnegut" ruefully observes that "every day my Government gives me a count of corpses created by military science in Vietnam" (210), deals with warfare as a deplorable constant in human history, and "Vonnegut," who learns to agree with his war buddy's wife, the nurse Mary O'Hare, that "wars were partly encouraged by books and movies" (15), takes care to debunk the popular macho image of heroic soldiers. He does so by contrasting what Mary O'Hare condemns as the mendacious Hollywood movies made by "Frank Sinatra and John Wayne or some of those other glamorous, war-loving, dirty old men" (14) with his own painful memories of the war experiences of such "foolish virgins . . . right at the end of childhood" (14) as himself and Billy Pilgrim. The mentioning of John Wayne contains an unspoken allusion to *The Green Berets*, the only American film that supported the US involvement in Vietnam, which was released a year before the publication of *Slaughterhouse-Five* with Wayne as codirector and star. This is confirmed when later

Billy Pilgrim's son, a juvenile delinquent, "joined the famous Green Berets. He straightened out, became a fine young man, and he fought in Vietnam" (24, see 189). Through such passing references, Vonnegut contrasts the jingoistic mass media version of romanticized warfare with its happy comradeship and manly self-fulfillment with the cruel reality of war as fought by frightened children expected to behave like men. And he adds that war always results in the senseless destruction of irreplaceable cultural monuments and once again stresses that this has happened throughout human history by quoting a passage about an earlier destruction of Dresden in 1760 from a 1908 book, Mary Endell's *Dresden, History, Stage and Gallery*. Moreover, it is certainly no accident that the fatal consequences of unending warfare are denounced by two women with the name of the mother of Christ.

The narrator's erratic reminiscences subtly unmask what the mass media disseminate as historical truth and reveal their patriotic rallying calls as a variant of what, more than a hundred years earlier, Charles Mackay had defined in 1841 as *Extraordinary Popular Delusions and the Madness of Crowds*. However, *Slaughterhouse-Five* is not only a committed "anti-war book," but in the story proper, it also exposes sundry other aspects of the American reality of the sixties through references to the injustices bred by the unwarranted belief in unhampered progress, the false pieties of institutionalized religion, and the social Darwinist tenets of a shirtsleeve capitalism. Thus, the abyss between seeming and being is repeatedly exposed as an opposition between pious Sunday sermons and ruthless everyday practice, and in the story proper, "Vonnegut's" unique instrument for the unmasking of fraud and greed, hypocrisy and corruption, is his daring introduction of the Martian perspective. The unheard-of combination of a massive historical tragedy with extraterrestrial aliens, which some conservatives found in bad taste but which Vonnegut meant to have the same function as "the clowns in Shakespeare" (Standish 94), makes his readers see the hectic scheming of Earthlings through the astonished eyes of the fatalistic Tralfamadorians. The Martian perspective, which was already successfully employed in previous novels (the Tralfamador-ians play a major role in *The Sirens of Titan* and are briefly mentioned in *God Bless You, Mr. Rosewater*), is a highly effective instrument for creating an alienation effect. It defamiliarizes events and attitudes the readers are used to and take for granted and makes them perceive these events in a new light. By combining this instrument with the motif of time travel, "Vonnegut" can also do what is simply impossible in mimetic fiction—namely, go beyond the traditional distinction between chronological and psychological time and manipulate chronological time itself.

Transitoriness and Death

As announced in its subtitle, "A Duty Dance with Death," *Slaughter-house-Five* explores the nature of time and human mortality, and once again, it is the opening chapter that slyly introduces these concepts and thereby prepares the readers for an adequate reaction to Billy Pilgrim's being "spastic in time" (23). At a first glance, the silly jingle about Yon Yonson from Wisconsin that can be repeated "to infinity" (3) seems to be a superfluous digression, but it playfully introduces the very endless-ness that Billy Pilgrim will gain by adopting the Tralfamadorian notion of death as a passing event in a nonlinear time continuum. The narra-tor's self-deprecatory reference to his failed plot outline—"One end of the wallpaper was the beginning of the story, and the other end was the end, and then there was all that middle part, which was the middle" (5)—stands in irritating opposition to the fact that it is undertaken by a man who "taught creative writing in the famous Writers Workshop at the University of Iowa" (18), and announces that a subject like the destruction of Dresden resists the chronological unfolding of mimetic storification. "Vonnegut's" recurring references to man's time-bound existence (for him it is "time to go, always time to go" [12], his wife "always has to know the time" [7], and he has "to believe whatever clocks said—and calendars" [20]) vary the central theme of human transitoriness. The mention of his visit to the World's Fair exhibitions, where they saw "the past according to the Ford Motor Company and Walt Disney, saw what the future would be like, according to General Motors" (18), slyly points to the insurmountable subjectivity of all perception and thus helps to prepare the readers for the recognition that an objective account of what happened in Dresden is impossible. And the three lines from Theodore Roethke's *Words for the Wind* (29), as well as the observation taken from Erika Ostrovsky's study that "time obsessed" Louis-Ferdinand Céline (21), give this concern additional dignity by showing that "Vonnegut" is not the only writer who wrestles with humanity's temporal limitations.

These and several other allusions to time and death that punctuate the opening chapter weave a tight net of unobtrusive cross-references between the frame and the inset tale. Thus, "Vonnegut's" introductory musings about "how wide [the present] was, how deep it was, how much was mine to keep" (18) prepare the readers for a protagonist who is an optician turned metaphysician and prescribes "corrective lenses for Earthling souls" (29). Since he is "unstuck in time" (23), Billy Pilgrim is as much concerned with time and death as "Vonnegut," and he provides an answer to the latter's musings by his proclamation of the Tralfamadorians' nonlinear time and his assertion that "it is just an illusion we have here on Earth that one moment follows another one" (27). Moreover, the Tralfamadorian notion of death as "just violet light— and a hum" (43, 143) experienced only "for a while" (143), which Billy offers as a remedy against Earthlings' mortality, is ironically enacted and turned into fictional reality when soldiers on maneuvers pretend to be only "theoretically dead" (31). And "Vonnegut's" concern in the opening chapter with "plain old death" (4) that makes "no art . . . possible without a dance with death" (21) is later ironically translated into fictional action when Billy Pilgrims runs from hostile bullets, performs "involuntary dancing" movements (33), and leaves tracks in the snow that look like "diagrams in a book on ballroom dancing" (39).

The willfully unsystematic and associative unfolding of the opening chapter prepares its readers for the unusual structure of an inset tale that replaces the linear progression of chronological narration with the circular spatiality of a fragmented action that moves erratically forward and backward. In the story proper, "Vonnegut's" failed attempt to unfold his story with a beginning, a middle, and an end as uselessly sketched on a piece of wallpaper is contrasted with the Tralfamadorian novels that are atemporal "clumps of symbols" (88) with "no beginning, no middle, no end, no suspense, no moral, no causes, no effects" but simply "the depths of many marvelous moments seen all at one time" (88). As early as 1766, Gotthold Ephraim Lessing had pointed out in *Laokoon oder über die Grenzen der Mahlerey und Poesie*, his groundbreaking essay on the limits of painting and poetry, that the former deals with the simultaneity of bodies in space whereas the latter is concerned with the succession of actions in time. Thus, Earthlings cannot create Tralfamadorian texts because human language unfolds as a temporal sequence of sounds and symbols. Vonnegut, however, tries very hard to approach the Tralfamadorian model by avoiding anything that might provide his tale with a conventional, logical progression. This also becomes obvious when he unabashedly destroys all suspense by quoting both the opening and the closing lines of the inset tale at the end of his opening chapter: "It begins like this: *Listen: Billy Pilgrim has come unstuck in time*. It ends like this: *Poo-tee-weet?*" (23), and when he prematurely reveals that "the climax of the book will be the execution of poor old Edgar Derby" (4). Thus, the opening chapter prepares its readers for a text that is radically fragmented, purposely avoids any logical cause-and-effect sequence, and offers no clear-cut moral. Instead, it is left to the readers to draw their own conclusions about the controversial reasons for the bombing of Dresden and find their own answers to the nagging question why humankind proves incapable of preventing history from repeating itself.

The Quest for Meaning and Purpose

Both the appearance-reality opposition and the conundrum of human transitoriness contribute to the central theme not only of *Slaughterhouse-Five* but of Vonnegut's whole oeuvre—namely, the quest for the meaning and purpose of a life that allows for an atrocity like the firebombing of Dresden or, on the individual level, the ludicrously unfair execution of Edgar Derby. In the inset tale, this concern, which varies the age-old theodicy problem, finds its most obvious expression in the many "why" questions that range from Billy's bewildered "Why me?" (76) through the title of the pamphlet "Why We Fight" (40) to an American POW's astonished "Why me?" (91). This theme, too, is carefully prepared in the opening chapter. The taxi driver's repeated phrase "if the accident will" (2), which is an unidiomatic translation of the German *wenn es der Zufall will*, becomes a handy label for the contingency of existence and gains additional irony from the fact that it is expressed on a Christmas card. The reference to Céline and the quotation from Roethke represent modern literature's obsession with the ineluctability of death. The film director Harrison Starr's insistence that "there would always be wars" (3) refers to the limitations of human reason. The absurdly illogical insistence of the air force that details of the bombing of Dresden are "top secret still" (11) varies the appearance-reality dichotomy. And the comically faulty observation of "Vonnegut," the erstwhile student of anthropology, "that there was absolutely no difference between anybody" (8) implies that all judgments are subjective and that there is no generally acceptable answer to the "why" question. In the story proper, however, a Tralfamadorian remedy is offered and all "why" questions are rejected as meaningless because "there is no why" (77), free will is an illusion, and Earthlings are misled when they act as "the great explainers, explaining why this event is structured as it is, telling how other events may be achieved or avoided" (85).

III.

For an effective presentation of his three major thematic concerns, Vonnegut uses four constitutive narrative strategies, with which he acquaints his readers in the opening chapter: the technique of the ingenious collage that establishes new and surprising connections; the postmodern play with competing realities that illustrates the subjectivity of all human perception and the limitations of human memory; the illusion-breaking interplay of fact and fiction that falsifies the traditional mimesis principle; and the creation of cross-referenced repetitions in ever new configurations that reveal human captivity in the ruling linguistic discourses.

The Technique of the Collage

It is the technique of the associative collage that allows "Vonnegut" to do what postmodern writers have perfected—namely, to arrange quotations from other works and seemingly unrelated phrases from the surrounding linguistic universe into new and meaningful patterns. The relevant items include:

- an unidiomatic Christmas card from the Dresden taxi driver Gerhard Müller with the important phrase "if the accident will" (2);

- a mildly dirty limerick about a "young man from Stamboul" (2);

- a circular jingle about Yon Yonson (3);

- a quotation from Horace's *Odes* (11), which can be identified as *Odes* 2.14.1–2: *Eheu, fugaces, Postume, Postume, / Labuntur anni*;

- a passage from Charles Mackay's 1841 book *Extraordinary Popular Delusions and the Madness of Crowds* (15);

- a passage from Mary Endell's 1908 book *Dresden, History, Stage and Gallery* (17);

- a quotation from Johann Wolfgang von Goethe's *Dichtung und Wahrheit* (18), which is taken from book 9 and given, in a Chinese-boxes variation, as a quotation within the quotation from Mary Endell;

- three lines from Theodore Roethke's poem *The Waking* (20) from his 1958 collection *Words for the Wind*;

- a statement by the French novelist Louis-Ferdinand Céline, as quoted from Erika Ostrovsky's study *Céline and His Vision* (21);

- a passage from *Death on the Installment Plan*, the English translation of Céline's 1936 novel *Mort à credit* (21);

- a passage from the Gideon Bible about the destruction of Sodom and Gomorrah (21), which is taken from Genesis 19:23–25; and

- a self-reflexive quotation of the first and last sentences of the novel within the novel (22).

The very number of these (sometimes unidentified) quotations signals their importance, and the twelve references that punctuate the first chapter blend parts from widely different discourses into a unique kind of intertextuality. Thus, a mundane postcard from a Dresden taxi driver is combined with a passage from the Bible, and a popular jingle and a dirty limerick are quoted side by side with an excerpt from Goethe's *Dichtung und Wahrheit*. In this irreverent way, "Vonnegut" makes it clear that he does not care for the traditional distinction between serious art and popular kitsch and that for him the customary gap between "highbrow" and "lowbrow" texts (the major reason for Vonnegut's early rejection by academic critics) is an artificial and obsolete distinction. And by offering some of the clippings he assembles as quotations within other quotations he shows that every statement is embedded in a multilayered network of previous statements. Since it is all too easy to overlook the subtle functionality of some of the oddly self-reflexive references that punctuate the opening chapter and point not only forward to characters and motifs in the story proper but also backward to previous and imaginatively recycled Vonnegut texts, one representative example may illustrate that what seems to be the ramblingly digressive monologue of a garrulous "old fart with his memories" (7) is really an artfully knit net of meaningful cross-references.

When, in the story proper, the fittingly named Roland Weary—he is certainly "weary" but definitely not the heroic Roland of French lore—flees from the unbearable reality of war into the fantasy world of Alexandre Dumas's *Three Musketeers*, he talks to himself about the great deeds of these famous heroes. The text reads: "He dilated upon the piety and heroism of 'The Three Musketeers,' portrayed, in the most glowing and impassioned hues, their virtue and magnanimity, the imperishable honor they acquired for themselves, and the great services they rendered to Christianity" (50). In the passage quoted in the opening chapter from Mackay's book, one reads: "Romance, on the other hand, dilates upon their [the crusaders'] piety and heroism, and portrays, in her most glowing and impassioned hues, their virtue and magnanimity, the imperishable honor they acquired for themselves, and the great services they rendered to Christianity" (15). Roland Weary's fantasies, then, are expressed in a word-for-word quotation from Charles Mackay's book. By making the dreams in which Weary indulges in 1944 identical to what Mackay identified in 1841 as the "popular delusions" of the crusaders, "Vonnegut's" subversive narrative strategy unmasks the individual fantasies of an incipiently insane soldier in World War II as a repetition of the delusions of the medieval crusaders and thus reveals them as a recurring and timeless human aberration. Once again, what seems a random digression in the opening chapter turns out to be a preparatory anticipation of what is to follow in the story proper. But Vonnegut is not content with this subtle, and hitherto overlooked, cross-reference, and he further undermines the patriotic heroism of the Three Musketeers. First, he makes a sensation-hungry secretary inquire about the death of a man in a gruesome accident while "eating a Three Musketeers Candy Bar" (9), and later, he has Billy's overweight fiancée sit at the bedside of her broken-down lover in hospital and munch on "a Three Musketeers Candy Bar" (107).

The Play with Competing Realities

The distinction between the historian's "discovery" of preexisting histories and the novelist's "invention" of newly made stories is a thing of the past, since "the historian [also] performs an essentially *poetic* act, in which he *pre*figures the historical field and constitutes it as a domain upon which to bring to bear the specific theories he will use to explain 'what was really happening' in it" (White x; italics in orig.). When told about and emplotted as a story, any reconstruction of a historical event must be subjective, and therefore postmodern writers see the difference between a historiography and a novel no longer as one of principle but one of accentuation, and they bridge the ontological divide between fact and fiction with the strategies of historiographical metafiction. Like E. L. Doctorow, who famously stated that "there is no history except as it is composed" (160), or T. C. Boyle, who admitted that "where historical fact proved a barrier to the exigencies of invention, I have, with full knowledge and clear conscience, reshaped it to fit my purposes" ("Apologia"), Vonnegut bends historical facts to his own aims and tells the idiosyncratic story of his personal Dresden experience as part of a self-reflexive inquiry into both the limitations of memory and the impossibility of recalling "how it really was." But this does not mean that his version is less "real" than David Irving's official book *The Destruction of Dresden*, with its biased forewords by British air marshal Sir Robert Saundby and US lieutenant general Ira C. Eaker, which Bertram Copeland Rumfoord reads in the hospital (186), a context that ironically undermines its authority.

With regard to narrative strategies, the presentational corollary of epistemological doubt is Vonnegut's use of the *regressus in infinitum* ("infinite regression"). This principle was most momentously employed by Jorge Luis Borges in his *Ficciones,* in which he demonstrates that there is no *prima causa* ("first cause"), that not only every cause of an effect is in turn the effect of a previous cause but that also every author of a fictional character can be understood as a character in the fiction of a previous author. And it was self-ironically summed up by John Barth, when, within one of his metafictions, he had the narrator muse about "another story about a writer writing a story! Another regressus in infinitum!" (114). Vonnegut made similar statements when he claimed in his interview with Patricia Bosworth that "nothing in this world is ever final—no one ever ends—we keep bouncing back and forth in time, we go on and on ad infinitum" (5), and when in another context he playfully stated that "I myself am a work of fiction" (*Wampeters* xix). In *Slaughterhouse-Five,* such an understanding is acted out when in his time travels Billy Pilgrim reenacts scenes from Kilgore Trout's *The Big Board*, and once again, the novel's readers are alerted to it in the opening chapter with the song about Yon Yonson that cannot only be endlessly repeated but already announces this principle through the protagonist's name (Yonson, after all, means "son of Yon"). It also lies behind the self-reflexive network of quotations within quotations. Thus, one of the novel's crucial messages—that in a contingent universe ("if the accident will") every answer that humans find in their unending quest for meaning and purpose only triggers yet another question—is subtly announced. This predicament had already found its most disillusioning presentation in Vonnegut's earlier novel *The Sirens of Titan* (1959), in which the greatest architectural accomplishments of humankind turn out to be nothing but encoded messages for a stranded Tralfamadorian. In *Slaughterhouse-Five*, the recognition of the limitations of human perception results in the insight that not even an eyewitness to the bombing of Dresden can provide any objective meaning for this wholesale slaughter of tens of thousands of civilians: "I thought it would be easy for me to write about the destruction of Dresden, since all I would have to do would be to report what I had seen. . . . But not many words about Dresden came from my mind then . . . And not many words come now, either" (2). Because "Vonnegut" has to accept that an orderly and meaningful reconstruction of his war experience is impossible, he must resort to other and more indirect means, and he resignedly admits that "So it goes" (2), a statement that will become a kind of refrain and punctuate the story proper more than a hundred times.

The Intermixture of Fact and Fiction

"Vonnegut's" third and most important strategy is the puzzling bracketing of the traditional ontological divide—namely, the openly acknowledged intermixture of fact and fiction. In its subtitle, *Slaughterhouse-Five* is classified as "a novel," but it begins with the surprising sentence "All this happened, more or less" (1). If the book is a novel, its action must be fictitious, but the traditional verification topos that "all this happened" claims that it is factual, only to be immediately subverted by the qualification "more or less." Thus, the very first sentence of the book disturbs the genre-specific expectations of its readers, and when the narrator goes on to say that at least "the war parts" of his story are "pretty much true" (1), even the ancient notion of poetic truth becomes entangled in the intermixture of fact and fiction. Since Vonnegut was an eyewitness to the bombing of Dresden, he thought he could deliver a firsthand account of "what really happened," but his pained admission that he had wrongly thought it would be easy for him to tell about his Dresden experience shows that an atrocity of the magnitude of the Dresden fire storm is beyond an individual's perception. It demonstrates what Robert J. Lifton aptly defines as "the increasing gap we face between our technological capacity for perpetrating atrocities and our imaginative ability to confront their full actuality" (23). Consequently, traditionally mimetic narration is incapable of dealing with such a subject. Therefore, "Vonnegut's" resigned admissions that *Slaughterhouse-Five* is a "lousy little book" (2) and that "this one is a failure" (22) must not be taken at face value since they refer to criteria of success that do not apply to the type of tale he tells and, being made in a fictional context, are relativized as to their factual meaning.

The irritating play with the intermixture of fact and fiction that is introduced in the opening chapter is taken up at the very beginning of the story proper. It opens with a direct reader address ("Listen") that transforms the distance of written text into the immediacy of oral communication and then offers the statement "Billy Pilgrim has come unstuck in time" (23). Once again, this surprising statement is immediately qualified by a twice-repeated "he says" (23); this not only makes the readers wonder whether Billy can really travel in time or whether he only says so, but also, together with the unusual choice of the present as a reporting tense instead of the past as a narrating tense, inspires speculation about to whom Billy (who seems to exist outside the narrated text) says this. Such a presentation creates another disruption of what readers have grown accustomed to expect. Because a traditional narrative reconstruction of a "real" event must arrange simultaneous events in a temporal succession, it must proceed from a beginning through a middle to an end. And since no narration can do without selection and any selection implies an evaluation, such a procedure is by definition a sense-making endeavor and would inevitably provide even an event like the Dresden massacre with coherence and meaning and thus domesticate it. But "Vonnegut" wants to convey the very opposite message: that "there is nothing intelligent to say about a massacre" (19). Therefore, he must discard all traditional strategies and do everything possible to change his readers from the passive recipients of a logically unfolding story into the active coauthors of a disrupted and constantly irritating tale.

The Human Imprisonment in Linguistic Discourses

To activate his readers, "Vonnegut" employs his fourth major strategy: he provides what at first glance seems to be a discontinuous and digressive tale with an artfully patterned subtext in which numerous repetitions plus variations in widely different contexts weave a subtle net of cross-references unveiling the degree to which human communication is limited by prevailing linguistic discourses. A typical example is the Dresden taxi driver's Germanism "if the accident will," which the narrator's comment "I like that very much" already marks as significant (2). When the narrator later mentions that he is thinking of writing a short story titled "If the Accident Will" (20), the significance of this phrase is underscored, and in the course of the tale, it turns into a formulaic comment on the contingency of human life. The limerick about the "young man from Stamboul" (2), which is a silly comment on human futility and transitoriness, and the endlessly repeatable jingle about Yon Yonson, which is a popular variant of the *regressus in infinitum*, become so firmly integrated into the narrator's discourse that later he can simply say, "I'm an old fart with his memories and his Pall Malls. My name is Yon Yonson, I work in Wisconsin . . ." (7). Likewise, a collage of previous references made without any comment—*"Eheu, fugaces labuntur anni*. My name is Yon Yonson. There was a young man from Stamboul" (11)—can function as a serious reflection on the limitations of human life.

Whereas the narrator's self-ironic characterization as "an old fart with his memories and his Pall Malls" (2, 7) occurs only in the opening chapter, his curious comparison of his alcoholic breath with "mustard gas and roses" (4, 7) is unexpectedly taken up in the inset tale when Billy Pilgrim imagines that he can smell "mustard gas and roses" (73) over the telephone, and it assumes deeper significance when Billy experiences the mountains of corpses in Dresden as stinking "like roses and mustard gas" (214). Thus, a small—and at first seemingly arbitrary—detail introduced in the opening chapter assumes a deeper significance and serves as an important bridge not only between the narrator and his protagonist, but also between the narrative present and the narrated past. The metaphorical description of the young American soldiers as "foolish virgins" (14) in the introduction becomes literally true in the story proper when the readers learn about Billy that "he had never fucked anybody" (34). When Pope Innocent the Third, whose name becomes highly ironical, praises the children who will go on crusades and die for a useless cause by saying, "These children are awake while we are asleep!" (16), his statement is not only subtly related to the lines from Theodore Roethke's "I wake to sleep" (20) in his poem *Words for the Wind*, but meaningfully disproved by Billy Pilgrim's behavior who can "scarcely distinguish between sleep and wakefulness" (34). And the third line of the quotation from Roethke ("I learn by going where I have to go" [20]) turns out to be a fitting description of Billy Pilgrim's random deterministic movement through the world. The onomatopoeic *"Poo-tee-weet?"* (19) of the birds, which is known from previous Vonnegut novels, is taken up in different contexts (22, 100, 215) and gradually accumulates an ever deeper meaning. The recurring references—to "blue and ivory feet" (28, 65, 72, 73, 75, 80, 148), to the "nestling like spoons" (31, 70, 71, 72, 78, 126, 144, 148), to the colors orange and black (69, 72), and to the baying of a hound as a "big bronze gong" (48, 82)—punctuate the text as chains of iterative images and reveal to the attentive reader an artfully constructed deep structure below a seemingly disorderly surface. And the cross-references between the clues planted in the opening chapter and the adventures of Billy Pilgrim in the story proper show that "Vonnegut" is haunted by the very traumatic experiences from which he makes his protagonist suffer.

IV.

The opening chapter of *Slaughterhouse-Five* is not, as some critics mistakenly think, an introduction to the novel but an integral part of it. The chapter introduces both the book's major thematic concerns and its basic narrative strategies in a seemingly casual, digressive, and dysfunctional monologue, the random surface of which hides a subtle and carefully constructed subtext that provides a kind of built-in "instructions for use" and prepares the readers for an appropriate reception of the story proper. The opening chapter also establishes the decisive contrast between "Vonnegut" and Billy Pilgrim. Kurt Vonnegut's position is not represented by Billy, the immature drifter who fatalistically accepts whatever happens and never becomes a grown-up Bill, but by "Vonnegut," who tells his sons "that they are not under any circumstances to take part in massacres" nor "to work for companies which make massacre machinery" (19) and who tries his very best to save historical atrocities from being forgotten. Therefore, *Slaughterhouse-Five* does not call for "Passivity. Acceptance. Resignation. Denial. Looking the other way" (Hendin 39) or teach that "one cannot control one's fate, so one should simply allow things to happen" (Hartshorne 25), but, on the contrary: it pleads for active commitment and human responsibility. And its constitutive tension between Billy Pilgrim as the representative of Tralfamadorian fatalism and "Vonnegut" as the representative of human responsibility is established in the opening chapter.

Works Cited

Allen, William Rodney, ed. *Conversations with Kurt Vonnegut*. Jackson: UP of Mississippi, 1988. Print.

Barth, John. *Lost in the Funhouse: Fiction for Print, Tape, Live Voice*. New York: Bantam, 1969. Print.

Bellamy, Joe David, and John Casey. *The New Fiction: Interviews with Innovative American Writers*. Urbana: U of Illinois P, 1974. 194–207. Print.

Bosworth, Patricia. "To Vonnegut, the Hero Is the Man Who Refuses to Kill." *New York Times* 25 Oct. 1970, sec. 2: 5. Print.

Boyle, T. Coraghessan. *Water Music*. New York: Penguin, 1983. Print.

Doctorow, E. L. "False Documents." *Jack London, Hemingway, and the Constitution: Selected Essays, 1977–1992*. New York: Harper, 1994. 149–64. Print.

Edelstein, Arnold. "Slaughterhouse-Five: Time Out of Joint." *College Literature* 1.2 (1974): 128–39. Print.

Fairfield, James C. "*Slaughterhouse-Five*: A Selected Guide to Scholarship and Resources, 1987–1999," *Bulletin of Bibliography* 58.1 (2001): 49–57. Print.

Greiner, Donald J. "Vonnegut's *Slaughterhouse-Five* and the Fiction of Atrocity." *Critique* 14.3 (1973): 38–51. Print.

Harris, Charles. "Time, Uncertainty, and Kurt Vonnegut, Jr.: A Reading of *Slaughterhouse-Five*." *Centennial Review* 20.3 (1976): 228–43. Print.

Hartshorne, Thomas L. "From *Catch-22* to *Slaughterhouse V*: The Decline of the Political Mode." *South Atlantic Quarterly* 78.1 (1979): 17–33. Print.

Hayman, David, David Michaelis, George Plimpton, and Richard Rhodes. "Kurt Vonnegut: The Art of Fiction LXIV." *Paris Review* 69 (1977):55–103. Rpt. in Allen 168–95. Print.

Hendin, Josephine. *Vulnerable People: A View of American Fiction since 1945*. Oxford: Oxford UP, 1979. Print.

Lifton, Robert J. "Beyond Atrocity." *Saturday Review* 27 Mar. 1971: 23+. Print.

Matheson, T. J. "'This Lousy Little Book': The Genesis and Development of *Slaughterhouse-Five* as Revealed in Chapter One." Mustazza 215–30. Print.

Mustazza, Leonard, ed. Slaughterhouse-Five: *Critical Insights*. Pasadena: Salem, 2011. Print.

Scholes, Robert. "A Talk with Kurt Vonnegut, Jr." Allen 111–32. Print.

Standish, David. "Playboy Interview." Allen 76–110. Print.

Todd, Richard. "The Masks of Kurt Vonnegut, Jr." Allen 30–41. Print.

Vonnegut, Kurt. *Armageddon in Retrospect and Other New and Unpublished Writings on War and Peace*. Introd. by Mark Vonnegut. London: Cape, 2008. Print.

___. *Palm Sunday: An Autobiographical Collage*. London: Cape, 1981. Print.

___. *Slaughterhouse-Five; or, The Children's Crusade*. New York: Dell, 1970. Print.

___. *Timequake*. New York: Putnam, 1997. Print.

___. *Wampeters, Foma & Granfalloons (Opinions)*. New York: Delta, 1974. Print.

Waugh, Patricia. *Metafiction: The Theory and Practice of Self-Conscious Fiction*. London: Methuen, 1984. Print.

White, Hayden. *Metahistory: The Historical Imagination in Nineteenth-Century Europe*. Baltimore: Johns Hopkins UP, 1975. Print.

Looking for Vonnegut: Confronting Genre and the Author/Narrator Divide_____

P. L. Thomas

"I keep losing and regaining my equilibrium, which is the basic plot of all popular fiction" confesses Kurt Vonnegut, "And I myself am a work of fiction" (*Wampeters* xix). Readers and students confronted with the wide range of texts produced by Vonnegut—from his early career focused primarily on short stories to his fame and critical success as a novelist, including his often overlooked but prolific work in nonfiction essays and speeches—can also be fairly described as losing and regaining their equilibrium. One of the central qualities found in Vonnegut's writing, across genres is that he works within *and* against the conventions of genre, medium, and forms that guide readers and writers (e.g., D'Angelo and Johns).

For readers and students of Vonnegut's work, the many and overlapping genres and forms Vonnegut employs create tensions that affect how readers and writers view the text. Some of those tensions include what counts as text (print, graphics, film), how to define various genres, how to distinguish among media, and how to identify the distinctions between the merging roles of author and narrator within distinct genres and forms. Over Vonnegut's career, these textual tensions and problems are represented in Vonnegut's canon and his biography (e.g., Shields), and recur each time readers and students confront a text by Vonnegut.

Vonnegut's autobiography, as it emerges in his fiction and nonfiction writing, offers readers and students repeated opportunities to confront the problems of genre seen in Vonnegut's complicated relationship with science fiction and the problems of the author/narrator divide in Vonnegut's blurring of fiction and nonfiction. Fictionalized autobiographies appear in several Vonnegut novels (*Mother Night*), contrived autobiography in his nonfiction (e.g., Shields), and finally the "autobiography of a novel" that makes up the central focus of

118

Critical Insights

Timequake (Klinkowitz 14). Below, these tensions and problems with genre and the author/narrator are examined within three contexts: Vonnegut's multi-genre works that challenge conventional definitions of text, genre, medium, and form; the problem of science fiction highlighted in his essays and novels; and the conventions of autobiography that are blurred throughout his work as an examination of author and narrative voice.

Confronting Text by and through Vonnegut

Readers and writers, informally and as students, come to develop conscious and unconscious expectations about text. Text is often assumed to be printed words on the page (or virtual print in electronic media), but readers and writers also come to recognize graphics (comic books and graphic novels, traffic signs, and product iconography, for example) as text. Film, as opposed to the essentially static form of text just noted, also presents a dynamic version of text.

While Vonnegut's works primarily conform to the traditional view of text as print, Vonnegut includes graphic text in some novels—for example, in *Breakfast of Champions*, which is in part an exploration of the rising iconography associated with marketing in the United States—and his somewhat crude line-drawings reinforce another tension in Vonnegut's work: the tension between humor and serious topics. But Vonnegut's own experimentation as a visual artist is significant in his writing and his life that it parallels the problems posed by his blurring genres as well as the author/narrator divide (*Bluebeard*, for example, serves broadly as a meditation on modern art as well as a fictional autobiography of an artist).

Readers and students confront in Vonnegut a wide range of ways to understand and negotiate the text, ways that include a variety of avenues to acquire "genre awareness" (Johns 238–39). Briefly discussed here, then, are some of the ways Vonnegut's texts help "prepare students for the academic challenges" (Johns 239) of reading, textual analysis, and writing before a discussion on the ways in which

Vonnegut complicates genre with science fiction and the author/narrator divide through his blurring of fiction and nonfiction.

Most of the ways texts are classified are less prescriptive than descriptive, although formal schooling tends to teach such distinctions as prescriptions (e.g., Johns 238–40). As well, once a reader, writer, or student comes to understand a way to classify a text, new experiences with texts tend to either reinforce those expectations or challenge them in ways that help to create new definitions. Vonnegut's works, for example, tend to do both simultaneously.

As noted above, one way to consider text involves what counts as text (print, graphics, and film), but another surface distinction includes whether a text is prose (composed primarily of sentence and paragraphs) or poetry (composed primarily of lines and stanzas). In Vonnegut, readers and students are confronted almost exclusively with printed text (with some graphics) and prose. These relatively simple textual distinctions, however, are important choices within which Vonnegut works, as his writing complicates other, more complex ways to identify texts.

Genre is far more challenging as a way to understand and classify text—both as "the most socially constructivist of literary concepts" (Johns 238), and as a structure for understanding Vonnegut's work. One key problem with the term "genre" is that it is a shifting concept itself, applied in a wide variety of ways, remaining a concept of controversy within the varied fields of literacy. Classroom examinations of genre have remained bound to narrow and misleading frames— description, narration, exposition, and argumentation—even though *"the nineteenth-century forms/modes of discourse confuse forms with modes"* (D'Angelo 347–48).

As Vonnegut's works exemplify, genre is a much more complex classification of text. Johns explains that genre is a "social and cognitive" construction (239). In other words, writers and readers are bound to identify texts in ways that are informed by the context of the wider society. One powerful example of this was the public and media anger over James Frey's *A Million Little Pieces*, a controversy that centered around genre (was Frey's work fiction or memoir?) as much as whether or not Frey misled Oprah Winfrey and her audience (e.g., Wyatt). Vonnegut's canon exemplifies a blurring of that exact distinction between fiction and nonfiction.

Further, Johns explains that determination of genre includes purpose (the writer creates a text with genre conventions in mind); characteristics identified by some authority (a critic or teacher); qualities that assist in grouping texts (elements that characterize science fiction, horror, or romance, for example); various conventions, which, according to Johns, include "text structure, the register, the relationships between the writer and the audience, the uses of non-linear material (e.g. graphs or charts), the common fonts, and even the paper type and quality" (241); and variations that cannot be defined or anticipated. "For the goals of genre awareness and student education, the most important of these are probably the possibilities for variation: that texts from genres can, and do, vary, sometimes radically, from situation to situation" (Johns 241). As explored more fully below, Vonnegut's works are examples of and challenges to this nuanced and complex understanding of genre within a reader's expectations for science fiction, autobiography, and author/narrative voice. As well, Vonnegut's texts provide readers and students with examples of how conventions and expectations of genre inform and mislead readers as they negotiate meaning from the text and create meaning with texts.

Parallel to the significance of how texts conform to or challenge the norms of genre, texts also confront readers and students with problems of fiction and nonfiction (as in the Frey controversy noted above). In Vonnegut, this tension is inseparable from how his texts complicate expectations for genre. While Vonnegut's antagonistic connection to science fiction highlights how his works complicate definitions of genre, Vonnegut's evolution as a novelist, as it is informed by his nonfiction work, reveals a powerful blurring of the expectations for fiction and nonfiction, for truth and fabrication. Vonnegut's biographer Charles

Shields even argues that Vonnegut created the autobiographical elements in his work as purposefully and methodically as he shaped his science-fiction narrations.

Critic Jerome Klinkowitz suggests that "the key to understanding Kurt Vonnegut's seemingly unconventional work has always been to address that work's accessibility" (1). While Vonnegut's novels are unconventional, a key step to confronting his fiction, then, may be to start with his nonfiction, specifically his unusual collections of essays, including *Wampeters, Foma & Granfalloons*, *Palm Sunday*, *Fates Worse than Death*, and *A Man Without a Country*. Klinkowitz recognizes that Vonnegut's unconventional style is consistent across genres and medium, and his fiction and nonfiction works share the same purpose, that is, "the desire to speak directly and convincingly to his audience" (1).

Genre expectations suggest that Vonnegut the man is the primary and real voice driving his essays, while some created narrator or persona is telling the fictional stories of his novels. Yet, in Vonnegut, that distinction falls apart. As Shields notes, Vonnegut worked purposefully and persistently to create an author persona that masked the real Vonnegut. Further, close examinations of Vonnegut's career reveal an evolving voice that was somewhat muted during his early phase as a short-story writer but that developed throughout his career as novelist and stood powerfully at the center of his essays, which was "beginning in 1964 the author's most consistent source of income" (Klinkowitz 5).

As a contrast to classroom messages about the essay as a mode of academic communication, Vonnegut's essays present many techniques associated with fiction writing, characteristics common in New Journalism, in which "writers made sense of a situation by placing themselves at its center and describing their own experience" (Klinkowitz 5). Klinkowitz argues, "Vonnegut's essays became an important mode of artistic expression and helped shape the revolutionary formats of his novels" (5).

Vonnegut's writing style proves to be grounded in conventional expectations for texts, genre, and medium while also "deliberately breaking conventional rules" (Klinkowitz 6). For example, readers and students experience tensions in Vonnegut's essays that do not conform to expectations about essay components (thesis, body, and conclusion), organization, and tone. Academic writing, like traditional norms for journalism, requires the writer to take an objective and authoritative stance by removing the writer from the text; Vonnegut as journalist, essayist, and novelist, however, insinuates himself directly into all of his writing, regardless of genre or medium. *Palm Sunday*, for example, is a collection of nonfiction described by Vonnegut as an "autobiographical collage"—at once calling to mind genre characteristics (autobiography, collage) and creating a genre unique to Vonnegut: "This theme is the power of writing, and the rhetoric involves Vonnegut's autobiographical experiences in living by the word" (Klinkowitz 11).

While Vonnegut's cultural and critical fame revolves around the success of *Slaughterhouse-Five*, a World War II novel drawn from Vonnegut's real-life experience as a WWII prisoner of war (POW), Klinkowitz explains:

> Kurt Vonnegut's novels during the decades of *Wampeters* and *Palm Sunday* parallel his evolving manner as an essayist. The author's tendency to introduce autobiographical elements into his fiction coincide with the self-apparent personal qualities in the essays and book reviews he began writing during this same period. . . . In both fiction and nonfiction, the author was not only drawing on his autobiography but using elements of his life to alter each genre's form. (12)

Vonnegut's authorial and narrative voices are bound to his blending of genres and manipulation of the conventions of fiction and nonfiction. As critic Bill Gholson notes, Vonnegut's "moral thinking and writing reflect a rhetorical orientation—one for which the self is never disembodied from the community, the history, and the discourses of which it is a part" (135). The version of himself that Vonnegut creates in his essays seems to be a persona that Vonnegut wants his readers to know—and possibly whom he wishes he could have been. In his novels, this persona serves as thinly veiled versions of Vonnegut, often as the narrator but sometimes as characters in the narrative; "Vonnegut blends genres, creating and recreating himself in the narrative" (Gholson 137). Vonnegut's essays and novels are artifacts of Vonnegut's self-consciousness and self-creation.

Finally, before looking more fully at science fiction and autobiography in Vonnegut's works, it is worth noting that readers and students are challenged by Vonnegut in terms of expectations of how to determine meaning from texts. Just as Vonnegut's essays and novels create tensions within the traditional definitions of genre, Vonnegut's quest to speak to and with his audience challenges the modernist view of textual meaning as defined by New Criticism (e.g., Daiches and Eagleton). New Criticism places meaning entirely in the text, decontextualized from the author's biography, the time and place of the text's writing, and the time and place of the reader. In short, New Criticism is a technical analysis of text that seeks to be objective. Vonnegut, however, embraces an authorial stance that is more closely associated with reader-response criticism (e.g., Rosenblatt), which views textual meaning as a discourse among reader, writer, and text: "Vonnegut invites readers to participate in the creation of his moral skeleton. Therefore, identity in Vonnegut's work is narrative and 'collaborative' (*Fates Worse Than Death* 49–50)" writes Gholson. Vonnegut's "work is his body" (Gholson 138).

Next, the many tensions created in the works of Vonnegut are highlighted in the intricate relationship that Vonnegut had with science fiction, a genre Vonnegut was closely associated with despite his own antagonistic relationship with the genre and his resistance to the popular and critical view that he was a science-fiction writer.

Vonnegut and the Problem of Science Fiction

In the opening essay of *Wampeters, Foma and Granfalloons*, after the preface, Vonnegut presents the essay "Science Fiction," originally printed in the *New York Times* in 1965, in which he explains his classification as a science-fiction writer: "I wrote a novel about people and machines, and machines frequently got the best of it, as machines will. . . . And I learned from the reviewers that I was a science-fiction writer" (1). Vonnegut then places himself squarely in the controversy concerning science fiction as a genre. "I have been a soreheaded occupant of a file drawer labeled 'science fiction' ever since," he explains, adding, "and I would like out, particularly since so many serious critics regularly mistake the drawer for a urinal" (1).

Despite the displeasure expressed in 1965 and almost a decade later when the essay was included in *Wampeters*, Vonnegut persisted in writing novels that included significant science-fictional elements—time travel, technology, science-based apocalypse, evolution. In "Science Fiction," Vonnegut offers a typically Vonnegutian way of determining what counts as science fiction and which writers are science-fiction writers, raising questions about George Orwell and Franz Kafka, for example. While Vonnegut's writing presents a running problem with genre, his antagonistic relation with science fiction presents an ideal opportunity to understand better science fiction through the debate surrounding the genre. As well, Vonnegut's science-fictional tendencies help to highlight how genre influences popular, scholarly, and critical perceptions of texts and authors.

Concerning a clear definition of science fiction, literary scholar Adam Roberts notes, "there is among all these thinkers no single consensus on what [science fiction] is, beyond agreement that it is a form of cultural discourse . . . that involves a world-view differentiated in one way or another from the actual world in which its readers live" (2). While attempts to define the genre of science fiction have produced more argument than clarification, Roberts notes that science fiction tends to include technology, aliens, space travel and time travel, synthetic life forms, and the like. Confronting Vonnegut's work as either science fiction or not science fiction helps to create a rich understanding of Vonnegut, genre, and science fiction.

Author of *The Handmaid's Tale*, *Oryx and Crake*, *The Year of the Flood*, and many other works spanning various genres and forms, Margaret Atwood entered into a debate over science fiction with highly revered science-fiction author and critic Ursula K. Le Guin. Atwood distanced herself from the science-fiction label much as Vonnegut had, stating that she did not want her works to be labeled as science fiction. As a result, she rekindled the debate over science fiction's merits and parameters, particularly in regards to the genres of science fiction, dystopian fiction, speculative fiction, and fantasy.

Like Vonnegut's antagonism over being treated as a science-fiction writer, Atwood's nuanced consideration of genre is often misinterpreted as a negative critique of science fiction itself. Vonnegut and Atwood, however, appear to be most concerned with the stigma associated with science fiction, not the genre itself. For readers and students, genre classifications often default to designations of quality. Literary fiction, which many so-called "serious" writers aspire to, is afforded critical consideration that science fiction is not, part of which includes the ironic stigma of being popular. If an author is popular, some conventions suggest that writer cannot be serious. Vonnegut and Atwood both produced serious works and extensive canons, so their problems with science fiction tend to rest on how the genre is marginalized and denigrated.

Atwood, then, offers a reasoned and complex consideration of science fiction, and any genre classification, and weighs in on the debate surrounding science fiction. "In short, what Le Guin means by 'science fiction' is what I mean by 'speculative fiction,' and what she means by 'fantasy' would include some of what I mean by 'science fiction'" clarifies Atwood, "When it comes to genres, the borders are increasingly undefended" (7). Further, Atwood recognizes science fiction as a narrative form that presents, creates, and examines *other worlds*, a broad but fair recognition that one science-fiction work exists in an alternate universe while another exists on alien planets and yet another exists in a world that appears to be here and now but with technological advances that certainly are not. And that brings Atwood specifically to a problem with science fiction and genre classifications found in Vonnegut's work and that of other writers. Atwood cites Bruce Sterling's 1989 essay "Slipstream" in which he assesses a number of contemporary, critically acclaimed writers who have been categorized as "science-fiction" authors. Atwood notes of these writers, "What they have in common is that the kind of events they recount are unlikely to *have actually taken place*" (8). Yet, for Vonnegut, his *Slaughterhouse-Five* stands as one of the most praised novels of the twentieth century *and* a work that combines elements of science fiction (time travel, aliens) with autobiographical details from his real-life experience as a prisoner of war during World War II.

The novel *Breakfast of Champions* opens with a preface, signaling a pattern in Vonnegut that would be repeated in much of his later work, where most novels include opening sections that blur the line between Vonnegut the writer and the narrator and characters of the novel, the line between fiction and nonfiction. Yet, with *Slaughterhouse-Five*, Vonnegut opens the work with "All this happened, more or less. The war parts, anyway, are pretty much true" (1). Therein lies the inherent tensions that characterize Vonnegut's work, tensions between tragedy and humor, fiction and nonfiction, author and narrator, and history and fabrication.

In paperback format, *Slaughterhouse-Five* proceeds for almost thirty pages without propelling the central plot forward or introducing the novel's characters (except for revealing *both* the opening and ending lines of the novel in the last few sentences of the first chapter). Chapter 1 of Vonnegut's signature novel is essentially a nonfiction essay about how Vonnegut came to write the novelization of his wartime experience and to add the subtitle (*Or, The Children's Crusade: A Duty-Dance with Death*) because of the fear expressed by Mary O'Hare, wife of a fellow vet, that his novel would glorify war. As Sumner states, "The opening chapter of *Slaughterhouse-Five* annihilates the boundary between fiction and autobiography" (126).

Now, is *Slaughterhouse-Five* rightfully classified a science-fiction novel, and if so does such a classification of genre truly matter in the negative ways suggested by Vonnegut (and even Atwood)? First, identifying *Slaughterhouse-Five* as a science-fictional novel appears equally as legitimate as autobiographical, satirical, or historical categorizations in that this novel has powerful elements of each of those genres. But the science-fiction designation does carry with it, as critic Lorna Jowett explains, both positive characteristics and significantly negative impressions, particularly in terms of critical reception:

> Science fiction can have immense temporal range, giving it epic range. One novel can deal with the whole of time; a time travel story can shift between many different time periods. . . . [But there is] a problem inherent in using the fantastic to comment on the real: people are often distracted by the medium and do not perceive the message.
>
> Another "problem" of science fiction, and something that causes it to be easily dismissed by those championing "real" literature, is that it may value the idea, the message, above the medium. (133)

Slaughterhouse-Five, as a time-travel narrative exploring the horrors of World War II, then, falls squarely into the problems identified by Jowett. The problem may become that this novel is either an autobiographical war novel with science-fiction elements or a science-fiction novel with autobiographical elements and a war setting and plot. As Elizabeth Abele explains, "Vonnegut's war novels are also significant for their quasi-autobiographical nature, which works to bring reality to the more fantastic elements of the narratives" (68)—specifically, those elements, such as aliens and time travel, that help classify the work as science fiction.

To classify a work as science fiction, a first step includes determining what characteristics that work demonstrates that conform to the genre; in other words, how is *Slaughterhouse-Five* a science-fiction novel? Then, once those elements are identified, the classification should rest on how essential those elements are to the novel as the work the writer intended. The first step with *Slaughterhouse-Five* is relatively easy, as Billy Pilgrim, the protagonist, is "unstuck in time" (*Slaughterhouse-Five* 29), and thus the narrative of the novel is a tour de force of Vonnegut's style—brief and disjointed sections that appear haphazard in the flow but fall into place as a coherent whole once the entire novel has been read.

Time travel is both an element of *Slaughterhouse-Five* and a defining characteristic of science-fiction novels. The time travel convention is also strongly tied, both thematically and narratively, to another characteristic typical of science fiction—aliens. In the novel, Billy Pilgrim confesses "that he had been kidnapped by a flying saucer in 1967. The saucer was from the planet Tralfamadore, he said. He was taken to Tralfamadore, where he was displayed naked in a zoo, he said. He was mated there with a former Earthling movie star named Montana Wildhack" (*Slaughterhouse-Five* 32). The question, then, with *Slaughterhouse-Five* is not whether or not Vonnegut incorporates significant science-fiction elements, but whether or not classifying the novel as science fiction is accurate.

The powerful and defining characteristic of Vonnegut's writing, regardless of genre, is his adept use of *tension*. Vonnegut, an avowed agnostic Freethinker, refers to and cites Jesus repeatedly. Vonnegut's style is often journalistic within a fictional narrative, and Vonnegut is also autobiographical in his fiction while taking creative license with his autobiography in his nonfiction essays, creating the Vonnegut he wants his readers to see, regardless of who he was in real life. Thus, Vonnegut blends satire and dark humor with the tragic, as he pairs historical fiction with science-fiction elements. These tensions are what make Vonnegut's writing distinctly challenging.

Vonnegut incorporating science-fiction elements and simultaneously taking a stance against being classified as a science-fiction writer represents exactly why *Slaughterhouse-Five*, and many of his other works, are fairly classified as science fiction. A central motif of

Slaughterhouse-Five is time—contrasting human perceptions of time with the Tralfamadorian perception of time, which is nearly incomprehensible or, within the constraints of human language, a concept that can be captured in Vonnegut's narration: "I am a Tralfamadorian, seeing all time as you might see a stretch of the Rocky Mountains. All time is all time. It does not change. It does not lend itself to warnings or explanations. It simply is. Take it moment by moment, and you will find that we all are, as I've said before, bugs in amber" (*Slaughterhouse-Five* 109).

The motif of time, the organization and style of the novel, and the science-fiction elements of time travel and aliens are inextricably intertwined in ways that make *Slaughterhouse-Five* a science-fiction novel. Now, as one more argument for this designation, *Slaughterhouse-Five* is often compared with Joseph Heller's *Catch-22*, as Heller and Vonnegut share many autobiographical details and the novels both combine the tragedies of World War II with satire. What distinguishes *Slaughterhouse-Five* from *Catch-22* are the science-fiction elements that ultimately make *Slaughterhouse-Five* the unique work of fiction, combining satire and history, that it is.

For readers and students of Vonnegut, *Slaughterhouse-Five* typifies how Vonnegut creates tensions through his use of genre elements. As a typical science-fiction novel, *Slaughterhouse-Five* would likely be less compelling, but as a science-fiction novel that uses the conventions of that genre against the conventions of satire and historical fiction, Vonnegut produces a work that is distinct as well as notable for its merging conventions and techniques adapted from a spectrum of genres, modes, and media. Like science fiction, Vonnegut's works depend heavily on another tension in his arsenal, the role of autobiography.

Autobiography as Metafiction/Nonfiction

In his biography on Vonnegut, *Unstuck in Time*, Gregory Sumner describes Vonnegut's 1987 novel *Bluebeard* as "an exploration of creativity and the possibilities of realism versus abstraction in communicating

---

the human experience" (261). One can imagine abstracting that comment to Vonnegut's career, recognizing that Vonnegut spent his entire existence as a human and as a writer trying to discover and create himself, both for and with the reader—an exploration of himself. *Bluebeard* appears to fictionalize the debate about whether artists such as Jackson Pollock were *true* artists—that tension between realism and abstract expressionism that is paralleled by Vonnegut's line drawings in *Breakfast of Champions* and his perpetual resistance to the science fiction label. Is a science-fiction writer a *real* writer? Are Vonnegut's line drawings and paintings consisting mainly of words *real* artwork?

At the core of Vonnegut's work, then, is Vonnegut the rule-breaker. To break the rules, the adage goes, one must first know the rules. Thus, in Vonnegut, readers discover journalism and historical narratives that reject objectivity and embrace the journalist as part of the story, as in New Journalism. Readers discover the fictional narrator and the narration disrupted by the author, who is insinuating himself into the story, which forces readers to consider whether or not the Vonnegut described in his nonfiction was in fact fabricating this persona as part of his artistic vision (as Shields has suggested in his biography).

Central to Vonnegut's writing is Vonnegut himself; as noted above, Vonnegut identifies himself as a work of fiction. But the autobiographical tendencies of Vonnegut, regardless of genre, are strongly linked with his need to challenge authority. As Shields notes, Vonnegut "demonstrates his love of debunking fixed ideas and institutions that are usually treated with reverence" (125). As a result, his nonfiction defies the traditional expectations for nonfiction, and his fiction comes to be a place where Vonnegut the man intrudes when modernist norms dictate the allure of the first-person narrator. In F. Scott Fitzgerald's *The Great Gatsby*, the novel's protagonist Nick is the reader's sole guide, although Fitzgerald clearly depends on his own life to inform his narrative; much is the same in the works of Ernest Hemingway. But in Fitzgerald and Hemingway, the author remains hidden, while

Vonnegut, over the course of his career, moves from the background to the introductions, and then to center stage.

As a companion to exploring Vonnegut through genre classifications, specifically science fiction, Vonnegut's work is examined below as it incorporates autobiography in a wide variety of ways that inform his unique approaches to genre conventions as well as to nonfiction and fiction more broadly. Autobiography in his nonfiction works becomes Vonnegut creating Vonnegut, while autobiography in his fiction evolves from fictional autobiography (a character presents the narrative as his personal autobiography) to Vonnegut inserting his biography into fictional works directly, and then to the autobiography of a novel itself, as in *Timequake* (e.g., Klinkowitz).

Breakfast of Champions was published four years after *Slaughterhouse-Five*, though Vonnegut has suggested that the works were significantly connected in their genesis. Part of that connection is the similarity between the nonfiction quality to Chapter 1 of *Slaughterhouse-Five* and the preface to *Breakfast of Champions*—a technique that suggests, as Shields claims, "*Breakfast of Champions* is the beginning of his second major phase as a novelist" (309–10), one that can be recognized in part by the more frequent use of direct autobiography in the novels.

This transition as a novelist overlaps with the publication of *Wampeters, Foma and Granfalloons*, which collects essays published from the mid-1960s through the early 1970s, when *Slaughterhouse-Five* and *Breakfast of Champions* were also taking shape. Vonnegut's evolution as a novelist is deeply indebted to his experiences as an essayist (as Klinkowitz has argued), particularly as his use of autobiography has informed both forms. But even the autobiographical elements in his work are characterized by tension: "I am not especially satisfied with my own imaginative works, my fiction. I am simply impressed by the unexpected insights which shower down on me when my job is to imagine, as contrasted with the woodenly familiar ideas which clutter my desk when my job is to tell the truth" (*Wampeters* xxv–xxvi).

Vonnegut's quest to define himself in his writing, then, may be seen as a quest to avoid "the woodenly familiar"—whether that includes the familiar details of his life used in his essays or the familiar details of his life incorporated directly into his fiction. Autobiography in Vonnegut's nonfiction accomplishes some key characteristics of his full canon: redefining the form (Vonnegut's essays are unlike traditional essays, just as his science-fiction novels redefine science fiction), creating tensions between his real-life experiences and ideologies and the norms of society (a Freethinker quoting Jesus, for example), and blurring the conventions of genre and form by turning to meta-genre (the speech becomes a speech about giving speeches, for example).

In *Wampeters* and *Palm Sunday*, autobiography leads readers to Vonnegut while simultaneously masking the "woodenly familiar" Vonnegut behind the nonfiction persona he carefully crafts in his essays, speeches, and interviews (e.g., Allen, McCartan). The essay as a writing form has traditional characteristics, especially in academic and scholarly settings that include a rigid organizational pattern, such as the five-paragraph essay (discussed by Johns), and the objective tone that includes the muted writer (the schoolhouse proscription against using the first-person voice in writing). In Vonnegut, however, the essay is an unwieldy thing.

Vonnegut's essay "Teaching the Unteachable," for example, features Vonnegut front and center in an essay that begins in its title and first sentence by creating tension: "You can't teach people to write well" (25), although here, Vonnegut is writing about being a teacher himself at writers conferences. The tone of this essay is similar to the autobiographical elements informing *Slaughterhouse-Five*, as with most of his other novels. In part, the Vonnegut presented in his essays, and other works, is a witness:

I tried to help those good students become what they were born to become. . . . I wanted to take hold of the end of a spool of ticker tape in the back of each student's throat. I meant to pull it out inch by inch, so the student and

> I could read it. The student's literary destiny, which had nothing to do with
> me or the University of Iowa, was written on the tape. (*Wampeters* 29–30)

Vonnegut is self-effacing and disarming, both in his role as witness to being unable to teach the "unteachable" and through his standard use of joke-telling to drive even his nonfiction essays.

Vonnegut as a work of fiction, as narrator and character in his novels, is paralleled by Vonnegut as a character in his essays, likely best captured in his carefully crafted association with the pseudonymous Mark Twain. Twain perfected the craft of fabricating an authorial self well before Vonnegut, but the association is worth noting since, as Vonnegut states himself, "I have meditated with Mark Twain's mind" (*Palm Sunday* 151), meaning perhaps that he collected and reshaped himself in a nonfiction genre Vonnegut labels "autobiographical collage."

Again, in his discussion of Twain, Vonnegut recognizes the inherent tension of his true self: "It hasn't always been convenient or attractive to comport myself as the purely American person I am" (*Palm Sunday* 151), introductory words leading to another form he manipulates, the speech. The speech that follows was delivered in 1979 to commemorate the anniversary of Twain's house being built. In typical Vonnegut fashion, he associates Twain with Jesus at the beginning of the talk, as an avenue to confronting the religious skepticism and bitterness Vonnegut shared with Twain.

In this speech, Vonnegut addresses the added tension of how and why writers present the truth, even when they distort facts or fabricate entire narratives:

> In Twain's time, and on the frontier, a person who calculated this or that
> was asking that his lies be respected, since they had been arrived at by
> means of arithmetic. He wanted you to acknowledge that the arithmetic,
> the logic of his lies, was sound. . . .
>
> This is the secret of good storytelling: to lie, but to keep the arithmetic
> sound. (*Palm Sunday* 153)

The larger irony of Vonnegut includes that he was a deeply moral writer, bound to foundational and even universal truths, functioning in a postmodern era as well as a postmodern paradigm for breaking conventions. Vonnegut sought to break the rules—whether he was working in essays, speeches, or novels—while always keeping "the arithmetic sound." Vonnegut ends with a nod to the power of myth; it appears he saw mythmaking as central to all of his writing, regardless of genre or form.

Vonnegut's work as an essayist and speechmaker is also reflected in another form—the interview (e.g., Allen, McCartan), possibly the logical extension of bringing autobiography to the forefront of any text. The role of the interview in understanding Vonnegut matches his public appeal as a speaker. In *Wampeters*, the collection ends with his famous *Playboy* interview. Later, in *Palm Sunday*, essays, speeches, and interviews became seamless in Vonnegut's own creation, the autobiographical collage, including Vonnegut's self-interview from the *Paris Review* in 1977. The self-interview also represents Vonnegut's genre-bending techniques: "This interview is purely written. Not a word of it was spoken aloud" (*Palm Sunday* 73). Just as Vonnegut protested that *Slaughterhouse-Five* is not science fiction, he creates an interview that is not an interview.

In the nonfiction genres and forms most common among Vonnegut's works—essays, speeches, interviews—the author/speaker divide and the role of autobiography are significant and often complicating factors within the expectations for the genre, although in nonfiction the author's voice is more often transparent than in fiction. Traditional and modernistic expectations for the author/narrator divide as well as the role of autobiography to inform fiction is expressed by a foundational concept from the novelist John Gardner: "Fiction does its work by creating a dream in the reader's mind. We may observe, first, that if the effect of the dream is to be powerful, the dream must probably be vivid and continuous" (31). One technique for accomplishing that dream is to mask the author behind a narrator. Gardner specifically rejected postmodern metafiction in which the author interrupted the narration, confronting directly that storytelling is taking place.

Four of Vonnegut's novels discussed below present representative examples of how Vonnegut as author incorporates autobiography and imposes himself into his fiction as a challenge to and redefinition of the novel. Further, Gardner's idea of the vivid and continuous dream appears central to science fiction, if not all fiction, but Vonnegut's commitment to himself as a work of fiction both contradicts and fulfills Gardner's traditional commandment.

"This is the only story of mine whose moral I know," opens the Introduction to Vonnegut's *Mother Night*, suggesting that Vonnegut embraces Gardner's call for moral fiction: "We are what we pretend to be, so we must be careful about what we pretend to be" (*Mother Night* v). Vonnegut's third novel, published in 1961, presents both the blurring of the author/narrator and the significant role of autobiography in Vonnegut's fiction. *Mother Night* opens with an Introduction (added in 1966) and an Editor's Note signed by Vonnegut.

The Editor's Note is a fictionalized explanation by Vonnegut as the editor of the fictionalized autobiography of Howard W. Campbell Jr., the fictional author of the fictional autobiography that is the novel *Mother Night*. The tensions in this novel help to create a foundation for the patterns that come to define Vonnegut's later fiction. One tension is that *Mother Night* is unlike many of Vonnegut's novels as his style is mostly masked by the commitment to this novel being an autobiography by the fictional Campbell. As well, the use of an Introduction and Editor's Note gives the novel some traditional qualities (autobiography informs the narrative but an author who remains mostly masked once the novel begins properly in Chapter 1), but also suggests the more overt blending of nonfiction and fiction along with the evolution of Vonnegut as an powerful voice and character in his novels—more directly seen in the transition of *Slaughterhouse-Five* and *Breakfast of Champions*.

While Vonnegut assumes the role of editor of an autobiography in *Mother Night*, Vonnegut presents both himself and his unique take on the novel with *Breakfast of Champions*, a transitional point in his career. Incorporating what would come to be Vonnegut's signature line drawings, Vonnegut replaces the nonfiction Chapter 1 of *Slaughterhouse-Five* with a preface signed by Philboyd Studge, who thinly disguises Vonnegut as himself, confessing: "I'm throwing out characters from my other books, too. I'm not going to put on any more puppet shows" (5). Characters created from Vonnegut's life, who mask Vonnegut himself, and Vonnegut as a speaker and character recur throughout Vonnegut's canon, notably Kilgore Trout who is central to *Breakfast of Champions*.

Trout, as a hack science-fiction writer, echoes many of the key elements of Vonnegut's confronting genre, form, and the author/narrator divide. *Breakfast of Champions* signals a shift in Vonnegut's approach to his fiction, as he increasingly incorporated autobiography into his work. By the late 1960s and early 1970s, Vonnegut had achieved recognition as a popular and possibly important writer, but he also had fostered a celebrity status that allowed him to intrude more directly into his work, and thereby, *simultaneously* breaking the conventions of traditional fiction and narration as well as fulfilling the "continuous and vivid dream" through his own cult of personality.

Bluebeard presents yet another overt fictional autobiography, this one of artist Rabo Karabekian:

> Having written "The End" to this story of my life, I find it prudent to scamper back here to before the beginning, to my front door, so to speak, and to make this apology to arriving guests: "I promised you an autobiography, but something went wrong in the kitchen. It turns out to be a *diary* of this past troubled summer, too! We can always send out for pizzas if necessary. Come *in*, come *in*." (1)

Highlighted in the novel's opening paragraph, Vonnegut again complicates genre (raising the tensions between autobiography and diary in a novel) and reveals the evolution of Vonnegut's style.

Bluebeard also more fully examines the merging of Vonnegut as writer and Vonnegut as visual artist, central to *Breakfast of Champions*. "It relates to the poles of his writing method, journalistic detail on the one end, experimental language, comedy, and scifi effects on the other, both approaches evident from his earliest fiction" (Sumner 262). *Bluebeard* draws Karabekian from *Breakfast*, suggesting that Vonnegut imbues his fictional world with the exact community that became central to his nonfiction motifs—themes he expressed in essays and speeches repeatedly throughout his career.

Regardless of the popular or critical success of *Timequake*, readers looking for Vonnegut find him fully demonstrated in this "autobiography of a novel" (Klinkowitz 14). In fact, *Timequake* serves as autobiography, an autobiography of the writing of a novel that is difficult to complete, and an autobiography that continues to redefine genres and form (autobiography, science fiction, and novel). The novelization about the original novel, more metafiction by Vonnegut, is bookended by Vonnegut himself in the book's Prologue and Epilogue. In the Prologue, Vonnegut speaks directly as himself to the reader, offering first an anecdote about Ernest Hemingway's novella *The Old Man in the Sea*. This builds to the author's confession about this novel: "And then I found myself in the winter of 1996 the creator of a novel which did not work, which had no point, which had never wanted to be written in the first place" (xiii–xiv). The solution came in the form of a novel about the novel that failed to take shape, with Vonnegut ending his novel-writing career with a science-fictional autobiography that includes Vonnegut as author and character as well as Kilgore Trout: "Trout doesn't really exist. He has been my alter ego in several of my other novels. But most of what I have chosen to preserve from *Timequake One* has to do with his adventures and opinions" (xv).

Echoing the iconic opening to *Moby-Dick*'s "Call me Ishmael," Vonnegut's last novel begins with "Call me Junior" (1). *Timequake* includes most of the qualities come to be associated with Vonnegut, but the Epilogue helps to draw a suitable end to the issue of the author/

narrator divide that Vonnegut always sought to close, the compulsion he felt to speak directly to his audience through himself regardless of the genre or form his writing took. The Epilogue focuses on Vonnegut's family, specifically the death of his brother Bernard. But toward the end of the book, Vonnegut's dark side emerges in "Extenuating circumstances to be mentioned on Judgment Day: We never asked to be born in the first place" (249). It is here that another warning from Vonnegut seems to echo in the background: "We are what we pretend to be, so we must be careful about what we pretend to be" (*Mother Night* v).

Vonnegut, to the end of his life and to the end of his writing career, took his own advice seriously, although he may not have fulfilled the purpose of his belief that his life was a work of fiction, meaning he had to be careful in what he pretended to be. In Vonnegut's work, writing, experimentation, and living are gradually and then fully merged by using genre to reform genre. Vonnegut grappled with both fiction and nonfiction to merge them into one, and he also worked on himself along with his writing so that he could stand at the center of his writing universe and, through his manufactured self, be who created the dream entertaining and instructing his audience.

Works Cited

Abele, Elizabeth. "The Journey Home in Kurt Vonnegut's War World II." *New Critical Essays on Kurt Vonnegut*. Ed. David Simmons. New York: Palgrave, 2009. 67–88. Print.

Allen, William Rodney, ed. *Conversations with Kurt Vonnegut*. Jackson: UP of Mississippi, 1988. Print.

Atwood, Margaret. *In Other Worlds: SF and the Human Imagination*. New York: Doubleday, 2011. Print.

Daiches, David. "The New Criticism: Some Qualifications." *English Journal* 39.2 (1950): 64–72. Print.

D'Angelo, Frank J. "Nineteenth-Century Forms/Modes of Discourse: A Critical Inquiry." *The Norton Book of Composition Studies*. Ed. Susan Miller. New York: Norton, 2009. 347–57. Print.

Eagleton, Terry. *Literary Theory: An Introduction*. 2d ed. Minneapolis: U of Minnesota P, 1996. Print.

Gardner, John. *The Art of Fiction: Notes on Craft for Young Writers*. New York: Vintage, 1983. Print.

Gholson, Bill. "Narrative, Self, and Morality in the Writing of Kurt Vonnegut." *At Millennium's End: New Essays on the Work of Kurt Vonnegut*. Ed. Kevin Alexander Boon. Albany: SUNY P, 2001. 135–47. Print.

Johns, Ann M. "Genre Awareness for the Novice Academic Student: An Ongoing Quest." *Language Teaching* 41.2 (2008): 237–52. Print.

Jowett, Lorna. "Folding Time: History, Subjectivity, and Intimacy in Vonnegut." *New Critical Essays on Kurt Vonnegut*. Ed. David Simmons. New York: Palgrave, 2009. 134–46. Print.

Klinkowitz, Jerome. "Vonnegut the Essayist." *At Millennium's End: New Essays on the Work of Kurt Vonnegut*. Ed. Kevin Alexander Boon. Albany: SUNY P, 2001. 1–16. Print.

McCartan, Tom, ed. *Kurt Vonnegut: The Last Interview and Other Conversations*. Brooklyn: Melville, 2011. Print.

Roberts, Adam. *The History of Science Fiction*. New York: Palgrave, 2005. Print.

Rosenblatt, Louise. *Literature as Exploration*. 5th ed. New York: MLA, 1995. Print.

Shields, Charles J. *And So It Goes. Kurt Vonnegut: A Life*. New York: Holt, 2011. Print.

Sumner, Gordon D. *Unstuck in Time: A Journey through Kurt Vonnegut's Life and Novels*. New York: Seven Stories, 2011. Print.

Vonnegut, Kurt. *Bluebeard*. New York: Delta, 1987. Print.

___. *Breakfast of Champions or Goodbye Blue Monday*. New York: Delta, 1973. Print.

___. *A Man without a Country*. New York: Seven Stories, 2005. Print.

___. *Mother Night*. New York: Delta, 1961/1966. Print.

___. *Palm Sunday: An Autobiographical Collage*. New York: Delta, 1981. Print.

___. *Timequake*. New York: Berkeley, 1997. Print.

___. *Wampeters, Foma & Granfalloons (Opinions)*. New York: Delta, 1974. Print.

Wyatt, Edward. "Best Selling Memoir Draws Scrutiny." *New York Times*. New York Times Co., 10 Jan. 2006. Web. 30 July 2012.

Vonnegut and Religion: Daydreaming about God_____
Susan E. Farrell

A self-proclaimed "Christ-worshipping agnostic" (*Palm Sunday* 298), Kurt Vonnegut's relationship to organized systems of religion was complex and nuanced. Raised in a family of German Americans who had considered themselves "freethinkers" for generations, Vonnegut told his listeners, in a 1979 speech given at the Mark Twain house in Hartford, Connecticut: "I am of course a skeptic about the divinity of Christ and a scorner of the notion that there is a God who cares how we are or what we do" (*Palm Sunday* 152). Vonnegut was particularly uneasy with conventional Christianity, especially in its fundamentalist forms, frequently reminding readers of Christianity's historical cruelties—the Inquisition, the Crusades—as well as what he considered to be the narrow-minded thinking of evangelical preachers and politicians of the later twentieth century. Yet, at the same time, he recognized that ordinary human beings need moral systems to help guide and shape their lives. Throughout his work, he professed a real love for Christ's message of mercy and redemption. He heartily admired the Sermon on the Mount, and viewed Christ's alliance with the poor, the meek, the hungry, and the peacemakers of the world as tantamount to an early form of socialism. In his 2005 essay collection, *A Man without a Country*, Vonnegut writes, "Christianity and socialism alike, in fact, prescribe a society dedicated to the proposition that all men, women, and children are created equal and shall not starve" (11).

The fundamental dilemma one sees over and over in Vonnegut's work, then, is how to retain a sound ethical system, what he calls a "heartfelt moral code" (*Palm Sunday* 185), in a contemporary world where conventional religions no longer offer people a sense of community or spiritual fulfillment. To this end, Vonnegut continuously depicts attempts to establish new religions in his novels, including Paul Proteus, who allows himself to become the "New Messiah" of the revolutionary Ghost Shirt Society in *Player Piano*; Winston Niles

Rumfoord, who engineers a Martian invasion of Earth in order to install a new religion known as the Church of God the Utterly Indifferent in *The Sirens of Titan*; the self-proclaimed phony religious prophet Bokonon in *Cat's Cradle*; poor, bewildered Billy Pilgrim in *Slaughterhouse-Five*, who imagines a heaven complete with a porn star Eve and alien gods shaped like toilet plungers;, and the establishment of the utterly bizarre Church of Jesus Christ the Kidnapped in *Slapstick*. Vonnegut's characters repeatedly work to create new moral and religious structures to give their lives meaning. Ironically, almost all of these invented religions are doomed to failure, subject to the same kind of cruelties and absurdities that plague the more traditional religions that Vonnegut frequently railed against. Nevertheless, this essay argues that Vonnegut admires these attempts to live moral lives, however mistaken they might ultimately be—it is the belief in one's ability to change, to shape one's life for the better, even if these beliefs finally prove futile or illusory, that makes an individual fully human.

Vonnegut's Critique of Contemporary Christianity

A lifelong advocate of the separation of church and state, Vonnegut suggests that the United States government has gone wrong when it places divine law above the civic laws of the nation. While covering the 1972 Republican National Convention for *Harper's Magazine*, Vonnegut was stunned by a sermon delivered by Dr. D. Elton Trueblood, a Quaker philosopher and college professor who argued for the "Divine Right of Presidents" (*Wampeters* 194). Trueblood later clarified his remarks by telling Vonnegut that because God alone is sovereign, the president has more responsibility to God than to citizens of the United States. Vonnegut believed this type of thinking was deeply ingrained in the country and served to explain why so many contemporary Americans refuse to respect the First Amendment's guarantee of free speech. At a fundraiser for the American Civil Liberties Union in 1979, Vonnegut proposed that the hierarchy of laws set down by Thomas Aquinas in the thirteenth century, in which divine law dominates natural law and "contemptible human law" comes in a distant third (*Palm Sunday* 9), is the real culprit eroding American freedoms. The problem with the Thomist hierarchy is that "no one really understands nature or God" (*Palm Sunday* 10). Nature, for instance, led people in Aquinas's time to believe that the world was flat, and "nature" seemed to teach eighteenth- and nineteenth-century Americans that black people were inferior to white people and that it was therefore acceptable to own slaves. Divine law, meanwhile, remains the province of an elite few—theologians who attempt to understand it and dictators who try to enforce it. As Vonnegut's recent biographers Charles J. Shields and Gregory D. Sumner have pointed out, Vonnegut's upbringing in Indianapolis, especially the excellent education he received at Shortridge High School, along with the city's free library system and its inexpensive cultural events, instilled in him an early public-spiritedness and desire to be a good citizen, which he never lost. Sumner, in fact, argues that Vonnegut remained a true American patriot throughout his life and that he retained "an almost corny faith in the very civic virtues that seemed to be disintegrating" at the end of the 1960s (4). In Vonnegut's view, placing divine law above civic law allows leaders to neglect the needs of citizens rather than design policies for their benefit, as President Franklin D. Roosevelt, whom Vonnegut greatly admired, did during the 1930s.

Vonnegut was appalled as well by the militarism of traditional Christianity, which, in his view, went hand-in-hand with the manic war preparations and build-up of weaponry that he saw as a sickness infecting the United States during the Cold War era and beyond. In a 1986 speech delivered to a Unitarian gathering in Rochester, New York, he assessed what he called the "religious revival" taking place in the country at the time. (Though he does not mention specific organizations, Vonnegut was referring to the rise of groups such as Jerry Falwell's Moral Majority, an evangelical Christian organization that became politically influential during the 1980s.) Informing the crowd that he has been able to distill two commandments from this new religious fervor—"stop thinking" and "obey" (*Fates* 158)—he compares these dictums to orders he had been taught as an infantry private during basic training. Even more, the new spirit of national religious fervor brings to mind Nazi Germany for him. When he fought the Germans during World War II, he noted that they had "crosses on their flags and uniforms and all over their killing machines, just like the soldiers of the first Christian Emperor Constantine" (*Fates* 158). Vonnegut despairs, as well, at the "sadistic" language of a sixteenth-century requiem mass he went to hear in 1985, the text of which promised listeners a paradise "indistinguishable from the Spanish Inquisition" (*Fates* 71). He went home that night and wrote new lyrics to the mass, pleading that humans be granted only eternal, peaceful respite from their sins rather than face a wrathful deity on judgment day.

The Value of Religious Systems

If organized religions, particularly Christianity, have caused so much trouble in the world, Vonnegut's readers might ask, why not do away with them completely? Would the world be better off without the systemized cruelties perpetrated by blind religious faith? Vonnegut's response to this question is complex. He recognizes the human desire for ethical and moral guidance, peoples' need to believe in something larger than themselves, even citing the philosopher Friedrich Nietzsche, who argued that "only a person of great faith could afford to be a skeptic" as Vonnegut paraphrases in *Fates Worse than Death* (157). While Vonnegut suggests that healthy skepticism, instilled by a good education, can help people identify "bad guesses" about what life is all about and to "destroy" those bad guesses "with mockery and contempt" (*Palm Sunday* 179), he does not believe that destruction of bad ideas is enough. In a speech delivered to the graduating class of Hobart and William Smith Colleges in 1974, he pleads that young people just graduating from college should also develop new theories about life that everyone can believe in. Vonnegut declares flatly, "we need a new religion" (*Palm Sunday* 181). With so many people in the 1970s experiencing the world as a chaotic and hostile environment, Vonnegut saw nihilism as a looming problem. Effective religions, he argues, allow people to make sense of their world and how they should behave in it. Yet, because traditional religions are too superstitious and too ignorant of science for contemporary people to swallow, perhaps what humanity needs instead of a religion per se is more of a "heartfelt moral code" (*Palm Sunday* 185) that would provide a coherent ethical structure to life. And the code he proposes is a simple one, a rule that would not need elaboration or interpretation by priests or theologians: "anything which wounds the planet is evil, and anything which preserves it or heals it is good" (*Palm Sunday* 185). Such a dictum, he argues, would shame those who harm the planet and earn them the contempt of their fellow man, a punishment Vonnegut believes people fear even more than the lurid threat of eternal hellfire and damnation.

Vonnegut's thinking in this speech was heavily influenced by his studies in cultural anthropology at the University of Chicago in the mid-1940s. In graduate school, he learned to appreciate cultural relativity, commenting in an interview that he believes this knowledge should come earlier than it came for him. Even a "first grader," he stresses, "should understand that his culture isn't a rational invention; that there are thousands of other cultures and they all work pretty well; that all cultures function on faith rather than truth; that there are lots of alternatives to our own society" (*Wampeters* 279). Such an understanding would logically involve a certain distancing from the beliefs individuals were brought up with, leading to less fanaticism and an increased respect for other cultures and systems of belief. Vonnegut was especially fascinated by the folk societies studied by Dr. Robert Redfield, one of his teachers at Chicago, who argued that such societies provided their members with a sense of belonging and self-worth. Relying on Redfield's theories, Vonnegut contended that humans are chemically programmed to live in such close-knit folk societies. The reason that modern humans "feel lousy all the time" (*Wampeters* 180) is because they are profoundly lonely. The nuclear family and the geographical mobility prized by contemporary Americans do not offer the stability and kinship ties they have evolved to need nor the unified spiritual vision that would give them a sense of belonging in the world.

While Vonnegut offered his simple rule about not harming the planet as one basis for a new, uniform ethical code, he also frequently rewrote and reinterpreted conventional Christian stories to give them what he considered better, more reasonable moral directives. Perhaps the best example of such a rewriting occurs in *Slaughterhouse-Five*, when Billy Pilgrim learns about the Kilgore Trout story, *The Gospel from Outer Space*. In Trout's story, a visitor from outer space comes to Earth to study Christianity in order to learn why Christians can be so cruel. The visitor concludes that "at least part of the trouble was slipshod storytelling in the New Testament" (*Slaughterhouse* 108). The gospel story as originally written teaches people not to harm those who are "well connected" (108)—meaning the son of God. In order to prevent other readers from making the same misinterpretation, the visitor writes a revised version of the story in which Christ is a nobody, a bum who is adopted by God to become his son only *after* the crucifixion takes place. The message of the new story? God "will punish horribly anybody who torments a bum who has no connections" (109). Vonnegut made a similar point in a speech given to a Unitarian church in Cambridge, Massachusetts, in 1980, in which he told his listeners about a new passion play he was composing, a work that "leaves God out entirely, but which manages to be spiritual anyway" (*Palm Sunday* 197). In Vonnegut's rewritten story, Roman soldiers behave as they do in the Bible: they torture Christ, strip him of his dignity, and leave him dangling on a cross to die. But a group of ordinary people gather around Jesus to sing to him and express their sorrow, eventually kneeling at the foot of the cross out of exhaustion. A wealthy Roman tourist, witnessing the scene, comments "My goodness! The way you are worshiping him, you would think he was the son of your God" (*Palm Sunday* 198). Mary Magdalene replies that if the tortured man were the son of God, he would not need them; it is because Jesus is a common human being exactly like themselves that the group is there comforting him.

These two rewritten versions of the Christian gospel story illustrate two major tenets in Vonnegut's religious thinking. First is the idea that humans crave to be treated with dignity. Dignity, however, is not something bestowed on humans by God; it is not an intrinsic quality humans are born with, but an extrinsic quality, granted only by other human beings. Vonnegut writes that dignity must be "given by people to people. If you stand before me, and I do not credit you with dignity, then you have none" (*Palm Sunday* 194). Dignity entails respecting one's fellow human beings. Vonnegut speculates that Christians would have been less "bloodthirsty" (*Fates* 158) through history had Jesus asked humans to respect rather than love one another, respect being a more attainable goal than love and more closely allied to human dignity. Vonnegut, in fact, often described himself as a humanist, someone who advocates a moral code that focuses on human beings and the world they live in rather than on the supernatural or the divine. In his final novel, *Timequake*, Vonnegut defines humanists as people who "try to behave decently and honorably without any expectation of rewards or punishments in an afterlife" (82). Because God is unknowable, humanists "serve as well as we can the highest abstraction of which we have some understanding, which is our community" (82). Again, for Vonnegut, being a good citizen trumps trying to serve an ultimately unknowable deity.

The Power and Importance of Language

The rewritten gospel stories also illustrate the importance Vonnegut accords language in his ethical universe. If "slipshod storytelling in the New Testament" or a mistranslation of the Aramaic word meaning "respect" as "love" is largely responsible for the cruelty Christians have exhibited over the last two thousand years, it follows that writers must be careful about the stories they tell and the language they use. Vonnegut takes this directive to heart in his own work. He overturns traditional narrative structure in his novel *Slaughterhouse-Five* in order to assure Mary O'Hare, the wife of his old war buddy Bernard

O'Hare, that the novel will not be made into a movie that glamorizes war. Similarly, in *Breakfast of Champions*, Vonnegut argues that Americans are able to behave so "abominably" because they are simply "doing their best to live like people invented in story books" (*Breakfast* 215). Traditional novels have falsely taught people that life has leading and secondary characters, significant details, lessons to be learned, and an orderly beginning, middle, and end. But Vonnegut visualizes a new art that will topple these dangerous ideas—he attempts to write a novel in which all characters are equally important, all facts are equally weighty, and life is presented in its chaotic, messy whole. Vonnegut's novels, which pay keen attention to their own narrative processes, can often be considered examples of metafiction, or fiction that takes as its subject matter fiction itself—the power of storytelling and language to shape the world we live in.

For Vonnegut, reading and literature become so important that they can even provide the kind of spiritual satisfaction some people find in religious faith. In the collection *Palm Sunday* he writes that "language" and "literature" as well as the "freedom to say or write whatever we please in this country" are all "holy" to him (150). In a speech delivered at Fredonia College in New York in 1978, he argues that reading and writing are "sacred" activities because, by reading well, any human being "can think the thoughts of the wisest and most interesting human minds throughout history" (*Palm Sunday* 163). Vonnegut makes a similar point when he describes dabbling in transcendental meditation at one point in his life. He gave up on Eastern forms of meditation, though, when he realized he had already been engaged in a Western form of meditation that allowed him to become a wiser human being by absorbing the wisdom of others: reading. Although he writes that books were initially invented as practical ways to transmit or store information, he argues that a "wholly unforeseen accident" of books is that they "can create a spiritual condition of priceless depth and meaning" that may finally be the "greatest treasure at the core of our civilization" (*Fates* 188).

Or, they can at least create the illusion of depth and meaning. While praising the acts of reading and writing as nearly sacred activities in some essays, elsewhere in his work, Vonnegut downplays the literary arts. Skeptical of viewing the writer as a person of exceptional genius, Vonnegut insists repeatedly that writing is a "trade," much like building a house or repairing an automobile. Writers, he points out, have only average intelligences; they are "mediocre people" who are "patient and industrious enough to revise their stupidity, to edit themselves into something like intelligence" (*Wampeters* xx). By pretending to be clever and working hard, would-be writers can actually grow into their artistic aspirations. For Vonnegut, pretending to be something one is not or holding onto illusions is not necessarily a bad thing. In his address to the graduating class of Bennington College in 1970, he advises students who want to improve the world to become "an enemy of truth and a fanatic for harmless balderdash" (*Wampeters* 165). While this may seem like odd advice to give to college graduates, Vonnegut wanted young people to maintain their idealism rather than allow themselves to be demoralized by the world they lived in. Above all, he begged the Bennington students to retain the superstition that "humanity is at the center of the universe, the fulfiller or the frustrator of the grandest dreams of God Almighty" (*Wampeters* 165). For Vonnegut, the primary purpose of the arts is to "make human beings seem more wonderful than they really are" (*Wampeters* 166), and therefore may be the best way to sustain this illusion. By placing humans at the center of the universe, whether they belong there or not, the arts imagine a saner, kinder, and more just world.

Religion in Vonnegut's Novels

Speculating that "works of the imagination themselves have the power to create" (*Wampeters* xxv), Vonnegut has great affection for utopian thinkers who use their imaginations to envision the world as better than it currently is. In many ways, he sees these figures as creative artists. While essays on mystics such as Madame Blavatsky, the nineteenth-century spiritual medium who founded the Theosophical Society, or Maharishi Mahesh Yogi, who developed the practice of transcendental meditation, at least partially satirize these figures, Vonnegut nevertheless found many of their beliefs, such as the idea "that man was not born to suffer" (*Wampeters* 31), or the idea that all human beings are brothers and sisters, "quite lovely" (*Wampeters* 139). His fourteen published novels are filled with characters who, like Blavatsky and the Yogi, imagine new and supposedly better worlds for human beings to inhabit. While these utopian experiments are almost always doomed to tragicomic failure, Vonnegut nevertheless admires his utopian strivers the same way he admired the loveable losers Laurel and Hardy, the comic slapstick duo from the 1920s and 1930s, whose movies he grew up watching. Laurel and Hardy, Vonnegut explains, were so endearing to him because they did their best to meet every test life gave them with optimism and the will to succeed: "They never failed to bargain in good faith with their destinies, and were screamingly adorable and funny on that account" (*Slapstick* 1). The second half of this essay briefly examines three Vonnegut novels in which characters invent either new religions or new moral systems that they believe will make the world a better place.

Player Piano, Vonnegut's first novel, published in 1952, does not depict a world devoid of religion so much as it depicts a world in which peoples' religious and spiritual longings have been redirected to the corporate marketplace and a worship of a machine-driven efficiency. An elite class of engineers, managers, and scientists inhabit one section of Ilium, New York, and serve as the theologians and priests of this new religion, while the masses of common, ordinary people live across the river in an area called Homestead, largely disenfranchised, useless, and with no sense of spiritual fulfillment. Paul Proteus is the manager of Ilium Works, an arm of the giant National Industrial, Commercial, Communications, Foodstuffs, and Resources organization, which was founded by his father, Doctor George Proteus. Paul is torn between continuing on his rising career path with the company and his uneasy conscience over the treatment of the Homesteaders, whose low IQ scores have tracked them into dead-end jobs with no hope of advancement or of securing a good future for their children. The Reverend James J. Lasher, a former Protestant minister and social scientist whom Paul meets in a bar in Homestead one night, serves as the novel's utopian prophet, inventing a new quasi-religious order, the Ghost Shirt Society, whose purpose is to foment a revolution that will destroy the machines and return ordinary people to the dignity of having meaningful work.

Set in the near future following a major war and a second Industrial Revolution, *Player Piano* depicts a United States that has mechanized not only industry, but love and spirituality as well. Paul Proteus's marriage to his wife, Anita, is based on duty and routine, not love. Anita is a social climber, concerned almost entirely with appearances. While she "had the mechanics of marriage down pat," any warmth she shows her husband is rationally thought out, a "counterfeit" of true affection (25). But Paul, who agreed to marry Anita only after she mistakenly claimed to be pregnant, is not blameless in the relationship either. Robotically replying, "I love *you*, Anita" (25) to his wife's brittle declarations of affection, Paul does not defend her when his friend Ed Finnerty claims he can design a machine—"stainless steel, covered with sponge rubber, and heated electrically to 98.6 degrees"—that can do everything Anita does and that will "show respect" (46). At the end of the novel, when Anita leaves Paul for his rival, Dr. Lawson Shepherd, one of her complaints is that she is "sick of being treated like a machine" (237). The novel depicts many other attempts to automate human interactions as well. Checker Charley, a machine designed by some of the young engineers at Ilium Works to outdo Paul as the company's checkers champion, threatens to do away with friendly game-playing competition; Paul invents a clean, hygienic mechanical saloon that eliminates the bad light, poor ventilation, and inefficient bartenders of ordinary drinking establishments; and the player piano of the novel's title erases the human element from music. But just like the Proteus' mechanical marriage, these attempts fail: Checker Charley experiences a loose connection that burns up its circuitry, Paul's saloon soon goes out of business, and listeners much prefer Ed Finnerty's piano playing to the automated music produced by the machine. People in Ilium still long for human connection and some deeper sense of spiritual fulfillment even as the machines eliminate the hard physical labor of ordinary work.

For the engineers, managers, and scientists who are Ilium's elite, this spiritual longing is fulfilled by the company itself. The corporation is set up as a religious entity, complete with a kindly father-god, a hierarchical clergy and laity, and rituals, ceremonies, stories, and myths designed to reinforce the religion's moral code. Vonnegut, highly conscious of these connections, frequently uses language that emphasizes the spiritual role the company plays. A photograph on the wall of Paul's office, depicting early employees of Ilium Works, testifies that these privileged, high IQ workers see themselves as a sort of secular clergy. The group displays "the attitude of a secret order, above and apart from society by virtue of participating in important and moving rites the laity could only guess about" (15). Matheson, Ilium's "manager in charge of testing and placement," the man who determines the future of all of Ilium's young people, is described as a "high priest" (36), and a rebellious employee such as Ed Finnerty is a "Freethinker" (52). Paul's boss, Anthony Kroner, is said to be an "evangelist" (45) for the company, a man who "personified the faith, the near-holiness, the spirit of the complicated venture" (49). It is no accident that Kroner speaks of himself as a father to all his employees, and has the young engineers refer to his wife as "Mom." Kroner is a godlike figure, and even Paul, with all his doubts about the company, cannot resist pouring "his heart out to this merciful, wise, gentle father" (128). The Meadows, where the engineers retreat for two weeks of game-playing and camaraderie, functions as an old-fashioned tent revival, where mythic stories such as the Sky Manager play renew the faith of true believers and convert skeptics to the cause. Nor does Vonnegut overlook the irony of the company linking itself to Native American spirituality. The tired old actor in a G-string, hired to perform the role of wise Indian, is as false as the history he presents, never mentioning the land theft and genocide that caused the Indian "braves" (213) to disappear from the island, giving way to the young men of the present time.

While the company religion satisfies the spiritual requirements of an elite few, those who do not fit in, such as Paul Proteus and Ed Finnerty, experience a profound loneliness. In a bar in Homestead, Finnerty complains to Paul about a sense of "not belonging anywhere" (88), and Paul clearly feels isolated and alone as well, both in his marriage and at work. But this sensation of not belonging is keenest among the Homesteaders themselves, men and women who cannot find meaningful work to do, and who feel like neglected outcasts in their own city. The Reverend James J. Lasher, whom Paul and Finnerty meet at the bar, explains that, when he was a minister before the war, he used to tell his congregation that their relationship to God was "the biggest thing in their lives" (92). The problem, however, is that, for generations, Americans had "been built up to worship competition and the market, productivity and economic usefulness . . . and boom! it's all yanked out from under them. They can't participate, can't be useful any more" (92). Lasher, like Vonnegut himself, had studied sociology and anthropology in graduate school, and he understands people's need to belong. He predicts that the Homesteaders are ripe for the emergence of a "phony Messiah" (93) who will restore their feelings of dignity. The phoniness of this predicted Messiah is not a comment on the low IQs of the Homesteaders, however; Lasher is wise enough to recognize, as Vonnegut himself does, that all religions are a matter of faith rather than truth. He points out to Paul that even the privileged elites of Ilium, who exhibit a "crusading spirit" and see their industrial work as a kind of "holy war" have started to believe the phoniness of their own advertising: "Yesterday's snow job becomes today's sermon" (93). As readers repeatedly see in Vonnegut's work, "we are what we pretend to be" (*Mother Night* v). Illusions are powerful and shape reality.

Recognizing peoples' need for a sense of group identity and a moral code to go along with it, Lasher forms his own religious organization, the revolutionary Ghost Shirt Society, with the purpose of helping Homesteaders to rediscover meaning in their lives. Vonnegut, however, is not naïve about this rebellious group; he does not romanticize them. Much like the company itself, the Ghost Shirt Society appropriates Native American spirituality, although in a somewhat less tawdry way, naming themselves after the Ghost Dance religion popular among western tribes in the late nineteenth century. The group, as well, is happy to use Paul Proteus's name and reputation for their own benefit, despite the cost. Paul even recognizes that his friend Finnerty would be willing to kill him for the cause. When the revolution actually begins, it turns out to be a dismal failure, the leaders unable to control the anger and desire for revenge of the Homesteaders, who begin to destroy *all* machinery—the power station and flush toilets as well as the automatic lathe controls that put so many people out of work. Perhaps most ironic of all, the last readers see of the Homesteaders is a group cheering on engineer Bud Calhoun as he repairs an Orange-O drink-dispensing machine. Vonnegut suggests a sense of futility here, as their love of gadgetry and mechanical tinkering causes the Homesteaders to begin to rebuild the very world that caused so much heartbreak.

Despite the failures of the Ghost Shirt Society, Vonnegut clearly sympathizes with Reverend Lasher and his doomed rebellion. Paul Proteus's finest moment in the novel comes when he refuses to inform on the members of the society, as Kroner had wanted him to, declaring himself from his prison cell, where he has been locked up as a potential saboteur, to be the group's Messiah. Paul's declaration is possible only after he has discovered that his rival for promotion in the company, Fred Garth, is locked up in a cell adjoining his. For the first time in his life, Paul shared "profound misfortune with another human being," which allows him to feel true warmth not only for Garth, but for all "the colorless, the nervous, the enervated," an affection that he had never felt for Anita, for Finnerty, for his parents, or for anyone else

(289). So, even though Paul's motives in joining the group may be somewhat tainted by a "sordid" (299) Oedipal rivalry with his largely absent father, his desire to help the Homesteaders is nevertheless authentic. Genuine feelings of empathy spur his acceptance of the Messiah role. In addition, Lasher is perceptive enough to know that his rebellion will fail from the beginning. Just as the ghost shirts used by nineteenth-century tribes did not repel bullets, Lasher recognizes that the modern incarnation of the movement will not do much to change the world. But Lasher, like Vonnegut, understands the value of symbolic action. While Vonnegut acknowledged that wars were as easy to stop as glaciers, yet wrote antiwar novels anyway, Lasher knows that humans will continue to devalue one another, but he still preaches against this devaluation. In what can be considered the Ghost Shirt Society manifesto, his group praises human imperfection, frailty, inefficiency, and "brilliance followed by stupidity" as virtues because, above all else, "Man is a creation of God" (286). At the end of the novel, after all, Lasher declares that he is, first and foremost, not a revolutionary, but a minister. For Vonnegut the humanist and freethinker, the idea that man is a creation of God might be only a hopeful illusion, but it is an illusion that can provide shape and meaning to human lives.

Bokononism and Tralfamadorianism

Vonnegut's fourth novel, *Cat's Cradle*, published in 1963, as well as his sixth and best-known book, *Slaughterhouse-Five*, released in 1969, both work to further develop the idea of hopeful illusions that make life meaningful. In *Cat's Cradle*, the Bokononist religion advocates that its adherents live by *foma*, defined in the novel's epigraph as the "harmless untruths" that can help people become more "brave and kind and healthy and happy" than they would otherwise be. Readers are introduced to Bokononism by a freelance journalist and convert to the religion named John, who is writing a book about the day the atomic bomb was dropped on Hiroshima. This pursuit leads him to explore the life of Dr. Felix Hoenikker, one of the bomb's creators, who, it turns out, had invented another doomsday device as well, a substance called *ice-nine* that can instantaneously freeze liquids into solids. John and Dr. Hoenikker's children eventually wind up on the small Caribbean island of San Lorenzo, where the *ice-nine* is accidentally unleashed into the ocean, freezing the entire world and leaving only a very small band of survivors. The plot of *Slaughterhouse-Five* revolves around an apocalyptic event as well: the fire-bombing of Dresden, Germany, during World War II. The novel tells the story of Billy Pilgrim, a tall, ungainly chaplain's assistant during the war who has become "unstuck in time" (23). Readers are unstuck in time as well as Billy's story is narrated in nonchronological order, his sufferings as a prisoner of war in Dresden interspersed with childhood memories, with scenes from his later life as a wealthy optometrist in Ilium, New York, and with his experiences on the planet Tralfamadore, where he claims to have been transported by flying saucer after having been kidnapped by space aliens. The hapless Billy Pilgrim lives by what might be considered *foma* as well, inventing an entire world that serves as a new Eden and allows him to cope with the war trauma he has experienced.

What these rough outlines of the novels' plots leave out, however, are the very things that made them cult classics, especially on college campuses in the 1960s and early 1970s: the elaborate belief systems Vonnegut invented as part of the Bokononist and Tralfamadorian worldviews. Both *Cat's Cradle* and *Slaughterhouse-Five* have long intrigued readers at least partially because Vonnegut's own attitude toward his invented religions is difficult to determine. While much has been written about each novel, critics strongly disagree on how to view Bokononism and Tralfamadorianism. Are we meant to reject Bokonon as a charlatan, a false prophet who cruelly and blithely leads human beings to commit mass suicide at the end of the novel? Or are we to see him as a kindly and wise spiritual leader who provides people with the hope they need to survive their harsh and unforgiving lives? The critic Lawrence Broer takes the first view, arguing that Bokonon's response to human suffering is fatalistic and morally corrupt and that

John's main challenge in the novel is to learn to reject the comforting illusions of Bokononist thought. Peter Freese, on the other hand, insists that while Bokononism is based on lies, it proves much more beneficial for human beings than its main opponent—natural science. Critics have been similarly torn about Tralfamadorianism in *Slaughterhouse-Five*. Critics Tony Tanner and Charles Harris suggest that Vonnegut promotes quietism in the novel, or a resigned passivity to life, while commentators such as Robert Merrill and Peter Scholl assert that Vonnegut rejects the Tralfamadorian passivity advocated by Billy Pilgrim, urging his readers instead to actively engage in humane behavior that can indeed change the world. This essay argues that Vonnegut's views actually lie somewhere in between the critical extremes—he certainly sees the flaws in Bokononism and even more so in Tralfamadorianism, just as he did in Reverend Lasher and the Ghost Shirt Society of *Player Piano*—nevertheless, he leans strongly toward a sympathetic portrayal of both Bokonon and Billy Pilgrim, as he does for all his utopian dreamers who try to help human beings cope in the world.

Perhaps the main objection critics raise to both Bokononism and Tralfamadorianism is that they offer a deterministic view of the universe, obviating the possibility of human free will. Good Bokononists, for example, believe that God has a plan for their lives and that, through the use of the *vin-dit*, or "sudden, very personal shove in the direction of Bokononism" (*Cat's Cradle* 69), God makes sure these plans are fulfilled. In addition, Bokonon himself appears to be a fatalist. The text of the fourteenth Book of Bokonon, titled "What Can a Thoughtful Man Hope for Mankind on Earth, Given the Experience of the Past Million Years," consists of the single word "nothing" (245). The very notion of man having a meaningful purpose in life, according to Bokonon, is invented by man, not by God. In the Bokononist creation story, God creates the earth and then, in his "cosmic loneliness," he creates man out of mud (265). When man first sits up and asks what the purpose of life is, God is surprised by the idea that everything must have a purpose. "Then I leave it to you to think of one," replies

God, and he goes away (265). While Tralfamadorianism is described in more secular terms than Bokononism, it nevertheless resembles the religion in its deterministic qualities. The Tralfamadorians, who can see all time at once rather than in small, lived segments the way Earthlings do, believe that the future is fixed and that nothing can be done to alter it. They even know how the world will end: a Tralfamadorian pilot experimenting with new flying saucer fuels will blow up the entire universe after pressing the wrong button on his spacecraft. When Billy Pilgrim finds this out, he is horrified and asks why the aliens do not try to stop the pilot. His Tralfamadorian guide replies that the "moment is *structured* that way" (117). When Billy suggests that the Tralfamadorians do not believe in free will, the aliens tell him that Earthlings are "the great explainers" of the universe; of the thirty-one planets the Tralfamadorians have visited, "only on Earth is there any talk of free will" (86).

Is Vonnegut then suggesting in these books that it is a fool's errand to search for meaning in the universe, that humans should give up and resignedly accept their predetermined fates? Alternately, does he want readers to completely reject Bokononism and Tralfamadorianism as morally corrupt philosophies that are presented satirically? Neither of these possibilities is quite right. Keeping in mind Vonnegut's 1970 address to the Bennington graduates, in which he argued that the arts can fraudulently place humans at the center of the universe, even if they do not belong there, both novels can be read to suggest that human beings have the ability to turn their lives into works of art in order to supply the meaning that is not inherent to human existence. In *Cat's Cradle*, Lionel Boyd Johnson and Earl McCabe, the cofounders on San Lorenzo of both Bokononism and the cruel dictatorship that outlaws the religion, do just this. Julian Castle, founder of a hospital for the poor in San Lorenzo, explains to John, the narrator, that even though McCabe and Johnson did not succeed in raising the standard of living on the island, they did increase the islanders' happiness by supplying them roles to play in an ongoing drama that pitted good against evil.

The islanders came to feel that they "were all employed full time as actors in a play they understood"; life on the island effectively "became a work of art" (174–75). And the Bokononist rituals invented by Johnson, such as *boko-maru*, or the rubbing together of the soles of the feet, really do provide comfort to the San Lorenzans, the pressing together of soles symbolically evoking the feeling of belonging from souls coming together. Even more, the novel suggests that there is a fine line separating illusion from reality; the pretenses invented by Bokonon have a way of coming true. Both Johnson and McCabe grow into the false roles of prophet and tyrant that they originally adopt as guises, and the legend of the golden boat that "will sail again when the end of the world is near" (109) is realized when Papa Monzano's body, ensconced in a golden lifeboat, crashes into the sea, unleashing the *ice-nine*. And while it is true that Bokonon does advise the San Lorenzans who survive the *ice-nine* apocalypse that they "should have the good manners to die" (273), it is also true that Bokonon had warned repeatedly that he is not to be believed, that his religion is made up of "shameless lies" (5). The contradictions that Bokonon espouses suggest that human beings must make up their *own* minds about what to believe: those who committed suicide are ultimately responsible for their own deaths because they selectively chose which tenets of Bokononism to act upon. Like Reverend Lasher, Bokonon recognizes the importance of symbolic action in the face of futility and impending destruction, handing John a piece of paper at the end of the novel in which he describes his desire to die while "thumbing [his] nose" at God (287).

Billy Pilgrim in *Slaughterhouse-Five* turns his life into a work of art in similar ways to the San Lorenzans. Billy creates the alien planet of Tralfamadore out of Kilgore Trout's novels and his own imagination, inventing a role for himself as a new Adam with former pornographic movie star Montana Wildhack as his Eve. While most peoples' idea of Paradise would not be a zoo on an alien planet, the Tralfamadorian fantasy works for Billy. His alien gods see him as a beautiful specimen of humanity; he is mated with a sexually experienced, yet demure young woman; his passivity is justified as all meaningful decisions are taken out of his hands; and most important, he no longer needs to fear the death as death is meaningless to the Tralfamadorians, who see it as just another moment in time. Yet, Billy, despite his overwhelming passivity, is one of Vonnegut's characters who, like Reverend Lasher and Paul Proteus, go to great lengths to comfort their fellow human beings. In order to deliver his message of hope to a wider audience, Billy writes a long letter to the newspaper about his Tralfamadorian experiences that brings him ridicule from his daughter, and he sneaks onto a radio program in New York City to spread his gospel. He sees himself as something like a Christ figure when he imagines a future in which he foretells his own death to his followers. The message he delivers to the masses—"it is time for me to be dead for a little while—and then live again" (142–143)—entails a Christ-like promise of eternal life. Billy truly believes that, if only people will trust his message, they too can live forever. While Vonnegut does not want all humans to adopt Billy's fatalistic attitude, he understands that Billy *needs* his Tralfamadorian fantasy to make life meaningful for him, and he has great sympathy not only for the imaginative processes that allow Billy to create a more agreeable world for himself but for the impulse that pushes him to share his vision with others.

In Billy Pilgrim, readers see a character who perhaps best represents a conflict Vonnegut returns to over and over again in his work: the difference between a Darwinian worldview and a Christian one. Vonnegut never cared much for the ideas of Charles Darwin, the father of modern evolutionary theory, because he believed that the popularization of Darwin's ideas, especially survival of the fittest, can make people more cruel (*Wampeters* 237). But "survival of the fittest," as Vonnegut knew, was a term coined not by Darwin, but by Herbert Spencer, an advocate of a theory called Social Darwinism, which suggests that people who are most successful in society deserve their success because they are more "fit," while those less fortunate deserve their misfortune. Social Darwinism was anathema to Vonnegut, who, throughout his work, advocated treating others compassionately, especially those people deemed worthless or useless by society. In the final chapter of *Slaughterhouse-Five*, the narrator reports to readers Billy Pilgrim's claim that "there isn't much interest in Jesus Christ" on Tralfamadore. "The Earthling figure who is most engaging to the Tralfamadorian mind," according to Billy, is "Charles Darwin—who taught that those who die are meant to die, that corpses are improvements. So it goes" (210). Billy serves as something of a paradox here: he advocates Tralfamadorianism, but he acts in a Christ-like manner, attempting to provide hope and solace to his fellow human beings. Never one to shy away from paradox, Vonnegut could declare himself an atheist and nonbeliever yet also refer to Jesus Christ as the "greatest and most humane of human beings" (*A Man* 432). He could critique the injustice and cruelty historically perpetrated by religion while declaring that contemporary Americans need a new religion. Most importantly, he understood that people go to church, not for "preachments," but to "daydream about God" (*Palm Sunday* 300) and to imagine better worlds for human beings to live in.

Works Cited

Broer, Lawrence R. *Sanity Plea: Schizophrenia in the Novels of Kurt Vonnegut*. Tuscaloosa: U of Alabama P, 1989. Print.

Freese, Peter. "Vonnegut's Invented Religions as Sense-Making Systems." *The Vonnegut Chronicles: Interviews and Essays*. Ed. Peter J. Reed and Marc Leeds. Westport: Greenwood, 1996. Print.

Harris, Charles B. "Time, Uncertainty, and Kurt Vonnegut, Jr.: A Reading of *Slaughterhouse-Five*." *Centennial Review* 20 (1976): 228–43. Print.

Merrill, Robert, and Peter A. Scholl. "Vonnegut's *Slaughterhouse-Five*: The Requirements of Chaos." *Studies in American Fiction* 6 (1978): 65–76. Print.

Shields, Charles J. *And So It Goes. Kurt Vonnegut: A Life*. New York: Holt, 2012. Print.

Sumner, Gregory D. *Unstuck in Time: A Journey through Kurt Vonnegut's Life and Novels*. New York: Seven Stories, 2011. Print.

Tanner, Tony. "The Uncertain Messenger: A Study of the Novels of Kurt Vonnegut, Jr." *Critical Quarterly* 11 (1969): 297–315. Print.

Vonnegut, Kurt. *Breakfast of Champions*. 1973. New York: Dell, 1999. Print.

___. *Cat's Cradle*. 1963. New York: Dell, 1998. Print.

___. *Fates Worse than Death*. 1991. New York: Berkley, 1992. Print.

___. *God Bless You, Mr. Rosewater*. 1965. New York: Dell, 1998. Print.

___. *Like Shaking Hands with God*. 1999. New York: Washington Square, 2000. Print.

___. *A Man Without a Country*. New York: Seven Stories, 2005. Print.

___. *Mother Night*. 1961. New York: Dell, 1999. Print.

___. *Palm Sunday*. 1981. New York: Dell, 1999. Print.

___. *Player Piano*. 1952. New York: Dell, 1974. Print.

___. *The Sirens of Titan*. 1959. New York: Dell, 1998. Print.

___. *Slapstick*. 1976. New York: Dell, 1999. Print.

___. *Slaughterhouse-Five*. 1969. New York: Dell, 1999. Print.

___. *Timequake*. 1997. New York: Berkley, 1998. Print.

___. *Wampeters, Foma and Granfalloons*. 1974. New York: Dell, 1999. Print.

Another "Atheist's Bible":
Knowledge Defeats *Hocus Pocus* _____

Lara Narcisi

In Kurt Vonnegut's 1990 novel, *Hocus Pocus*, the narrator Eugene Debs Hartke refers to John Bartlett's *Familiar Quotations* as "the Atheist's Bible" (180). While Hartke uses the term sarcastically for the book, Vonnegut's novel itself might legitimately deserve that title. Despite its seeming morbidity, the novel offers a protagonist who attempts to act as sincerely and ethically as he can in a world of futility and chaos. The novel inveighs against the racism, environmental devastation, and systems perpetuating poverty of its dystopian near-future universe, but it proposes that widespread ignorance of these ills is the most pervasive danger of all. Hartke moves out of the small-mindedness of his society into a larger vision of moral responsibility, specifically by dedicating his life to education. While *Hocus Pocus* is not exactly optimistic, it does demonstrate ethical patterns of behavior outside of organized religion. *Hocus Pocus* can help the attentive reader to discern truth amidst the pervasive societal "hocus pocus" Vonnegut critiques.

How to Think Freely

Vonnegut made no secret of his beliefs, claiming that his study of anthropology "confirmed my atheism, which was the faith of my fathers anyway. Religions were exhibited and studied as the Rube Goldberg inventions I'd always thought they were" (*Current Biography*). Throughout his works, Vonnegut suggests that all religions can mislead. Bokononism, a fictional religion described in Vonnegut's 1963 novel *Cat's Cradle*, is one particularly farcical example, as even the narrator refers to his chosen religion as "bittersweet lies" (2). In Vonnegut's novel *Breakfast of Champions* (1973), Dwayne Hoover takes Kilgore Trout's novel as a message from God and becomes violently abusive to everyone around him. The narrator of Vonnegut's novel *Galápagos* (1985), set one million years in the future, observes, "Back when childhoods were often so protracted, it is unsurprising that so many people got into the lifelong habit of believing, even after their parents were gone, that somebody was always watching over them— God or a saint or a guardian angel or the stars or whatever" (122). In the 1979 novel *Jailbird*, the atheist narrator comments wryly about a fellow inmate, "He had so opened himself to the consolations of religion that he had become an imbecile" (78). While many events in Vonnegut novels appear miraculous or supernatural, the author clearly refutes the idea that any particular religion supplies answers or solutions.

Hocus Pocus holds a unique niche, however, because of its focus on the ways in which an atheist can lead an ethical and meaningful life. Eugene Debs Hartke calls himself an atheist outright, and informs us early on that in his memoir "There are no dirty words in this book, except for 'hell' and 'God'" (4). The novel's title itself can in fact be read as an indication of the importance of atheism, as John Wilson observes in his review of the novel: "One theory holds that the expression 'hocus-pocus' originated as a travesty of a phrase in the Mass ('hoc est corpus,' meaning 'this is [my] body'). In the novel, Vonnegut travesties Christianity as the ultimate con-game." I would argue that the title and the book are not targeting Christianity in particular, but rather any dogma that may impede the search for truth. While Vonnegut does not necessarily imply that an objective "Truth" is out there, he does emphasize the importance of combating falsehoods with as much rationality as possible. The novel's primary concern is less about attacking religion and more about considering alternative approaches to making sense of the world: in this surreal near-future where nothing makes sense, where might one find other models for objectively seeking truth and meaning?

Distinguishing truth from its opposite is no easy feat; here and in other works, Vonnegut destabilizes our notions of truth by suggesting that nothing is what it appears or claims to be. The novel is set in a dystopian 2001—a decade in the future at the time of the novel's publication. This future America, closely paralleling the present, parodies and exaggerates the deceptive qualities of American society. Hartke describes the small college for the learning disabled where he taught as "Oz or City of God or Camelot." Throughout the novel, beautiful women conceal hidden genes for madness; brilliant businessmen conceal dyslexia; caskets conceal living convicts. Rabid soldiers morph into peaceniks; ammunition becomes beautiful carillon bells; a man can be shot while ice-skating or survive an atomic bomb while retrieving a ball. A picturesque scene that Eugene assumes must look "like Paradise" (79) to outside observers conceals a miserable tale of isolation, infidelity, and suicide. A motorcycle cavalcade that appears to be either Hell's Angels or "a regular military operation" (174) is actually a grand entrance for an eccentric billionaire. Each of these instances subtly undermines a dedicated belief in anything—war, America, capitalism, or religion. What, then, in the near-future of *Hocus Pocus*, or even in the incomprehensible present, can one trust? The novel's myriad uncertainties reveal the folly of ever believing one knows the truth, and especially of anyone claiming religious authority.

Hartke presents one alternative to religion in the form of the Freethinkers, who, he says, believe "that science had proved all organized religions to be baloney, that God was unknowable, and that the greatest use a person could make of his or her lifetime was to improve the quality of life for all in his or her community" (183). For Hartke, the greatest enemy is, consistently, ignorance. Therefore, improving the quality of life in his community means fighting ignorance as honestly and consistently as he can. Hartke dedicates his entire postwar life doing exactly this; he finds fulfillment in teaching nontraditional students at Tarkington College, and when he loses this job, he finds fulfillment in teaching even less traditional students, from the prison across the lake. Improving the quality of life in one's community is no easy task, however, particularly in the novel's future setting. As society becomes increasingly bleak, beset by a growing roster of social ills, there is no easy secret to living a good and valuable existence. The "Atheist's Bible" that is *Hocus Pocus* merely suggests some approaches to being a sane and humane human being, a good fellow citizen, and a lifelong soldier in the war on ignorance.

How to Read, or, Words Can Lie

Hocus Pocus, like Hartke, takes education as its primary directive. The novels attempts to educate the reader from the beginning by consistently warning that one can never take anything at face value, as writing and language can deceive. As literary critic Lawrence Broer puts it, the novel presents "fact and fiction as interchangeable or indistinguishable realities" ("Hartke's Hearing" 192). The book itself is labeled "pure fiction" on the dedication page, but we have no way of knowing who assigned this description: was it the real Kurt Vonnegut, the editor known only as "K.V.," the fictional Hartke? For that matter, can it be called fiction when so much of it appears to be autobiographical, detailing as it does the life of a curmudgeonly Midwestern soldier-turned-teacher with a haunted past? Vonnegut suggests from the beginning that while language can provide truth, it is often contingent on the interpretation and intelligence of the reader. Throughout his works Vonnegut presents fiction as problematic, with the potential to lead to good or evil. Broer observes that in Vonnegut's works "artists have a moral obligation to produce art that discourages aggression and promotes awareness and compassion. He saw all wordplay or fiction—'hocus pocus'—as practical joking, albeit with the power to encourage compassion and engagement as well as cruelty and violence" (*Vonnegut* 127). As *Breakfast of Champions* demonstrates, the effect of fiction depends largely on the reader. It is therefore essential to become as educated a reader as possible.

Hocus Pocus makes a similar point about the importance of careful reading through the absurd story "Protocols of the Elders of Tralfamadore," also presumably penned by Kilgore Trout. This work, published in a porn magazine, lampoons the similarly titled anti-Semitic tract, "The Protocols of the Elders of Zion," by presenting a nihilistic view of humanity as a mere Petri dish for creating heartier space-traveling germs. Hartke muses that the story has a surprisingly strong impact on him—"deep down" it is working "like a buffered analgesic" (203). But it would be a mistake to assume that its effect on him or its purpose in the novel is to encourage a sense of fatalistic futility. Throughout Vonnegut's fiction, the character of Kilgore Trout can appear—notably in the 1965 novel *God Bless You, Mr. Rosewater*—as a figure of wisdom and humanistic compassion, but the reader learns not to take his stories at face value, as the fake author is as capable of being as ironic as his real-life creator. Vonnegut's most famous novel, *Slaughterhouse-Five*, critiques the Tralfamadorian philosophy as fatalistic and passive; it enables the novel's protagonist, Billy Pilgrim, to drift through his life without taking any action or even experiencing any real emotion. The Tralfamadorians mock humanity's sense of its own greatness, providing a kind of antidote to the hubris that men and nations exhibit in war. The Tralfamadorians' real effect, however, is to dissuade readers from the temptation of seeing themselves as inert victims of fate. In the larger context of *Hocus Pocus*, the "Protocols" story suggests that one should attempt to create positive change in the world rather than meekly accept fate—and that this message needs a close reader to uncover its meaning.

Vonnegut repeatedly subjects his readers to the lesson that one needs to be alert rather than passive, to constantly interrogate what others say, by demonstrating language's inherent subjectivity and ambiguity. Eugene Debs Hartke is named for the Socialist union leader who championed the lower classes, and yet he temporarily becomes part of the "ruling class" his namesake fought to abolish. Exotic-sounding locales frequently turn out to be Midwestern towns: Lima is in Ohio, Cairo is in Illinois, and both Peru and Brazil are in Indiana. Tarkington College is originally named the Mohiga Valley Free Institute, though it became quite expensive and was eventually converted to a prison, and thus is not "free" in either sense of the word. The prison itself is named Athena—surely a more appropriate title for the institution of higher learning across the lake. At Athena Prison, the convicts rename the lethal disease of AIDS with the comical abbreviation "the PB" for "parole board" because death through AIDS appears to be the only way they will ever leave the prison. Hartke takes the joke one step further into absurdity by labeling these acronyms "Alphabet soup!" (68). In each of these instances, Vonnegut trips up unwary readers, forcing them to examine language closely rather than taking it at face value.

Deceptive language is of thematic importance throughout the novel, but it shifts to a central plot point when Tarkington's Board of Trustees fires Hartke from his teaching position. The board claims that Hartke is a bad influence on children, predominantly due to his pessimistic worldview; Hartke is thus essentially (ostensibly) fired for the crime of language. The evidence against him comes from his "dimwit" (96) student Kimberley Wilder, who trails him and records his every word. Inevitably, some of his comments appear damning when taken out of context. All of the previous (and usually comedic) instances of linguistic instability crystallize in the inability of the board members to understand that Hartke's words might not mean what they assume. Vonnegut's subtle and persistent cautioning against such linguistic misreading has thus primed the reader to experience outrage at the board's decision. In the most preposterous instance, Kimberley accuses Hartke of declaring that all Jews should be incarcerated in concentration camps in Idaho, because she has heard him repeating a joke—that the Jews are "trying to get through life with only half a Bible," which is "like trying to get from here to San Francisco with a road map that stops in Dubuque, Iowa" (95). This example is fascinating for its many layers of misreading: attribution (the words were not originally Hartke's); tone (a joke); basic facts (Iowa becomes Idaho); and of course the entire meaning, which is bungled beyond belief. Kimberley gives these tapes to the Board of Trustees; while the board sees them as proof that Hartke is a nihilist rather than a Nazi, they are ready and willing to pillory him for his decontextualized words.

Remarkably, after Hartke's colleagues on the Board of Trustees fire him for statements taken out of context, they then proceed to commit the same sin themselves. While Kimberley's misunderstanding is particularly egregious and humorous, Vonnegut demonstrates that taking words out of context is a near-ubiquitous practice among brainiacs and morons alike. This is the importance of the oft-mentioned book that Hartke has at hand in the prison library, Bartlett's *Familiar Quotations*, in which seemingly educated individuals frequently use the book to cite beautiful passages of literature or oratory without any idea of the actual or intended meaning. At Hartke's firing, the illiterate chair of the board, Robert Moellenkamp, quotes Mercutio's death speech from *Romeo and Juliet*, ending dramatically and absurdly with, "A plague on both your houses!" (148). The speech in the original Shakespeare decries the meaningless feud that has brought destruction upon both the Montagues and the Capulets; here, the allusion is incongruous to the point of absurdity. As Hartke wryly comments afterwards, "I have lifted this speech from Bartlett's *Familiar Quotations*. If more people would acknowledge that they got their pearls of wisdom from that book instead of the original, it might clear the air" (149). The final clause is a classic Vonnegut understatement, as the whole episode indicates that using language clearly and honestly is of critical importance. Quoting Shakespeare gives a nice rhetorical flourish, but decontextualizing it can cause the type of dangerous misinformation that cost Hartke his career. In contrast, famous literary allusions can bring power and depth when used correctly, as Hartke demonstrates by suggesting at the end of the chapter that a more apt comparison might be between the feuding of *Romeo and Juliet* and the pointlessness of the Vietnam War. In what could be considered a primary tenet of *Hocus Pocus* as the Atheist's Bible, Vonnegut shows how easy and yet damaging it is to be fooled by false language. Misleading language is more than simply dishonest: it prevents us from facing reality.

How to Self-Improve, or, Hartke's Progress

Hartke, a self-described "genius of lethal hocus pocus" during the Vietnam War, learns to speak honestly and confront reality; his transition from soldier to teacher represents his progression from military con artist to academic mentor, and from self-delusion to a frank acceptance of his past. In Vietnam, Hartke colossally failed to fulfill the part of the Freethinker credo that advocates doing good for the community; as a civilian, it becomes his life's mission. As a soldier, he is an automaton; as a writer, he shows originality of thought in such small ways as using numerals instead of written numbers, avoiding swearing, and writing on paper fragments. Through the protagonist's progress, the novel demonstrates the possibility of personal growth and positive change even in a chaotic and misleading world.

Reviewers often miss this transformation, reading the novel's darkness as an indication that its protagonist and message are both dismally pessimistic. In an unflattering review of the novel printed in *Time* magazine, critic J. Skow's asks, "Why, for instance, has the author named him after Eugene V. Debs, the great U.S. socialist? Merely, or so it appears, because Vonnegut likes the contrast of Debs' nobility ('While there is a lower class I am in it . . . while there is a soul in prison I am not free') with the grubby hopelessness of Hartke's world" (73). But as Hartke reflects back on his life with relentless judgment, it becomes clear that he knows exactly where he has failed to live up to his namesake, specifically during his time in Vietnam: "You know who was the Ruling Class that time? Eugene Debs Hartke was the Ruling Class. Down with the Ruling Class!" (250). Hartke thus explicitly separates his previous self from his new and improved one. Later, as he considers the despicable inhumanity of crucifixions he muses, "What kind of animal would do such a thing? The old me, I think" (188). The old Hartke might have been bestial, but the reflective and honest man penning his memoir in 2001 is indeed someone who might make his namesake proud. As Broer discusses at length, Hartke's progress over his lifetime enables him to transcend the depression and stasis that haunt other Vonnegut characters: "No Vonnegut . . . protagonist chose to explore his shadowy inner world so directly or to nurture awareness and moral responsibility more avidly than Eugene Debs Hartke" (*Vonnegut*

126). Indeed, Hartke eventually takes responsibility for all his actions, from self-pity to adultery to murder. Andrea Wakefield, the wife of the president of Tarkington College, goes so far as to call him a "Saint" (169) for refusing to abandon his wife and mother-in-law after they have gone insane. If Freethinkers had "saints," Hartke might be a contender given this evidence of his kindness, compassion, and loyalty.

Given the novel's emphasis on the importance of truth-telling, the most significant transformation may be that Hartke learns to admit the truth about himself, unflattering though it may be. In this he distinguishes himself from many other Vonnegut characters, notably Howard Campbell, the narrator of *Mother Night*, who first ignores the encroachment of Nazism by focusing on his own advancement and then convinces himself that his successful propaganda work for the Nazis actually contributes to the Nazis' eventual destruction. Even when the latter proves true and he is confirmed as a spy for the Americans, he cannot face his own lifetime of duplicity and commits suicide, deciding, "I think that tonight is the night I will hang Howard W. Campbell, Jr., for crimes against himself" (192). Because of the similarity in the protagonists' artistic inclinations, unintended professions promoting unpopular wars, and eventual attempts at confessional memoir, *Hocus Pocus* can be seen in part as a rewriting of *Mother Night*, in which the former propaganda expert is able to atone for his wrongs by spreading information rather than disinformation. Campbell never creates a new life that he feels can atone for his role in the Nazi Party, and he is never able to confront his past directly. Hartke is able to do so, as he establishes early on in the novel: "I used to find it easy and even exhilarating to lie that elaborately. I don't anymore" (27). He seems to confess honestly, at least to the reader, all of his former crimes, whether of word, thought, or deed.

Hartke's honesty about his own past contrasts with that of characters who, like Howard Campbell, are incapable of either admitting what they have done or living with the consequences. Lyle Hooper, the town's fire chief in *Hocus Pocus*, runs a bar that enjoys unprecedented success because he allows prostitutes to pick up clients and take them to his parking lot. He refuses to acknowledge this, however, and insists to the end that he runs "a nice, clean place" (215). It is only in his final words, just before his execution at the hands of the escaped convicts from Athena, that Hooper confesses the truth: "OK, I admit it. It really was a whorehouse" (216). Hartke does not see anything particularly unusual or contemptible about Lyle's profession—he even observes darkly that these last words could be the epitaph for most contemporary Americans—but Lyle is unique in his moment of honesty, albeit at the very end of his life. Hartke takes his cue from this and owns up to all his metaphorical whorehouses. The drawings of little men and women at the beginning and ending of the book, respectively, are a confession: each drawing represents one man he killed or one sexual partner, all of whom he openly discloses throughout his narrative. He never attempts to exculpate his wartime violence with the famed Nuremberg defense that he was "just following orders." He is honest about having committed adultery before Margaret went insane. While he claims to have loved all of his paramours, he does not use this as an excuse for his behavior. In confronting all of his immoral actions, past and present, Hartke indicates his active, internal conscience and his desire to do good for himself and others.

How to Fight the Complicated Futility of Ignorance: Hartke as Teacher

Teachers generally receive positive treatment in Vonnegut's novels—Mary Hepburn of *Galápagos* is one notable example—but only if they, like Hartke, are able to think unconventionally and encourage their students to do the same. As a teacher, Hartke's conscience enables him to develop and adhere to his own moral code and encourage others to do the same, in sharp contrast to his regimented military service. He respects the unconventional Tarkington students enough to treat them as freethinking adults, whereas the Board of Trustees prefers to see them as children in need of protection from the truths of the world. In a particularly eloquent speech, Hartke defends his view of teaching: "I argued that it was a teacher's duty to speak frankly to students of college age about all sorts of concerns of humankind, not just the subject of a course as stated in the catalogue. 'That's how we gain their trust, and encourage them to speak up as well,' I said, 'and realize that all subjects do not reside in neat little compartments, but are continuous and inseparable from the one big subject we have been put on Earth to study, which is life itself'" (145). The board objects to Hartke teaching anything beyond the field of physics, but this is something of a joke as Hartke has no real qualifications to be a physics teacher, and was simply hired out of a kind of reparation by the officer-turned-peacenik who recruited him to serve in Vietnam. As Hartke's words aptly demonstrate, compartmentalization is a danger: it represents the mentality of an automaton soldier rather than that of a freethinking individual.

The board, like the military, wants to convey a single message of patriotism and self-confidence, and so Hartke's battle with the board in some ways represents a struggle against his former self. Kimberley's father, Jason Wilder, claims that by failing to feign optimism and patriotism at all times Hartke has become an "unteacher" (125). This is a comically unapt accusation, as "unteaching" seems to suggest some kind of mind erasure; a student can forget or be reeducated, but not untaught. Wilder's valuation of chirpy positivity over the truth is equally unsound. Present-day Hartke, in contrast, chooses the truth, recognizing that the feel-good bromides of his previous "hocus pocus" encouraged a false belief in America's omnipotence, which led to enormous casualties in the unwinnable Vietnam War. Hartke's disagreement with Wilder culminates over the beautiful but useless perpetual-motion machines in the library, which Hartke had rescued from cobwebs in the attic and labeled "THE COMPLICATED FUTILITY OF IGNORANCE" (14). Although the American education system deems Wilder brilliant and his daughter uneducable, Jason and Kimberley share a thoroughly literal mindset and inability to interpret or analyze. Wilder asks Hartke, "What could be a more negative word than 'futility'?"

When Hartke replies "Ignorance," Wilder triumphantly states, "There you are," as though Hartke has "somehow won his argument for him" (125). To Wilder the mere presence of the two words "futility" and "ignorance" is defeatist; he is incapable of seeing that in the context of the actual sentence Hartke is underscoring the importance of education.

Those who read *Hocus Pocus* as a pessimistic tale of woe may be similarly guilty of missing the larger message. David Montrose, like many reviewers, found the novel "replete with . . . guilt and futility: life as a cruel joke." Clearly the novel opposes optimism-at-any-cost, as we see in the absurdity of Wilder's belief that the students should be taught they can do the impossible, even if that means encouraging them to violate the laws of physics through an attempted perpetual-motion machine. Vonnegut's version of the Atheist's Bible teaches instead that in order to see the world as it really is, rather than accept tragedy, one must be dedicated to fighting ignorance. This is not a message of hopelessness, because while perpetual-motion machines are impossible, understanding physics is not.

Losing his job has potentially drastic repercussions for Hartke, but it does not cause him to abandon his commitment to education and truth. Virtually unemployable at the age of fifty-one with two children and two mentally unstable dependents, Hartke could easily forsake his calling as teacher. Instead, he chooses to teach even though the only position open to him is at the prison. He then chooses to treat the black inmates of Athena prison exactly as he treated his privileged white students at Tarkington. In doing so he sets himself apart from most of society, as the novel's 2001 setting is characterized by, among other social ills, a regression to the era of segregation. As a soldier, Hartke did exactly as he was told, even if it violated his conscience; as a teacher he follows his own moral code, which requires him to treat everyone equally, regardless of race, age, or social status. He lives with the unfortunate consequences of this attitude, as he becomes infected with tuberculosis from the prisoners because he would not separate himself from them as the other prison employees do: "I refused to wear gloves and a mask. Who could teach anybody anything wearing such a costume?" (115). Hartke's tubercular "cough, cough" periodically punctuates his narrative, serving as a reminder of his selfless commitment to teaching, and his ongoing dedication to avoiding the kind of compartmentalization the board required at Tarkington.

Hartke eliminates the socially prescribed boundaries between himself and the prisoners in an even more substantial way by resolving to answer any question as truthfully as possible. Here again he goes against common practice, as the prison parallels Tarkington (and by extension many of our own institutions) in its desire to protect its charges from any potentially upsetting news of the outside world. Unlike the college, the prison has the ability to filter the inmates' knowledge, so wardens play old news tapes on constant replay to avoid any infiltration of relevant current events. Hartke instead tells the convicted felons the truth about everything from environmental destruction to class distinctions:

> I simply described the truth of the inquirer's situation in the context of the world outside as best I could. What he did next was up to him.
>
> I call that being a teacher. I don't call that being a mastermind of a treasonous enterprise. All I ever wanted to overthrow was ignorance and self-serving fantasies. (88)

This statement is a succinct summary of Hartke's defense against the charges of treason for which he awaits trial at the novel's end; the novel as a whole supports his defense by demonstrating his commitment to improving the quality of life of his community. His lawyer wants to prove him insane, a kind of shortcut for exoneration; but Hartke clearly knows right from wrong, as he unflinchingly condemns his previous actions as a soldier. It is not Hartke whom the novel has put on trial, but society itself—a society not so far from the novel's present day, and one beset by problems familiar to the reader. Rather than despair, however, the novel teaches the value of education, learning, and knowledge. Ignorance is, indeed, the most negative word.

The Complicated Optimism of Knowledge

For all its seeming negativity, *Hocus Pocus* offers at least the possibility for optimism. Vonnegut repeatedly uses the phrase "Yes, and," to begin his paragraphs, giving the choppy fragments a continuous flow and providing an ongoing, quiet affirmation. The phrase lacks the tedious repetition implicit in his oft-used fragment from other novels, "And so on," or the fatalism of "So it goes," and instead echoes James Joyce's exuberant "Yes I said yes I will Yes" at the conclusion of *Ulysses*, though far more tentatively. "Yes, and" offers just a hint of hope and possibility, with the implication that the reader must fill in the blank. The novel reminds its readers to always follow the "yes" with an "and"—that one should always keep questioning.

With real knowledge, optimism is earned rather than false, and this optimism allows one to appreciate the true beauty of science and humanity rather than perpetuate delusions with comforting falsities. Hartke's mentally unstable mother-in-law, Mildred, catches a "humongous" (85) fish and exclaims, "It's God! It's God!" (82). This is perhaps not as crazy a response as it appears. The novel suggests that nature and science can be reliably worshipped because they are real; or, as Vonnegut suggests in *Cat's Cradle*, "Science is magic that *works*" (218). Remembering Mildred's response to the miraculous fish prompts Hartke to offer an easily overlooked and rather lovely aside about the human eye:

> People who are wary of what they might find in a book if they opened 1 are right to be. I have just had my mind blown by an essay on the embryology of the human eye.
>
> No combination of Time and Luck could have produced a camera that excellent, not even if the quantity of time had been 1,000,000,000,000 years! How is that for an unsolved mystery?" (81).

This passage suggests that evolution can be poetic and awe-inspiring; it also focuses attention specifically on sight. Jason Wilder theatrically and childishly closes his eyes (and covers his ears) to shut out Eugene's descriptions of the miserable prisoners across the lake; the novel urges us, in contrast, to keep that miraculous eye open, literally and metaphorically, to the world around us.

Hartke finds that humanity can prove as happily surprising as science. During the siege of Scipio, nothing is more precious than gasoline, which can facilitate escape, so it vanishes along with the fleeing citizens. The only vehicles left unscathed are the fire engines, which still have full tanks. Hartke, attempting to get a volunteer firefighting force together, observes this humane miracle and notes, "Every so often, in the midst of chaos, you come across an amazing, inexplicable instance of civic responsibility. Maybe the last shred of faith people have is in their firemen" (293). Volunteer firemen appear frequently in Vonnegut's work as symbols of pure selflessness (prominently in *God Bless You, Mr. Rosewater*), and his other novels include additional examples of the incredible kindness humans can sometimes show to others. In *Slaughterhouse-Five* the prisoners in the Nazi baggage car offer their limited rations to one another: "When food came in, the human beings were quiet and trusting and beautiful. They shared" (90). *Cat's Cradle* concludes with the narrator praising "meaningful, individual heroic acts" after the global apocalypse (285). In *Jailbird* the narrator reflects that he has "encountered almost nothing but kindness since leaving prison" (214), and all these kindnesses are handsomely rewarded by the story's conclusion. Throughout all his dark skepticism about the fate of the planet and humans' intrinsic avarice and stupidity, Vonnegut consistently shows glimmers of hopes. He might say, like Albert Camus wrote in his essay "The Unbeliever and Christians," "If Christianity is pessimistic as to man, it is optimistic as to human destiny. Well, I can say that, pessimistic as to human destiny, I am optimistic as to man" (55). Or, as Robert T. Tally Jr. aptly puts it, Vonnegut evinces a "misanthropic humanism," because "if the basic humanity is then the problem, it is perhaps the quirky, oddball humans in whom the best hope lies" (170). Vonnegut's novels consistently demonstrate the possibility that the individual may morally transcend the species.

While both individual and species appear damned in other Vonnegut works, *Hocus Pocus* does not envision any clear endpoint for its protagonist or for humanity. Hartke survives the Vietnam War, the ensuing post-traumatic stress disorder, his disgraceful firing, and the siege of Scipio; it seems probable he will also survive his tuberculosis, which is easily controlled by medication. Humanity survives, too; while Vonnegut's 2001 is a bleak time indeed, marking the end of America's power and prosperity, it does not depict the near-decimation of the human race that occurs in *Cat's Cradle* and *Galápagos*. Indeed, while "The Protocols of the Elders of Tralfamadore" describes the Second World War as the "Finale Rack of so-called Human Progress" (202), Hartke notes that this is only because it was written before the subsequent wars (Korea and Vietnam). The term "finale rack," as he explains, comes from the huge explosion at the end of a fireworks show: the massive pyrotechnics following the apparent conclusion of the show. This novel suggests the folly of believing we have ever seen the finale rack; there is no sudden apocalyptic judgment day here, but rather continuation.

How to Laugh like Hell, or, The Lighter Side of Reality

Seeing the world as it really is can open our eyes to an often harsh reality. *Hocus Pocus* suggests that one of the most important ways of dealing with this reality is not to ignore it, as does Jason Wilder, but to develop the ability to laugh at the world and at oneself. Vonnegut himself obviously possesses this trait; he mocks himself throughout his fiction, whether in the absurd caricature of Kilgore Trout, or in the doodling self-portraits in *Breakfast of Champions*. Humor is a central point of pride for Vonnegut. In his 1963 essay "Why I am Funny and Original," incomplete and unpublished, he observes that his writing is "authentically fresh and hilarious," although his novels have not sold well because they are "too funny, too irreverent, too original, really, for a mass market" (8). Vonnegut is self-deprecatingly humorous even in describing his own humor. Given the tragedies Vonnegut experienced throughout his life—from his mother's suicide to surviving the bombing of Dresden—the ability to laugh in (and about) his fiction must have been a crucial survival technique. Of course, not everyone finds Vonnegut funny; *Hocus Pocus* was widely denounced as depressing when first published and given scant critical attention since then. Phoebe-Lou Adams wrote in a review for the *Atlantic*, "It is strange that Mr. Vonnegut . . . should not have realized that savage denunciation, unrelieved by any contrasting material, can eventually become quite meaningless" (137). In an even more critical review for the *New York Times*, Christopher Lehmann-Haupt writes that "darkness and despair seem to have inched ahead in *Hocus Pocus*" (16). Vonnegut may well have felt like Hartke, who is surprised to find himself fired while his far more blatantly pessimistic friend, Damon Stern, goes unpunished. The difference, Hartke muses, is that "he was a comedian, and I was not" (113). As Hartke is in fact highly comedic at times, the difference appears to be more in the reception. Vonnegut's and Hartke's dark and subtle humor appear to be similarly misunderstood.

One cause for confusion may lie in equating Hartke's affection for his deceased war buddy, Jack Patton, with an acceptance of Jack's fatalistic philosophy. Just as Hartke's fascination with "Protocols of the Elders of Tralfamadore" should not lead the reader to take the story at face value, Hartke's friendship with Jack should not imply that he sees the world through Jack's eyes. After all, Jack himself notes that he probably has a "screw loose" (72), an idea Hartke supports by observing that Jack, like the sociopathic character Alton Darwin, uses only one tone of voice for everything, as though "nothing mattered more or less than anything else" (73). This is, in fact, Jack's most salient (or perhaps only) characteristic: he responds to every event the same way, stating, "I had to laugh like hell" (46) without laughing, thus indicating the simultaneous humor and gloom of all situations. Jack's anaesthetization to the world recalls Billy Pilgrim's, both of which receive sympathy but never validation from Vonnegut. However, Hartke is able to take Jack's words and apply them appropriately; he, unlike Jack, knows when to laugh. One example occurs when Hartke is playing the carillon at Tarkington, which he describes as providing him with the "happiest moments in my life, without question" (7). In the midst of this joyous experience, he realizes that the acoustics of the lake make it appear as though a phantom carillonneur in the prison is playing the bells back at him in mimicry and mockery. Hartke's response to this could be one of annoyance or anger, but instead he says, "I would yell into the mad clashing of bells and echoes, 'Laugh, Jack, laugh!'" (58). Hartke evokes his friend but demonstrates emotions—euphoria, humor, irony—that Jack never could. While Jack is completely desensitized, Hartke can respond to both nuances of happiness and sorrow.

Hartke is also distinct from many of the other characters in his ability to laugh at himself. At the very end of the novel he meets his illegitimate son, Rob Roy, and confesses that he is filled with happiness at the encounter because "I had always wanted to be a General, and there I was wearing General's stars. How embarrassing to be human" (309). Even at this emotional moment, Hartke mocks his own natural reaction. In contrast, Pamela Ford Hall, one of his many paramours, demonstrates an inability to see any humor in her own pain, and becomes an alcoholic as a result. Pamela's first major art show, "Bagladies," is destroyed when her figurines, all made from weightless polyurethane, blow onto heating pipes and melt, releasing the smell of urine. Nationwide news stations all cover this as a light and funny human-interest story, but Pamela cannot appreciate the publicity because she is too overcome with self-pity to find the humor in her situation. To Hartke's credit, he never laughs at her, even though his own problems are so much larger. He does, however, contrast her to another lover, Zuzu, of whom he observes, "The prognosis for her was a lot better than for Pamela . . . she could see the humorous side of things. She said, I remember, that the loss of the Venice dream had left her a walking corpse, but that a zombie was an ideal mate for a College President"

(194). Zuzu, Pamela, Hartke, Lyle Hooper, and most of the other characters in the novel lose their dreams. The world has plenty of darkness, but ignorance and delusion, whether imposed or chosen, is never the solution. The ability to see humor even in the grimmest realities of both themselves and the world gives characters like Hartke and Zuzu the highest probability of leading sane and relatively happy existences.

Yes, And . . .

Choosing the life of a freethinker is not necessarily an easy path; opening one's eyes to all the world's horrors can easily bring despair, and the novel indicates that the temptation to give responsibility over to a deity is ever-present. Twice in the novel Hartke asks the question, "How much longer can I go on being an atheist?" (205, 295), but both moments simultaneously suggest his resolve to remain so. In the first instance, Hartke realizes the backhoe at Tarkington is the only vehicle besides the fire trucks that still possesses gasoline. While the miracle of gasoline in the fire truck was an example of human public-spiritedness, this one is far more venal: the backhoe uses diesel fuel, which has a much lower value on the black market. Simple human avarice, not divine intervention, explains why all the vehicles save this one have been emptied. The other, more significant, time that Hartke rhetorically questions his atheism is when he is shocked that the length of his two lists—the men he has killed and the women he has loved—will end up being identical. This, however, is a matter of mere bizarre coincidence. In order to avoid the possibility that some readers "will turn to the end to learn the number" and judge the book by the number rather than the content, Hartke provides a final moment of education by constructing an absurd math problem that he claims will lead the reader to the correct answer using facts from the book. However, the problem really requires just two facts, only the latter of which even appears in the novel: the year in which Thomas Jefferson died and the greatest number of babies born to one woman. The resulting number (eighty-two) has no specific meaning, and so the math game is mere hocus pocus itself.

The overall lesson, however, is not: there are no easy answers, and we must avoid the temptation to believe otherwise. Vonnegut foreshadows this conclusion with a previous numerological chart that Hartke uses to teach students the perils of using "facts tailored to fit a thesis" (253). The chart spells "Christ" using the first letter of all the names of WWII leaders, but only if you choose to call Mussolini "Il Duce"; it gives numbers that add up to the year the war ended, but only if you choose specific facts and then halve the final number. In other words, Hartke understands that seemingly impressive numerology often adds up to random coincidence, and no more.

These examples suggest that the novel's myriad other coincidences be viewed as just that; they are not meant to suggest some overarching divine hand, but rather the way that humans often interpret the "hocus pocus" of their lives as something that must have a greater plan. Jack Patton shares a surname and the position of class "goat" with the famous General George Patton (no relation); Mildred mangles a perch's eye while fishing, throws it back, and catches the same fish again; the Tarkington students are all away on vacation during the two life-threatening events that hit campus (the diphtheria epidemic and the Siege of Scipio). It is not unusual to see red herrings of this type in a postmodern novel, and it is not surprising that these clues and coincidences do not provide the reader with some magical key to the text. As Tally observes, however, Vonnegut is really a "reluctant postmodernist" (168); he is not just throwing in tantalizing connections to befuddle the reader, but rather to prove a larger point: that although life will always include the inexplicable, artificial explanations dangerously enable individuals to avoid the challenges of interrogating their behavior toward others. One may want to believe that all coincidences have greater meaning, but the novel asks the reader to accept the absence of a larger pattern and still seek a productive contribution to the world.

Hocus Pocus is by no means as dark a novel as many critics initially presume it to be; instead, it attempts to do what Hartke dedicates his life to doing: educate, even if the truth is inconvenient or unpalatable.

The last sentence reveals this message in a clever anagram; "just because some of us can read and write and do a little math, that doesn't mean we deserve to conquer the Universe" can be rearranged to spell, "A masquerade can cover a sense of what is real to deceive us; to be unjaded and not lost, we must, then, determine truth" (Calhoun). The actual concluding line demonstrates pessimism about humanity; the anagrammed version reveals hope for humans' abilities as rational thinkers. Vonnegut's world lacks a divinity, but not a sense of sacredness. The novel, like Vonnegut's work as a whole, retains a quiet humanism; people may be dumb, as he states repeatedly, but if there is any hope for humankind, it rests in the ability to learn, to teach, and to think freely.

Works Cited

Adams, Phoebe-Lou. "HOCUS POCUS (Book)." *Atlantic* 266.4 (1990): 137. Print.

Beidler, Phil. "Bad Business: Vietnam and Recent Mass-Market Fiction." *College English* 54.1 (1992): 64–75. Print.

Broer, Lawrence R. *Vonnegut and Hemingway: Writers at War*. Columbia: U of South Carolina P, 2011. Print.

___. "Hartke's Hearing: Vonnegut's Heroes On Trial." *The Vonnegut Chronicles: Interviews and Essays*. Westport: Greenwood, 1996. 179–203. Print.

Calhoun, Cory. *Anagram Hall of Fame*. Wordsmith, n.d. Web. 21 Aug. 2012.

Camus, Albert. *Resistance, Rebellion, and Death*. New York: Mod. Lib., 1960. Print.

Lehmann-Haupt, Christopher. "Books of the Times; Familiar Characters and Tricks of Vonnegut." *New York Times* 8 Sept. 1990. Web. 10 June 2012.

McInerney, Jay. "Still Asking the Embarrassing Questions." *New York Times Book Review* 9 Sept. 1990, late ed.: 12. Print.

McMahon, Gary. *Kurt Vonnegut and the Centrifugal Force of Fate*. Jefferson: McFarland, 2009. Print.

Montrose, David. "Life as a Cruel Joke." *TLS* 4569 (1990): 1146. Print.

Skow, J. "And So It Went." *Time* 136.10 (1990): 73. Print.

Tally, Robert T. "A Postmodern Iconography: Vonnegut and the Great American Novel." *Reading America: New Perspectives on the American Novel*. Ed. Elizabeth Boyle and Anne-Marie Evans. Newcastle: Cambridge Scholars, 2008. 163–78. Print.

"Vonnegut, Kurt, Jr." *Current Biography* 52.3 (1991): 52. *EBSCOhost*. Web. 15 July 2012.

Vonnegut, Kurt. *Breakfast of Champions*. 1973. New York: Delta, 1999. Print.

___. *Cat's Cradle*. 1963. New York: Dial, 2010. Print.

___. *Galápagos*. New York: Delacorte, 1985. Print.

___. *God Bless You, Mr. Rosewater*. 1965. New York: Berkley, 2006. Print.

___. *Hocus Pocus*. 1990. New York: Berkley, 1997. Print.

___. *Jailbird*. 1979. New York: Dial, 2011. Print.

___. *Mother Night*. 1961. New York: Laurel, 1996. Print.

___. *Slaughterhouse-Five*. 1969. New York: Delta, 1999. Print.

___. "Why I am Funny and Original." 1963. MS. Lilly Lib. Indiana U, Bloomington.

Wilson, John. "Hocus Pocus." Magill Book Reviews (1990). *EBSCOhost*. Web. 10 June 2012.

Anthropology across the Universe: Folk Societies in the Early Novels of Kurt Vonnegut_____

Shiela Ellen Pardee

Kurt Vonnegut began his graduate study of anthropology in 1945 on what he called the happiest day of his life. His army experience, especially witnessing the aftermath of the firebombing of Dresden when he was detained as a prisoner of war, had been emotionally devastating. He had seen the worst and best of the world, but what he saw did not correspond to his midwestern ideas of good and evil. He had studied science, but science seemed to end in bombs. Studying anthropology at the University of Chicago seemed like a way to process the past and affirm a human future. "At last! I was going to study man!" (*Wampeters, Foma & Granfalloons* 177). After trying and rejecting physical anthropology and archaeology, he turned to cultural anthropology, characterized by his advisor Sydney Slotkin as "poetry which *pretends* to be scientific" (178). Vonnegut immersed himself in a field of study that would influence the next three decades of his life with humanist philosophy and cultural relativism. Although he left the University of Chicago without a degree, it is no secret that Vonnegut's study of anthropology had a profound influence on his fiction. This essay will focus primarily on the anthropological significance of Vonnegut's early fiction, written in the years after his unfinished graduate training at the University of Chicago, but clearly the insights gained from Vonnegut's formal and informal anthropological studies affected his work throughout his long career.

Vonnegut's coursework was shaped by two pioneers in the field who were each mentioned by his advisor: Ruth Benedict and Margaret Mead. Benedict had been largely responsible for making the term "culture" a common word in educated speech. Benedict's *Patterns of Culture* (1934) demonstrates her perception of how each group of people she studied seemed to elaborate particular character traits as a group so that each culture could be represented as a kind of "personality writ large" (Mead xiii). Originally a student of literature, Benedict felt "that each primitive culture represented something comparable to a great work of art or literature" (Mead viii), and she insisted on the "internal consistency" of each culture, expecting that the religion, mythology, and everyday ways of men and women would all be interrelated and meaningful in the group's own terms (vii–ix). In all of his fiction, but particularly in his early novels, Vonnegut takes this vision of cultural relativism and abbreviates its habits, characterizing both the otherworldly cultures he creates and the earthly cultures he recreates in broad strokes and placing characters in cross-cultural encounters to demonstrate the contingent nature of our ideas about what is normal.

Benedict had been strongly influenced by her Columbia University professor Franz Boas, the most influential American anthropologist of the early twentieth century. Boas rejected the concept of racial limitations and believed that knowledge of other cultures was important to determine the "parts of our mental life that are common to mankind as a whole and those due to the culture in which we live" to enable us "to view our own civilization objectively" (qtd. in Bunzel 5). In her introduction to Boas's *Anthropology and Modern Life*, Ruth Bunzel adds that Boas "sought to use anthropology to free men's minds of the yoke of traditional patterns of thought by confronting audiences with different and coherent styles of life" (5–6). Vonnegut made that mission his own as a fiction writer and was conscious of its importance throughout his career. In an interview with *Playboy* in 1973, he goes back to his childhood to explain the impact cultural relativism had on him as a young man, as he insists on its importance in education:

> I've often thought there ought to be a manual to hand to little kids, telling them what kind of planet they're on, why they don't fall off it, how much time they've probably got here, how to avoid poison ivy, and so on. . . . And one thing I would really like to tell them about is cultural relativity. I didn't learn until I was in college about all the other cultures. . . . A first-grader should understand that his culture isn't a rational invention; that

there are thousands of other cultures and they all work pretty well; that all cultures function on faith rather than truth; that there are lots of alternatives to our own society. (*Wampeters* 278–79)

Vonnegut learned that cultures are not only flawed constructions to be criticized; culture also gives humans a vital and necessary connection to others, and the respect accorded to local culture was in harmony with attachment to his own midwestern roots. The professor who most influenced Vonnegut was Robert Redfield, the head of the Anthropology Department at the University of Chicago, who specialized in the study of "folk societies." Vonnegut downplays Redfield's academic accomplishments, referring only to his article "The Folk Society," published in the *American Journal of Sociology* in January 1947, and calling his ideas "a lovely dream." Redfield's work actually included extensive fieldwork and significant contributions on social science education as well as anthropology. As Vonnegut acknowledges, Redfield's ideas continued to resonate in his fiction throughout his career. He credited Redfield for his thematic emphasis on the human need to belong to a small, supportive social group. Vonnegut often explores this theme by demonstrating the extremes of foolishness and depravity people will resort to when deprived of a role in such a group. According to John Tomedi, Vonnegut felt "strongly about the anthropological need to belong to a folk society and the vulnerabilities human beings face without it" (82). He believed that the need for belonging to a group small enough for everyone to be known and to have roles to play was innate and biological. "We are full of chemicals which require us to belong to folk societies," Vonnegut told the National Institute of Arts and Letters, "or, failing that, to feel lousy all the time" (*Wampeters* 180).

Redfield's work also made an important contribution to Vonnegut's art by framing his discipline's conflicts about the role of local culture versus that of innate human nature in shaping individuals. Redfield's article in the *Journal of General Education*, "The Universally Human and the Culturally Variable," posits a cyclical alternation in the focus of anthropology over the years, with attention given to differences between cultures succeeded by increased focus on universal traits. According to Redfield, James Frazer's *Golden Bough*, written to bring attention to worldwide human similarities, instead brought renewed attention to human differences by its detailed recording of worldwide customs. During Redfield's own student years, dominated by work like Benedict's, he says, "particular cultures were everything; uniformities of human development got small attention," but more recently, emphasis had shifted, moving back "toward the common elements, the resemblances among peoples" (Redfield 152). Vonnegut confirms this new focus in his own education in the first chapter of *Slaughterhouse-Five* (1969), writing that when he was a student of anthropology, "they were teaching that there was absolutely no difference between anybody" (8). This alternation of focus within the discipline of anthropology is worked out in Vonnegut's novels by employing the additional breadth afforded by science fiction to view humanity from a feigned intellectual distance impossible to achieve by ethnocentric humans. Vonnegut's work pries apart the two sides of the issue, insistently highlighting both the importance of community identity and the need for a transcendent moral framework from which to view the whole human enterprise.

Vonnegut has said that his own "prettiest contribution to [his] culture" was his master's thesis in anthropology, which was rejected by the University of Chicago (*Palm Sunday* 285). The thesis has disappeared, but based on his own abbreviated reconstruction, he appeared to be applying a form of structuralism to literature and folktales. Vonnegut's simplistic graphs of story structures were based on "good" and "ill" fortune, charted simplistically as ups and downs along the line of the narrative. He reaches toward a theory with his observation that the Christian story of creation and the fall (in common with other creation myths worldwide) graph was similar to that of Cinderella in its accumulation of favors leading to disobedience and an abrupt fall from grace. Vonnegut saw that "the rise to bliss at the end was identical with the expectation of redemption as expressed in primitive Christianity" (*Palm Sunday* 288). He appears to have been groping toward an analysis of stories similar to those by the Russian philologist Vladimir Propp, beginning with *Morphology of the Folktale* in 1928; it is probable that Vonnegut got the germ of Propp's ideas, if not more, from his academic study of folktales. Vonnegut's 1963 novel *Cat's Cradle*, eventually accepted by the University of Chicago as an MA thesis for an honorary degree in anthropology, is considerably more subtle as a study of the comforts found in moral tales. In *Cat's Cradle*, the sacred literature is invented. Vonnegut learned to use imagination to illustrate the patterns shown so poorly by his graphic representations as an academic. Meanwhile, Vonnegut left Chicago in the late 1940s to work in public relations at General Electric, which, in those days of paternalistic corporate culture, gave him a new angle on the comforts, irritations, and limitations of small-group support. While at General Electric, he published enough short stories to quit his job and write full time.

In his first novel, *Player Piano* (1952), Vonnegut satirizes corporate culture and its dehumanizing cult of efficiency. Engineer Paul Proteus sees the banality of his self-congratulatory colleagues and the injustice in the combined corporate and government power that valorizes production so much that most workers are replaced with machines, stripping ordinary people of dignity and autonomy. Paul's conscience nags him for working toward more mechanization, but he fears losing security in the only community he has known. He is let go for a lack of enthusiasm before he quits, and as he says "goodbye to his life so far, to the whole of his father's life," a "wave of sadness" washes over his thoughts: "He was understanding now that no man could live without roots—roots in a patch of desert, a red clay field, a mountain slope, a rocky coast, a city street. In black loam, in mud or sand or rock or asphalt or carpet, every man had his roots down deep—in *home*" (*Player Piano* 237). Vonnegut shows how a corporate imperative has perverted the natural family support structure. Engineers and managers in the company town of Ilium participate in an artificial community of empty rituals, while former workers and ordinary townspeople are cast adrift without any cultural identity at all; the two groups are literally divided by a river. The Reverend James J. Lasher, a character whose education as an anthropologist enables him to take an outsider's view and speak for Vonnegut (Freese 54), contrasts the two communities. The "crusading spirit" of the managers and engineers was "cooked up" by public relations and advertising "folklore" to make big business popular (*Player Piano* 91). Now, the engineers and managers "believe with all their hearts," and "yesterday's snow job becomes today's sermon" (92). Freese notes that the setting for ritualized team spirit was based on Association Island, where morale-building camps were offered by General Electric to their most deserving young men. Vonnegut told Charles Reilly in a 1980 interview, "They closed down their Association Island shortly after the novel began to circulate" (199). As for the workers in the story: "Their whole culture's been shot to hell" (Freese 91), leaving the situation "ripe for a phony Messiah . . . with some new magic" to help them regain "the feeling of participation, the feeling of being needed on earth" (*Player Piano* 92).

Proteus finds a new family in the opposition Ghost Shirt movement, which was directly inspired by Vonnegut's anthropology research (Freese 41). Vonnegut had wanted to study "exactly what it took to form a revolutionary group" (Klinkowitz 13). He wrote to S. Miller Harris about this research in February 1951, explaining that he got interested in the notion of artistic schools at the instigation of his advisor. When the faculty insisted on something "more strictly anthropological," he turned his attention to the American Indian Ghost Dance Rebellion of 1894 (*Look at the Birdie* 3–4). In *Player Piano*, the Ghost Shirt movement of rebellious displaced workers illustrates the craving for small-group identity, the need for a charismatic leader, and the limited effectiveness of such groups, especially when they come in conflict with one another in the industrial world. The most craven need for inclusion is represented by Luke Lubbock, a member of various lodges and artificial societies that help fill the empty days of the displaced workers. Luke changes out of one tawdry, elaborate costume into another as he participates in different groups. As he puts on a jacket with "ponderous epaulets, Luke was growing again, getting his color back, and as he strapped on his saber he was talkative again—important and strong" (*Player Piano* 95). Yet, Lasher comments, "that sort of business wears thin pretty quick" (95). The people need a more inspiring leader, and here Vonnegut draws on his research on artistic "schools." In his letter to Harris, Vonnegut says he learned that a "school" provides "the fantastic amount of guts it takes to add to culture. It gives him morale, esprit de corps, the resources of many brains, and—maybe most important—one-sidedness with assurance" (*Look* 4). "Fire and confidence and originality and fresh prejudices," Vonnegut recalls, "As Slotkin said, these things are group products. It isn't a question of finding a Messiah, but of a group's creating one" (*Look* 4–5). In *Player Piano*, the group creates Paul Proteus as their leader before he is brave enough to participate.

When the revolution of the workers finally comes, the costumed artificial communities meld into one dedicated mob: Scots with bagpipes, Indians, Arabs, and "gold-epauleted Royal Parmesans" (*Player Piano* 318–22) waiting for their "reinforcements"—the VFW, the Knights of Pythias, and the Masons (325). The cobbled-together community cannot hold onto its ideals, and the disaffected engineers who led them return to face punishment in the corporate community on their own side of the river.

In his first novel, Vonnegut does not resort to characters from beyond the planet to provide social commentary from a distance, but he writes in the dystopian genre with a near-future setting to the same effect. Proteus's nonconformist friend Ed Finnerty says: "I want to stay as close to the edge as I can without going over. Out on the edge you see all kinds of things you can't see from the center" (*Player Piano* 84). Vonnegut is already describing his own times in the anthropological mode so that "the stuff of American culture is assumed to be so foreign that it needs to be drawn" (Tomedi 76). As Richard Giannone puts it, "By drawing the fruits and worries of our daily life as if they were the dinosaurs, he brings us to confront the fatal consequences of our ignominy: we are faced with, as an accomplished fact, the oblivion we are making" (qtd. in Tomedi 77). At the same time, this attempt at objectivity is balanced with respect for the bravery and effectiveness of a local culture supporting "one-sidedness with assurance."

The Sirens of Titan (1959) is also a dystopia set in the near future, "The Nightmare Ages" between the Second World War and the "Third Great Depression" (2), a formula that places it in the midst of the consequences of the folly of his own times. People have pushed "ever outward" instead of finding the meaning of life within (*Sirens* 1), but "the bounties of space, of infinite outwardness" were only "empty heroics, low comedy, and pointless death" (2). Empty heroics and low comedy show how we are bullied by assumptions about progress that extend even to our notions of speed and direction; a spaceship is stuck on Mercury because it has been designed to descend during hostile fire into the "deepest hole it could find" (192). It uses elaborate sensing systems to move down the branching passages of a large cave, but the designers did not anticipate "problems going up" (196), so the ship keeps blundering against the walls and sides until the harmoniums of Mercury suggest that they turn the ship upside down. The idea of reversing course to make progress was apparently alien to the average human mind.

Extraterrestrial settings and characters tell a story of human affairs controlled from outside their knowledge, let alone understanding. In particular, the artificial perspective of extended space travel is used to critique the human tendency to equate success with divine approval. The words of antihero and protagonist Malachi Constant lead off the novel: "I guess somebody up there likes me" (*Sirens* 1). He believes this, even though his pool looks "like a punchbowl in hell" after an extended, depraved party (50), simply because his father has been lucky and left him rich. Crediting God as a source for luck seems reasonable in the case of his father, who used the letters in the Bible to choose bank stocks and make a fortune (70–71). Constant, however, is cruelly used by the forces of the universe in return for his desire to replicate his father's luck, to deliver "a first-class message from God to someone equally distinguished" (12). Winston Niles Rumfoord—with authority based on old money and his accidental encounter with the *chrono-synclastic infundibula*, which brings him back to earth for brief, periodic materializations—sends Constant on his way, and Constant is offered "an opportunity to see a new and interesting planet, and an opportunity to think about [his] native planet from a fresh and beautifully detached viewpoint" (90). This dangled opportunity to experience cultural relativism is just a lure; instead, the Martians clean out his memory and insert antenna to control him as the army prepares to invade earth. Rumfoord has arranged the whole war to unite the diverse people on earth but has himself been used "ruthlessly" and to "disgustingly paltry ends" (60–61) to arrange the events of earth to procure a spare part for a spaceship from Tralfamadore. Constant also eventually realizes "that he was not only a victim of outrageous fortune, but one of outrageous fortune's cruelest agents as well" (163).

The *chrono-synclastic infundibula* provides a spatial immersion in the cultural relativist perspective. In an invented definition for a child's encyclopedia, it is defined as a place where the smartest daddies from different places can all be right at the same time, even though they all disagree. "The Universe is an awfully big place . . . there are so many different ways of being right" (8–9). Vonnegut has used this imaginary location in space to resolve the contradiction between the comforts of folk society prejudice and the irrepressible impulse to find a basis for worldwide unity.

Rumfoord uses the power given him by his perspective from the *chrono-synclastic infundibula* to found a new religion called the Church of God the Utterly Indifferent, which teaches the people to take care of each other because "Puny man can do nothing at all to help or please God Almighty, and Luck is not the hand of God" (183). "Luck," Rumfoord claims, "is the way the wind swirls and the dust settles eons after God has passed by," (257). The universal desire to enter Paradise with your family and best friends proves impossible to eradicate in the case of Malachi Constant, however. Despite an intergalactic collection of evidence against the possibility of meaning in life and God's power to convey favor, Constant dies dreaming that his best friend Stony Stevenson has come to take him to Paradise, where his wife awaits, thus showing that our earliest illusions about life are formed together with our early relationships and stubbornly, perhaps not unfortunately, rooted in our natures.

The dangers that await a person who tries to live life from a neutral position are exposed in *Mother Night* (1961), whose main character, Howard W. Campbell Jr., is without a culture, "a nationless person by inclination" (1). He is like the man in the novel's epigraph by Sir Walter Scott "with soul so dead, / Who never to himself hath said, / 'This is my own, my native land!'" Lack of patriotism makes him an ideal double agent who poses as a Nazi while broadcasting coded messages to the British military (Freese 165). His lack of loyalty also reflects the isolationist and family-centered world of post–World War II and post-Depression Americans. He wishes to retreat to "a nation of two" with his wife, Helga, but their life together illustrates the limits of life lived by the principle that personal love conquers all. They give each other "uncritical love" (42), hear "only the melodies in [their] voices" (43), and refuse to think about what is happening in the world. "Away from the sovereign territory of our nation of two, we talked like the patriotic lunatics all around us . . . And when that nation ceased to be, I became what I am today and what I always will be, a stateless person" (*Mother Night* 42–43).

Campbell had been uprooted from his Schenectady, New York, home at age eleven when his father was transferred. As in *Player Piano*, Vonnegut blames a lack of community values on the replacement of hometown culture with a corporate substitute. Campbell's father was an engineer whose "mission . . . was to install, maintain and repair General Electric heavy equipment" worldwide so he "was rarely home" and "had scant time and imagination left over for anything else. The man was the job and the job was the man" (*Mother Night* 25). After his transfer to Berlin, Germany, Campbell says, "my education, my friends, and my principle language were German" (27).

His dual citizenship is exploited by an American espionage agent who recruits him in 1938, as Hitler is consolidating his power before World War II. Campbell reveals his lack of moral indignation and patriotic fervor in conversation with his recruiter. When asked about "the things going on in Germany . . . Hitler and the Jews and all that," he replies, "It isn't anything I can control . . . so I don't think about it" (*Mother Night* 34–35). He also says, "Nationalities just don't interest me as much as they probably should" (35). Even after the war, his sentiments are the same. Commenting that it would be as "silly" to love America as to hate it, he explains: "I can't think in terms of boundaries. Those imaginary lines are as unreal to me as elves and pixies. I can't believe that they mark the end or the beginning of anything of real concern to a human soul. Virtues and vices, pleasures and pains cross boundaries at will" (133). His disregard for citizenship eventually backfires, when it is cited by several countries as eligibility for his execution.

As a writer, he had been asked to write and deliver broadcasts of Nazi propaganda with inserted codes (whose content is unknown to him) transmitted by means of "mannerisms, pauses, emphases, coughs, seeming stumbles in certain key sentences" (*Mother Night* 29). He takes the job because he is "a ham" and being a spy would give him "an opportunity for some pretty grand acting" (39). Although he is not a Nazi, his diatribes are utterly convincing. As in the case of his father, "the man was the job and the job was the man." Even his recruiter comes to believe that despite his service to the Allies, he was "certainly" a Nazi because of the zeal he had given to the role (188). Campbell acknowledges that if Germany had won the war, he might have become the good Nazi he had played.

The limits of cultural relativism are suggested in the swastika, the hammer and sickle, and the Stars and Stripes that Campbell drew as he argued "the meaning of patriotism to, respectively, a Nazi, a Communist, and an American" (*Mother Night* 81). "Hooray, hooray, hooray," he would say, concluding his argument (81), no closer to improving life or preventing war. Despite insisting on the need for humans to learn about cultural relativism and respect for other cultures, Vonnegut also recognized the need to remain grounded and claimed by one's own, and the tension between those two needs is an important theme in his body of work. People should respect the cultures of others but should not don another culture like a coat or speak in someone else's voice as a matter of everyday practice. "I myself find that I trust my own writing most, and others seem to trust it most, too," he wrote, "when I sound most like a person from Indianapolis, which I am" (*Palm Sunday* 70).

As an actor and writer, Campbell represents the artistic community. Vonnegut challenges the idea that life is short but art is long, so artists should eschew involvement in politics to create ideal, beautiful forms. Campbell's friend George Kraft sermonizes on the importance of the arts, saying, "Future civilizations . . . are going to judge all men by the extent to which they've been artists" (*Mother Night* 56) and "if some future archaeologist finds our works miraculously preserved in some city dump, [they] will be judged by the quality of [their] creations" (56). By this scheme of judgment, Campbell's Nazi father-in-law would be a champion of civilization because he scolds a "nameless, ageless, sexless ragbag" of a slave for careless handling of a "luminously beautiful" vase (95). "Close to unashamed tears, he asked us all to adore the blue vase that laziness and stupidity had almost let slip from the world" (96). He had made a slave, already condemned and helpless, "to feel like a fool. She had been given her opportunity to participate in civilization, and she had muffed it" (96). He has reversed the values of life and art, choosing representation over life. He proposes to shoot his daughter's living dog because he has "no interest in it" (97). Then he praises another slave carrying a hideous Chinese carved-oak dog "as carefully as though it were a baby," explaining, "That's the way to handle precious things" (100). Kraft and Campbell become spies and hypocrites in fear of perishing along with their art, which they, like Campbell's father-in-law, value more than the lives of others.

As for the fate of art and artifact, Campbell's complete writings survive the war. Ironically, though, they become known as the writings of a Russian interpreter who translated and published them as his own: "a trunkful of instant career" (200). Campbell's private journal of his sexual relationship with his wife is anonymously published and widely distributed in Russia. Campbell complains, "The part of me that wanted to tell the truth got turned into an expert liar! The lover in me got turned into a pornographer! The artist in me got turned into ugliness such as the world has rarely seen before" (206). Sacrificing his political responsibility to protect his personal life and continue writing has been useless. Once let loose in the world, his works are no more loyal than he is.

The closest Campbell ever comes to understanding the value of community is when he glimpses the "little Eden formed by joined back yards" (23) from the window of his Greenwich Village hideout after the Germans are defeated. From that walled-off park, where children play, he sometimes hears the voice of community forgiveness for one of its own: "the sweetly mournful cry that meant a game of hide-and-seek was over, that those still hiding were to come out of hiding . . . 'Olly-olly-ox-in-free.' And I, hiding from many people who might want to hurt or kill me, often longed for someone to give that cry for me" (24). He dies with no connection to the kind of community, as close as a set of interconnected backyards, which could claim him for its own.

The title and unifying image of the 1963 novel *Cat's Cradle* may have germinated from a seed sown by Professor Redfield in one of his lectures. In "The Universally Human and the Culturally Variable," Redfield discusses "two contradictory aspects" or ways of looking at human nature—"that men in every tribe or nation are all very much alike and the differences among peoples are great and perhaps limitless"—that "come to men at different times, for different reasons, and with varying emphasis on the one or the other" (151). As an illustration of the view of universal humanity, he gives the example of

> instructions to airmen who might find themselves unexpectedly landed in some remote primitive community of the South Seas. Such an American, if he saw a native coming toward him about whose ways he knew nothing, was told to sit down quietly by the path and begin to make string figures. People are enough alike so that this conduct would be reassuring to the native—and, besides, the chances would be great that he too would know how to make string figures. (150–51).

Although it might be soothing for two humans with no other way to communicate to make string figures, it would do little to further understanding. String figures are meaningless, though they have traditional names that suggest something familiar in their patterns. Cradle is not a universal concept, however, and a cat in a cradle takes it a step further into whimsy. Making a string figure like a cat's cradle represents motion without motive or meaning. In Vonnegut's novel, it is a symbol for the *karass*, a concept he invents for the imaginary Bokononist religion. A *karass* is a team (everyone supposedly belongs to one) whose members together "do God's Will without ever discovering what they are doing" (12). The association with the cat's cradle image is strengthened with the first quotation from the *Books of Bokonon*: "If you find your life tangled up with somebody else's life for no very logical reasons . . . that person may be a member of your *karass*" (12). The narrator of *Cat's Cradle*, John, has a *karass* that includes a former Auschwitz physician doing penance in the jungle and the children of Felix Hoenikker, one of the inventors of the atomic bomb, among other unlikely companions (127).

Cat's Cradle challenges the assumption that string figures are inherently soothing. When John sends a letter to Newt Hoenikker to learn what his celebrated father, Felix, was doing on the day the bomb dropped, Newt relates that besides terrifying the world with his satanic invention, his father had scared the hell out of him with a cat's cradle he made while idly toying with some string. Although he had never played with him and hardly spoken to him, he got down on the floor, "waved that tangle of string in my face," and sang "Rockabye catsy" (17–18). The appearance of his real father affected Newt more than the abstract arrangement of string, despite his father's efforts to create familiar associations with a nursery song. Newt wrote: "His pores looked as big as craters on the moon. His ears and nostrils were stuffed with hair. Cigar smoke made him smell like the mouth of Hell. . . . I ran out of the house as fast as I could go" (17–18).

Newt never recovers from the trauma of his father's attempt to communicate with an inadequate model. As a grown man on the island of San Lorenzo, he reproduces the empty, bewildering tangle in a painting John describes as "scratches made in a black, gummy impasto" that "formed a sort of spider's web" like "sticky nets of human futility hung up on a moonless night to dry" (113). Rejecting the notion that "it means something different to everyone who sees it," Newt bluntly calls it a cat's cradle (113). He suggests the anthropological source of Vonnegut's motif, adding that it is "one of the oldest games there is . . . even the Eskimos know it" (114). "For maybe a hundred thousand years or more, grownups have been waving tangles of string in their children's faces. . . . No wonder kids grow up crazy. A cat's cradle is nothing but a bunch of X's between somebody's hands, and little kids look and look and look at all those X's" and see "*No damn cat, and no damn cradle*" (114; italics in orig.).

This suggests the role of religion in making children afraid of the father and offering a complex but empty pattern for their lives based on belief in something unseen. Newt snorts, "Religion!" and asks, "See the cat? . . . See the cradle?" (124). The political implications are shown in the performance of San Lorenzo's Bokonon religion. A pretense of persecution keeps the people involved in a game of opposition to the government. "The truth was that life was as short and brutish and mean as ever. But people didn't have to pay as much attention to the awful truth" (118) and their happiness grew as they participated "in a play they understood, that any human being anywhere could understand" (119).

A poem from *The Books of Bokonon* downplays the importance of an accurate model while asserting the importance of experiencing shared meaning:

> Tiger got to hunt,
> Bird got to fly;
> Man got to sit and wonder, "Why, why, why?"
> Tiger got to sleep,
> Bird got to land;
> Man got to tell himself he understand. (124)

The Books of Bokonon cheerfully admits that its stories of origin are *foma*, "harmless untruths" (129–30), which, according to Vonnegut in the preface to *Wampeters, Foma, and Granfalloons*, are "intended to comfort simple souls" (xiii). Despite its levity, *Cat's Cradle* is a serious exploration of what religion and local culture might mean in a postmodern world and the dangers of relying on "objective" science as a substitute. It was eventually accepted as a graduate thesis for an honorary degree in anthropology from the University of Chicago in 1971.

An anthropological fieldwork approach toward understanding the urban poor is reflected in *God Bless You, Mr. Rosewater* (1965). Eliot Rosewater has ten thousand dollars a day of inherited wealth to spend, thanks to his father, Senator Lister Ames Rosewater, who saw to it that the Rosewater family fortune was "stashed into a foundation" so "predators not named Rosewater might be prevented from getting their hands on it" (1). After attending Harvard and serving in World War II, Eliot administers his foundation responsibly. "Rosewater dollars fought cancer and mental illness and race prejudice and police brutality and countless other miseries, encouraged college professors to look for truth, bought beauty at any price" (17).

Eliot cannot stop drinking, though, and he goes off on regular jaunts and benders in search of community. Crashing a science-fiction convention, he proclaims: "I love you . . . You're the only ones with guts enough to *really* care about the future" (*God Bless* 18; italics in orig.). His favorite author is Kilgore Trout, a neglected science-fiction writer (and recurring character who appears for the first time in this novel). "Trout's favorite formula was to describe a perfectly hideous society, not unlike his own, and then, toward the end, to suggest ways in which it could be improved" (21). This is the technique of defamiliarizing one's own society for purposes of reform that Vonnegut has already used in his novels. Eliot tells the science-fiction writers that someone should write a book about money. "You don't have to go to the Planet Tralfamadore in Anti-Matter Galaxy 508G to find weird creatures with unbelievable powers. Look at the powers of an Earthling millionaire!" (23). Writing checks for everybody, he adds, "It's insane that I should be able to do such a thing" (23). Vonnegut has handed over to his character the technique of defamiliarizing his own culture with science-fiction comparisons.

Still searching for a welcoming version of a folk community as well as a meaningful place to spend his money, Eliot starts visiting volunteer fire departments. Claiming to have belonged to a volunteer fire department himself, he proclaims: "We few, we happy few, we band of brothers—joined in the serious business of keeping our food, shelter, clothing and loved ones from combining with oxygen" (*God Bless* 24). Even his identification with this community is based on his privileged childhood, when "sycophants among the townies had flattered little Eliot by making him mascot of the Volunteer Fire Department of Rosewater" (25). Instead of aiding firefighters in their work, he had accidentally murdered three of them in a smoke-filled building he thought was occupied by SS troops during his war service.

These attempts to find community end in the drunk tanks and then psychoanalysis, where his analyst pronounces him incurable because he dreams about history and social reformers instead of parental issues. His wife, Sylvia, goes insane as well. Ironically, her insanity is not found in the destructive distance between the rich and the poor, but rather in her failure to adapt in a "balanced" way to this reality. Sylvia's "hysterical indifference" was attributed to an "overactive conscience" that has been unable to improve the outside world by unselfish acts (*God Bless* 52).

Eliot finds his mission in Rosewater, Indiana, where the original family fortune was made, intending "to *care*" about people" who "have no *use*" (*God Bless* 43; italics in orig.) because they are no longer needed by the factories, farms, and mines that had given meaning to their lives. This is similar to the mission of Paul Proteus and the Ghost Shirt society in *Player Piano*, although Eliot acknowledges in advance that the people are not going to be able to take responsibility for their own problems. He cares for them only because they are human, while living in a grubby office, answering the phone himself in a voice "as humane as the lowest note of a cello" (74). His usual remedy is a little money and some focused concern. He listens and responds in a pitch-perfect imitation of the "client-centered" counselor, echoing each person's concerns and injecting short, comforting comments to bolster self-esteem. When the character Eliot Rosewater reappears in the novel *Slaughterhouse-Five*, as a mental patient in a veteran's hospital, he is described as "a big, hollow man . . . so full of loving echoes" (103).

He confesses to "communistic thoughts" but insists that "nobody can work with the poor and not fall over Karl Marx from time to time . . . . The least a government could do, it seems to me, is to divide things up fairly" (*God Bless* 121). He believes that the poor feel shame because they do not know how to get to "The Money River, where the wealth of the nation flows" (122). He reminds his father that they "were born on the banks of it—and so were most of the mediocre people we grew up with, went to private schools with, sailed and played tennis with. We can slurp from that mighty river to our hearts' content," taking "slurping lessons" from lawyers and tax consultants "so we can slurp more efficiently" (122). When his father points out that poor people should stop "believing in crazy things like the Money River" and get to work, Eliot replies, "If there isn't a Money River, then how did I make ten thousand dollars today, just by snoozing and scratching myself, and occasionally answering the phone?" (123).

Eliot narrows his philosophy down to one essential, which he intends to pass on at a baptism: "There's only one rule that I know of, babies—: 'God damn it, you've got to be kind'" (*God Bless* 129). Vonnegut takes on the forces that would divide us into communist and capitalist, struggling to find one potent universal rule. Eliot treats the poor who come to him with all their bad reasons for ill luck, with all the unattractive differences of the culture of the poor, with all the decency his resources allow. Eliot's mad plan to provide everyone in Rosewater County with a familial community is an apt example of Vonnegut's commitment to the ideals of folk society that had so entranced him as an anthropology student two decades earlier.

These themes continued to be heard throughout his career, but in his early novels, we may see Vonnegut sounding them with increasing urgency, as he finds the baleful effects of American individualism more and more intolerable. Readings of Kurt Vonnegut's novels vary greatly, of course. Although he prefers stories with a moral when possible and understands that readers crave certain patterns, he insists on opening up those patterns to questioning by the breadth of plot and characters across the body of his work. He believes deeply in the beneficial effect of communities of limited size, but proposes, in his utopian schemes, that all Americans should be provided "with artificial extended families of a thousand members or more. Only when we have overcome loneliness can we begin to share wealth and work more fairly. I honestly believe that we will have those families by-and-by, and I hope they will become international" (*Wampeters* xxii). To balance the insular and provincial concerns of the local community, he proposes over and over in his fiction that communities should have all of the attributes of the local community without the constraint of keeping its members in the same location. To retain the spirit of love and support that used to be provided by folk societies without accepting their provincial limitations in perspective, Vonnegut dreams of recombining people in new groups: everybody similar, brought together for a purpose; everybody different, from a different place.

Vonnegut undercuts his most meaningful observations with jokes and ironic commentary, and this contingent style was influenced by the cultural relativism of his anthropological studies. Vonnegut does not abandon meaning or morality even though he probes their nature deeply and often gleefully. In the framework of his early novels and in his intergalactic search for patterns, we find a sometimes desperate search to illustrate his favorite professor's insistence that "morality is both relative and universal" (Redfield 159).

Works Cited

Bunzel, Ruth. Introduction. *Anthropology and Modern Life*. By Franz Boaz. New York: Dover, 1986. 4–10. Print.

Freese, Peter. *The Clown of Armageddon: The Novels of Kurt Vonnegut*. Heidelberg, Ger.: Winter, 2009. Print.

Klinkowitz, Jerome. *Vonnegut in America: An Introduction to the Life and Work of Kurt Vonnegut*. Columbia: U of South Carolina P, 2009. Print.

Mead, Margaret. Preface. *Patterns of Culture*. By Ruth Benedict. Boston: Houghton, 1961. xiii–xvi. Print.

Rackstraw, Loree. *Love as Always, Kurt: Vonnegut as I Knew Him*. Cambridge, MA: Da Capo, 2009. Print.

Redfield, Robert. "The Universally Human and the Culturally Variable." *Journal of General Education* 10.3 (1957): 150–60. Print.

Reilly, Charles. "Two Conversations with Kurt Vonnegut." *Conversations with Kurt Vonnegut*. Ed. William Rodney Allen. Jackson: UP of Mississippi, 1988. Print. 196–229.

Richter, David H. "Vladimir Propp." *The Critical Tradition: Classic Texts and Contemporary Trends*. New York: St. Martin's, 1989. 791–802. Print.

Tomedi, John. *Great Writers: Kurt Vonnegut*. Philadelphia, Chelsea, 2004. Print.

Vonnegut, Kurt. *Cat's Cradle*. New York: Bantam, 1963. Print.

___. *God Bless You, Mr. Rosewater*. 1965. New York: Dell, 1998. Print.

___. Letter to Miller Harris. 11 Feb. 1951. *Look at the Birdie*: *Unpublished Short Fiction*. New York: Dial, 2010. 3–6. Print.

___. *Mother Night*. 1961. New York: Random, 2009. Print.

___. *Palm Sunday*. New York: Dell, 1981. Print.

___. *Player Piano*. 1952. New York: Random, 2006. Print.

___. *Sirens of Titan*. 1981. New York: Random, 2009. Print.

___. *Slaughterhouse-Five; or The Children's Crusade*. 1969. New York: Rosetta, 2010. Print.

___. *Wampeters, Foma & Granfalloons*. New York: Random, 2006. Print.

Whitlark, James S. "Vonnegut's Anthropology Thesis." *Literature and Anthropology*. Ed. Philip A. Dennis and Wendell Aycock. Lubbock: Texas Tech UP, 1989. 77–86. Print. Studies in Comparative Literature 20.

The Myth of the Two Monsters in
*Breakfast of Champions*_____

Gilbert McInnis

> There were two monsters sharing the planet with us when I was a boy, however, and I celebrate their extinction today. They were determined to kill us, or at least to make our lives meaningless [. . .]. They inhabited our heads. They were the arbitrary lusts for gold, and God help us, for a glimpse of a little girl's underpants.

> —Kilgore Trout, *Breakfast of Champions*, 25

Kilgore Trout introduces the central subject of this chapter: how the humans presented in Kurt Vonnegut's novel derive their values from materialism. Vonnegut's characters believe that their values provide happiness and fulfillment, and they seek to authenticate these beliefs through material gains or pleasures of the body. Deriving values from materialism is nothing new, but, after a closer examination of the materialism in *Breakfast of Champions*, one can conclude that it is validated by the "scientific" ideas and "materialism" of Charles Darwin. Therefore, the novel wants readers to believe that scientific materialism is what forms those human values and what creates an emerging mythology.

In agreement with this, in "Kurt Vonnegut and the Myth of Scientific Progress," Sallye Sheppeard states:

> That the values fostered by science and technology prove more detrimental than beneficial to mankind also finds expression in Vonnegut's other early novels, but of these, *Breakfast of Champions* (1973) contains their grimmest exposé. Its setting and narrative clearly reflect the debilitating effects of contemporary American society, via science and technology, upon the human spirit. (17)

While Sheppeard thus argues that contemporary American society lives according to "values fostered by science and technology," in *Myth and Reality* Mircea Eliade states more precisely that myths "narrate [how and why] man became what he is today—mortal, sexed, organized in a society, obliged to work in order to live, and working in accordance with certain rules" (11). If one agrees with Eliade, when humans live in accordance with "certain rules," or the ethos of scientific materialism, then myth is operating on their lives too. Similarly, the American values depicted in Vonnegut's *Breakfast* come from the laws of evolutionary science. The "debilitating effects" of those rules on society are revealed in the form of "popular" materialism. Hence, analyzing Vonnegut's *Breakfast* can lead one to conclude that if material facts are the only source of truth for evolutionary science, then it is possible that people of this time, who live according to those certain rules, will attempt to consume meaning in a similar material fashion. First, this essay will briefly examine materialism as another aspect of the theory of evolution. Second, the essay will examine how, according to the dogma of an evolutionary mythology, the human mind is transformed by this "scientific materialism." Lastly, this essay will explore how the characters have a prior commitment to materialism and how they fail to achieve their metaphysical goals because of this particular commitment.

Materialism as an ideology has been applied in many different areas of Western culture, as its advocates have attempted to construct a complete, unified theory that would apply to all aspects of life. In the face of its wide application, in his *Dictionary of Philosophy*, Dagobert Runes succeeds in providing a thorough definition:

(1) A proposition about the existent or the real: that only matter [. . .] is existent or real; that matter is the primordial or fundamental constituent of the universe [. . .] that the universe is not governed by intelligence, purpose, or final causes; [. . .] (2) a proposition about explanation of the existent or the real: that everything is explainable in terms of matter in motion

or matter and energy [. . .] that the only objects science can investigate are the physical or material (that is, public, manipulable, non-mental, natural, or sensible); (3) a proposition about values: that wealth, bodily satisfactions, sensuous pleasures, or the like are either the only or the greatest values man can see or attain; (4) a proposition about the explanation of human history: that human actions and cultural change are determined solely or largely by economic factors. (189)

As Runes upholds that materialism (like the theory of evolution) espouses the doctrine that "the universe is not governed by intelligence, purpose, or final causes," it is to be noted that according to Darwin's theory of evolution by natural selection, "human actions and cultural change" (Runes) are determined by these material factors, and in Stephen J. Gould's view, this "new take" on evolution raised a fear in Darwin himself. He was afraid of the radical philosophical implications of the principle of natural selection, or "his take on evolution, his own theory of about how evolution occurred, not of evolution itself." Moreover, Darwin "was afraid to expose his belief in materialism . . . that the mind is a product of the material substrate of the neurology of the brain" (*Revolution in Thought*). Hence, the operation of our mind and our consciousness, which influence our values, functiona according to matter or material substrates.

Both materialism and the theory of evolution are codependent in the construction of an evolutionary worldview, or a mythology (see, e.g., McInnis). In *Biology as Ideology*, the evolutionist Richard Lewontin states that "Darwin's whole theory of evolution by natural selection bears an uncanny resemblance to the political economic theory of early capitalism as developed by the Scottish economists" (10). Lewontin's theory gained support from Gould, who identified Douglas Steward and Adam Smith as the Scottish economists in question. In fact, Gould argues that Darwin formulated his theory of natural selection with the help of Smith's ideas of the "invisible hand" and laissez-faire: "natural selection is, in essence, Adam Smith's economics transferred to nature" (122). Thus, Smith's economic theory of the invisible hand can be seen as having allowed Darwin to construct an analogy between human society (via economics) and nature. This "scientific" and "materialistic" analogy finally manifested its true colors in the twentieth century, and especially in post–World War II American culture, under the guise of sociobiology, what Phillip E. Johnson has called "the inherent potential biological theories of human behavior to provide support for those who think the existing distribution of wealth and power is 'natural'" (39). Thus, according to Lewontin, Gould, and Johnson, Darwin's "scientific" and "materialistic" theory of evolution by natural selection can be seen as providing a rationale for a new type of value system in Western culture. In addition, Johnson concludes from this that "Darwinian evolution (beyond the micro level) is materialistic philosophy disguised as scientific fact" (69), and he calls this new materialism "Scientific Materialism." Moreover, he adds that Darwin's nineteenth-century "scientific materialism" is the blueprint for the later economic consumerism of the twentieth-century (39); this observation coincides with what Michael Aeschliman affirms: "With the growth of scientism has come a massive increase in the powers of technology and applied science to change and manipulate not only the physical landscape but the mental and human landscape too" (78). We can conclude from what Lewontin, Gould, Aeschliman, and Johnson have written that it is possible for an evolutionist to find meaning or values in materialism, and if so, then it is also possible that, from the principles of evolution, a new mythical reality in the form of a popular materialism emerges.

In *Breakfast of Champions*, Vonnegut gives readers a fictional picture of all these philosophical, sociological, and biological notions of materialism, evolution, and natural selection at work. He demonstrates Darwin's notion of natural selection governing the human mind, and therefore contemporary society as well. Vonnegut has the human mind and contemporary society call into question the idea of evolutionary growth and expansion in order to depict those who achieve pre-eminence in natural selection. Referring to one of the novel's main characters, the car salesman Dwayne Hoover, the narrator says: "Dwayne's incipient insanity was mainly a matter of chemicals, of course. Dwayne Hoover's body was manufacturing certain chemicals which unbalanced his mind" (14). Hence, Dwayne's mind, which reminds readers of the "big brains" in Vonnegut's *Galápagos*, suffers from a kind of "big brain" engendered by the irrational bad chemicals that cause him to consider suicide. "Here is what the last night of that weekend was like for Dwayne: his bad chemicals . . . made him take a loaded thirty-eight caliber revolver from under his pillow and stick it in his mouth" (49). Apart from unbalancing his mind and provoking him to commit suicide, the chemicals also make Dwayne violent. "Dwayne dragged Francine Pefko out of Dwayne's showroom and onto the asphalt. Dwayne wanted to give her a beating in public, which his bad chemicals made him think she richly deserved" (272). These bad chemicals have also caused evil in others:

> Dwayne certainly wasn't alone, as far as having bad chemicals inside of him was concerned. He had plenty of company throughout history. In his lifetime, for instance, the people in a country called Germany were so full of bad chemicals for a while that they actually built factories whose purpose was to kill people by the millions. The people were delivered by trains. (133)

The narrator points out that these "bad chemicals" are completely natural in that they come from the body, and therefore they are continuous with the ideology of evolutionary biology. "It was a dangerous place to be. The whole city was dangerous—because of chemicals and the uneven distribution of wealth and so on. A lot of people were like Dwayne: they created chemicals in their own bodies which were bad for their heads" (70). If the whole city is dangerous because of "bad chemicals," it is also dangerous because of an "uneven distribution of wealth." According to the sociobiological approach of the novel, the "existing distribution of wealth and power" (that has caused the unevenness) is in accordance with the natural sciences, because it is justified according to the scientific and materialistic ideas of Darwin. Hence, Darwin's theory provides the narrator, who believes that bad chemicals and the "uneven distribution of wealth" are the roots of all evil, with a psychology that is continuous with biology. Likewise, Vonnegut's interest in the evolutionary theory of degeneration (rather than progression) implicit in the narrator's description may be in fact linked to how Darwin portrayed the human race in his *Descent*. According to Gillian Beer, "In *The Descent* a double, contrary, story is indicated forthwith in the title—the genealogy of man. 'Descent' may imply his fall from his Adamic myth or his genetic descent (ascent) from his primate forebears" (108). For Vonnegut's part in *Breakfast of Champions*, he seems to be musing on man's genetic "fall from his Adamic" state because the notion of original sin in man is replaced with the materialistic and deterministic counterpart of bad chemicals operating in the human mind.

In his criticism of *Breakfast of Champions*, Wayne McGinnis goes so far as to include the novel's readers as part of the world Vonnegut describes. He asserts that in *Breakfast*, the human mind is programmed to behave like a mechanistic object, and "This reductive effect is also aided by Vonnegut's message that we are all robots or machines. . . . We as readers look around, and people do seem to be programmed to the routine monotony and even insanity of daily life" (8). It is true in the novel that there are "programmed" characters, and Vonnegut clearly emphasizes the devastating consequences of this conditioning even on himself. He says from within *Breakfast*, "As for myself: I had come to the conclusion that there was nothing sacred about myself or about any human being, that we were all machines" (219). Therefore, Vonnegut would have his readers understand that when they allow their "sacredness" and "humanness" to be diminished, they are going to be vulnerable to someone's program to convince us to behave like machines. In the case of *Breakfast*, people have been programmed to behave mechanically by the routine monotony of daily life, as can be seen when the novel's other main character, Kilgore Trout, converses with a retired miner:

> He asked an old, old man on a stool next to him at the table if he had worked in the coal mines. The old man said this: "From the time I was ten till I was sixty-two."
>
> "You glad to be out of 'em?" said Trout.
>
> "Oh, God," said the man, "you never get out of 'em—even when you sleep. I *dream* mines." (125)

The mind of the retired miner is programmed to the extent that the routine monotony of the mining life has not left his mind. The effects of the routine are buried deep within his psyche, and although he physically has left the mine, it remains present in his dreams. The psychological effects of being programmed by his conditioners are noticeable further on in the conversation as well. The retired miner complains to Trout about his employers: "The rights of the people on top of the ground don't amount to nothing compared to the rights of the man who owns what's underneath" (126). "[W]hat's underneath" the ground refers literally, of course, to the minerals. However, this "underneath" also refers to the state of the worker's psyche; he cannot escape the effects of the mine even in the comfort of his bed, where he still dreams about it. The owners of the mine have "mined" his "mind" as well, with the routine monotony of mining life. This procedure of "mecha-humanization" can be argued to have mythological meaning: the conditioners have transformed the human psyche to imitate the pattern or ideology of technology, and have led it to accept a sort of mechanistic image of human existence as the real visible model of life on earth.

John B. Watson has documented how the human brain can be conditioned in the mechanistic fashion of the miner in Vonnegut's novel, and Stanley Jaki has discussed Watson's conclusions at length in *Brain, Mind, and Computers*:

The task of establishing the traits of one's personality was in such a framework equivalent to knowing what kind of organic machine he was. The "parts" of that machine were the "habit systems" [i.e., the simpler and more routine decisions] which in turn resulted from the [machine-like?] "situations" that imposed on the individual a deterministic course. (150)

To scientific materialists, the human mind is an organic machine. While being the fundamental seat of our personalities as Watson has argued, it can reveal how our "habit systems" impose "on the individual a deterministic course." Vonnegut's interest in how the human mind is conditioned in *Breakfast* suggests how the human organ, or "part," is more pertinently an investigation of a "whole Brain" of America, and how the habit systems of the American "Brain" impose on the individual "brain" a deterministic course. As such a study of the individual and society, Vonnegut's novel shows how the human brain is conditioned by material mechanizations by exploring how the evolutionary program operates within the collective psyche, or the whole of contemporary American society.

How deeply Vonnegut is concerned with conditioning is made apparent by how Jaki agrees with him. Jaki contends that any anti-materialist would argue in favor of personal characteristics that would differentiate humans from machines. Vonnegut's narrator does not provide much evidence to support his assertion, but he provides some nevertheless. Jaki states that "Man cannot be accounted for by those [materialistic] methods precisely because he is more than a machine. He has what no machine has, the ability to think and the ability to make free decisions" (5). Vonnegut's narrator implies that Dwayne Hoover has the ability to "think and the ability to make free decisions," but that in spite of this, ironically as he exercises some free will he also concludes that he is a machine. The narrator of *Breakfast* informs the reader moreover that Dwayne is the only character having free will in the universe depicted in the novel:

Of all the creatures in the Universe, only Dwayne was thinking and feeling and worrying and planning and so on. Nobody else knew what pain was. Everybody else was a fully automatic machine, whose purpose was to stimulate Dwayne. Dwayne was a new type of creature being tested by the Creator of the Universe. Only Dwayne Hoover had free will. (14–15)

Readers know from this description that Dwayne "was thinking and feeling" and "had free will"—thus "free" from the dictates of natural selection, too. In contrast, the remaining characters are not free. For instance, the narrator says, "The premise of the book [Trout's *Now It Can Be Told*] was this: Life was an experiment by the Creator of the Universe, Who wanted to test a new sort of creature He was thinking of introducing into the Universe. It was a creature with the ability to make up its own mind. All the other creatures were fully programmed robots" (173). Taken literally, Dwayne is that created creature and all the "other creatures were fully programmed." But understood figuratively, these "other creatures" are "freely" programmed robots, like the miner discussed earlier, when they live according to the materialist ontology, or by the "popular" manifestation of materialism.

If Dwayne's programming is essentially accomplished by *Now It Can Be Told*, it can be observed nevertheless that the book is not solely responsible. It is Dwayne himself who decides that the book's ideology or evolutionary mythology is valid enough to live by. But on the whole it is Trout's book that determines what he will think, or at least reflects what he commits himself to. Shortly before Dwayne's violent outbreak, as the narrator informs us, "Dwayne didn't notice the restraints. He thought he was on the virgin planet promised by the book by Kilgore Trout" (272). Again, "Dwayne Hoover read in that book that robots all over the world were constantly running out of fuel and dropping dead, while waiting around to test the only free-willed creature [Dwayne] in the Universe" (269). Even earlier in the novel, the narrator mentions that Dwayne read from the book: "'Dear Sir, poor sir, brave sir:' he read, 'You are the only creature in the entire Universe who has free will. . . . Everybody else is a robot, a machine'" (253). So Trout's book, conforming to the ideology of scientific materialism, does inform Dwayne that everybody is a machine and therefore can be exploited like any other machine or raw material. But the narrator adds, pointing to Dwayne's other quality to direct himself:

> But Dwayne, like all novice lunatics, needed some bad ideas, too, so that his craziness could have shape and direction. Bad chemicals and bad ideas were the Yin and Yang of madness [. . .]. The bad ideas were delivered to Dwayne by Kilgore Trout [. . .]. Here was the core of the bad ideas [like those of scientific materialism] which Trout gave to Dwayne. (14)

Dwayne's bad chemicals are "naturally" "selected," but he has a kind of control, however feeble, about what they produce. Readers also discover that his "bad chemicals and bad ideas" (that are also continuous with biology) are selected in a kind of willed way by him "so that his craziness could have shape and direction." If Trout's "evolutionary" mythology provides the "shape and direction" for such an ideology, the material bad chemicals and the bad ideas of evolutionary materialism somehow religiously yoke in the Yin and Yang notion that obtains his assent.

In *Breakfast*, the characters have an a priori commitment to materialism, and they comply with this commitment in the hope that it will bring them happiness. However, in doing so, they end up reducing human happiness to the acquisition of material possessions, and, as one can imagine, adapting their behavior accordingly. Richard Chase, in "Notes on the Study of Myth," claims that "when science is psychologically adequate, it can be shown to have much in common with myth" (68). The world Vonnegut paints in *Breakfast* is a portrait of Chase's comment on the real life of fiction. In *Breakfast*, scientific materialism is "psychologically adequate" when materialism influences the characters' behavior. Trout offers an excellent example of how materialism has captivated the human mind when he claims: "'There were two monsters sharing the planet with us when I was a boy . . . They were determined to kill us, or at least to make our lives meaningless . . . They inhabited our heads. They were the arbitrary lusts for gold, and God help us, for a glimpse of a little girl's underpants'" (25). At first glance, the two monsters of sex and money are Freudian constructs that reflect the human path to power. However, beyond the analytical interpretation, there is another explanation, which involves the doctrine of social Darwinism and Darwin's notion of natural selection. The characters' will to survive is arbitrarily selected, and consequently, their materialistic behavior can be argued to derive from Darwin's notion. The norms of materialistic sex and money portrayed critically in *Breakfast* are consistently validated by Darwinism and the notion of natural selection, and when science is used to rationalize these materialistic norms for the society, it functions as myth.

The mythology of the two monsters prevailing in *Breakfast of Champions* is such that its characters believe it will somehow bring them ultimate happiness, and it is infinitely perpetuated by their unconscious drives. Bonnie MacMahon, the waitress who works for Dwayne at the Holiday Inn, and her husband live their lives according to the rules of this belief. "Bonnie had only two goals in life now. She meant to recoup all the money her husband had lost in the car wash in Shepherdstown, and she ached to have steel-belted radial tires for the front wheels of her automobile" (211). Bonnie's happiness is reduced to her increasing her wealth, or by obtaining "steel-belted radial tires." Her desire to increase her wealth is just another form of that materialistic monster, or "arbitrary lust for gold," inhabiting the planet. If Runes's definition of materialism is applied to them, Bonnie and her husband are materialists because their values of wealth and pleasure are, as Sheppeard states, "fostered by science and technology" (17). Notwithstanding the importance that materialism plays in our quest for happiness, Dupré argues, "it is often taken to necessitate some kind of reductionism" (87); Bonnie and her husband's mundane state validates Dupré's opinion because they have reduced their human desire for happiness to goals of consumption. However, in their decision to fulfill their metaphysical ache for happiness by physical things, they perpetuate the reality, or mythology, of that "arbitrary lust for gold" in their lives, which will eventually destroy their dignity and make their lives meaningless.

With Bonnie and her husband in mind, *Breakfast* makes readers aware of the authority of materialism and its mythological implications, i.e., its power to structure people's lives. If Vonnegut's *Breakfast* is an accurate portrayal of how Darwin's theory has changed human nature's vision of itself, then the Darwinian notion for struggle for existence has transformed, as Frederick Engels predicted over a century ago, into a struggle for pleasure. After reading the *Origin of Species*, Engels, in a letter to Darwin, attempted to warn him of how Darwin's "method" would eventually lead to illogical associations, if Darwin continued to make analogies between the "animal kingdom" and human society, because the "struggle for existence—if we permit this category for the moment to be valid—is thus transformed into a struggle for pleasures, no longer for mere means of development, socially produced means of development" (303).

Other characters in *Breakfast of Champions* besides Bonnie and her husband reveal to readers this "struggle for pleasures" and its influence on their behavior as well. Such characters do not often realize the trouble they are in, and instead of achieving a deep sense of happiness from their materialism, they reap only fleeing benefits, if even that. Readers are made aware of this when Trout and a truck driver converse about Trout's past job of installing aluminum siding on houses, and to what extent this profits homeowners. When the trucker asks Trout how long the happiness of "people who get aluminum siding" lasts, Trout replies, "About fifteen years" (107–108). Trout's response illustrates Vonnegut's parody of how limited the happiness available to those who behave according to this materialistic world view is, wherein happiness is proportional to the life span of the material objects that they possess—or, should we say, that possess them.

The characters' material quest for happiness and fulfillment, while dependent on the observable or tangible feeling of possession, appears to have a supernatural and therefore mythic power as well. In the scene between Dwayne and Patty at the Burger Chef, for example, Vonnegut's allusion to the Cinderella tale sheds some light on how American materialism has appropriated this simple fairy tale, which is the requisite element required for the creation of myth. "The Cinderella story," according to Tennessee Williams, "is our favorite national myth, the cornerstone of the film industry if not of the Democracy itself" (99). It is pertinent to American society, and Patty and Dwayne's life, because it is the archetypal rags-to-riches tale. A poor individual like Patty, as the fairy tale goes, and also as the tenets of American materialism require, can rise above her humble beginnings to achieve fame and success in terms of the doctrines of materialism. In *Narratives of Human Evolution*, Misia Landau observes how the Cinderella myth reminds us of Darwin's narrative in *The Descent of Man*. "Though the details," according to Landau, "of *The Descent of Man* differ greatly from those of the Cinderella tale, the moral is not very different" (60). The moral shared by *The Descent of Man* and the Cinderella myth is:

Man may be excused for feeling some pride at having risen, though not through his own exertions to the very summit of the organic scale; and the fact of his having risen, instead of having been aboriginally placed there, may give him hopes for a still higher destiny in the distant future. But [. . .] we must acknowledge, as it seems to me, that man with all his noble qualities [. . .] still bears in his bodily frame the indelible stamp of his lowly origins. (Darwin, *Origin* [1871] 405)

In Vonnegut's character of the modern world, Dwayne (and Patty to an extent) supports Landau's parallel between the Cinderella tale and Darwin's narrative of human evolution because Dwayne has risen to a "higher" material "destiny." For her part, Patty adores Dwayne because he embodies her hopes of the same "higher destiny in the distant future." That "higher destiny" is best explained as that future state of comfort and pleasure, because both Dwayne and Patty believe in a materialistic world view that is derived from the materialistic theory of evolution. Hence, stories like the American dream that incorporate fairy tale or supernatural elements present the characteristics and functions of myths.

Despite the godlike aura conferred on him, Dwayne too is enslaved by the monster of materialism. The mythological power that materialism confers on him isolates him from any meaningful relationship with his community.

> Dwayne Hoover sat in the used Plymouth Fury in his own vacant lot for an hour, listening to West Virginia. He was told about health insurance for pennies a day, about how to get better performance from his car. He was told what to do about constipation. He was offered a Bible which had everything that God or Jesus had actually said out loud printed in red capital letters. He was offered a plant which would attract and eat disease-carrying insects in his home [. . .]. All this was stored away in Dwayne's memory, in case he should need it later on. He had all kinds of stuff in there. (62)

Although Dwayne's life is "stuffed" full of material objects and his measure is great, his memory too is stuffed full. His mind is reduced to nothing more than an infinitely growing shopping list of things to possess. And, despite his material wealth, he fails to fulfill his basic human need for affection. Paradoxically, his wealth and power are monsters keeping him from other humans, so he is left empty to suffer loneliness and despair, without any resort to human comfort. Robert Merrill argues this point as well when he claims that, "Like Pilgrim [of *Slaughterhouse-Five*], he is a successful entrepreneur [. . .]. But Hoover is also like Pilgrim in that he suffers terribly despite his apparent prosperity" (158). The social commentator Jaki provides at least one reason for this sort of human suffering.

He claims that although the human body may be a mere machine, the soul, or mind, insofar as it has an inalienable dignity, "reveals a dimension that transcends the material" (7). If what Jaki says is true, Dwayne suffers because his materialistic world view negates the transcendence that his soul really desires. When his relationship with Francine Pefko is taken into account, Dwayne's suffering does "reveal a dimension that transcends the material [whatever is material in him]." For instance, shortly after he and Francine have sex, readers are given an "immaterial" reason for his suffering: "Here was the problem: Dwayne wanted Francine to love him for his body and soul, not for what his money could buy. He thought Francine was hinting that he should buy her a Colonel Sanders Kentucky Fried Chicken franchise" (157).

Another implication of the materialistic mythology is observed when Trout visits a New York cinema. However, the tragic consequences are more devastating than in the scene between Dwayne and Francine because the mythology in which the scene's characters are involved as actors is perpetuated by the mass media. In Vonnegut's investigation of the role of American entertainment, specifically the cinema, in perpetrating materialism, the film industry functions not as an art form, but as a commercial enterprise to profit laissez-faire capitalists. Moreover, the profits from these films are gained at the expense of those humans who take part in its production, because they must sacrifice their dignity in order to be successful.

> The movie theater where Trout sat with all his parcels in his lap showed nothing but dirty movies. The music was soothing. Phantasms of a young man and a young woman sucked harmlessly on one another's soft apertures on the silver screen [. . .]. And Trout made up a new novel while he sat there [. . .]. The big topic of conversation was censorship. The cities were blighted with motion picture theaters which showed nothing but dirty movies. The humanoids wished they could put them out of business somehow, but without interfering with free speech. (59)

The monstrous behavior of the young man and woman is projected into the memories of those who view it. As such, paradoxically, the story inspires Trout to think up a new novel. Obviously, Trout's book will be a parody of what is occurring on the screen in front of him. Like Trout's book, in which humans have been reduced to "humanoids," Vonnegut's *Breakfast* describes humans as machines so that a double parody is at work. Trout, like Vonnegut, is wise enough to understand the implications of such materialism and the mythology it prefigures. In this creation of parodies, the film industry serves to propagate materialism and its mythology; it hides behind the mask of art to avoid censorship. Yet, once the metaphor of the screen is deconstructed, the face of materialism, or the myth of two monsters, is discovered behind it.

Shortly after the movie scene of "soft apertures," Trout goes to the washroom, and when he returns, he finds the house lights up and the movie over. It is at this moment that Vonnegut parodies materialism as mythology most profoundly. The narrator explains:

> Trout didn't protest. Neither did he leave immediately. He examined a green enameled steel box in the back of the auditorium. It contained the projector and the sound system and the films. There was a hole in the front of the box. That was how the pictures got out. On the side of the box was a simple switch [. . .]. It intrigued Trout to know that he had only to flick the switch, and the people would start fucking and sucking again [. . .]. Trout took his leave of the machine reluctantly. He said this about it to the manager: "It fills such a need, this machine, and it's so easy to operate." (68–69)

In this scenario, human sexual parts are dehumanized when they are reduced to machine-like behavior. But what did Vonnegut intend when he chose the word "box"? Did he intend it to be a euphemism for the female vagina, since the box is placed in the context of a "dirty" movie? Also, what does he mean by "It fills such a need?" Is the "it" the machine or the female genitals? His ambiguity is purposely constructed to reveal how our perception of human sexual organs can be dehumanized to a point where we do not perceive a great difference between them and machines anymore. If this is true, then according to evolutionary mythology, humans are only materialistic constructs who themselves created this machine (because it fills such a need), and the humans who buy its service (because they have an ache for this need) have been victimized by a monstrous mythology. What is the worth of this mythology in *Breakfast*? It seems to be one that promotes material pleasure as being the only true road to happiness, that maintains that human affection can be reduced to the material consumption, and that to be ultimately happy, to progress personally, one must seek material pleasures or consume things for the sake of fulfilling one's own needs.

In their quest to build their paradise on earth, Vonnegut's characters barter away their humanness. Dwayne, Francine, Patty, and Wayne believe in that doctrine of scientific materialism. Dwayne attempts to fulfill the desires of his soul by having a physical relationship with Francine, hoping with futility to increase his faith in the belief that human affection will bring him ultimate happiness. In this way, Francine's affection becomes his paradise on earth. However, he is seduced into deception the very moment he believes a physical or sexual act could provide him with the metaphysical affection he so desires. In his pursuit of happiness, the act of sex is reduced to a utilitarian function. His physical act becomes a fleeting product exchange instead of suggesting even vaguely any form of a spiritual exchange. Worse, Dwayne discovers that Francine is guilty of the same. Like Dwayne, Francine approaches their human relationship in a utilitarian fashion, prostituting herself in order to free herself from being "a machine made of meat—a typing machine, a filing machine" (188). Ironically, her expectations are not fulfilled because, in her attempt to gain material freedom, she hastily, like Dwayne, reduces love to just another kind of machine. Her "humanness" is dehumanized in that exchange, the same humanness that Dwayne sought in the first place. Viktor Frankl, in "Reductionism and Nihilism," claims that when love is reduced to "goal inhibited" sex, the result is reductionism. "Now love, to the reductionist, is derived from sex; it is conceived as a sublimation of sexual instincts or, as Freud has put it, 'goal-inhibited' sexuality" (402). If this is so, like Dwayne, Francine resorts to material means to achieve a non-material paradise, but Vonnegut shows his readers the dehumanizing effects of their goal and how they have dehumanized not only each other, but themselves.

Apart from the psychological interpretation of Francine and Dwayne's actions, there is a Darwinian element present in their love scenario that reflects a sexually obsessed society. Beer claims that:

"Darwin's theory of development depended to a large extent upon that 'rampancy of insatiable unmeasured longing', on the unassuageable passion of the sexes for each other, on the vigour of survival, on the profusion of production and on the insurgency of growth. To that extent his is a daemonic theory, emphasising drive, deviance and the will to power." (115)

This description fits Francine and Dwayne. They have "unassuageable passion of the sexes for each other," "the vigor of survival," and "the will to power," but as Beer mentions, these "drives" or behaviors have "origins" in a mythology that combines science and materialism, or that "daemonic theory." Francine and Dwayne's "Darwinian" behavior, if one chooses to call it that, is typical of many other couples who resort to this type of ritual to achieve their goals. Clyde Kluckhohn, in "Myth and Ritual," argues that myths "are symbolic representations of the dominant configurations of the particular culture. Myths, then, may express not only the latent content of ritual but of other culturally organized behavior" as well (38). In *Breakfast*, this "culturally organized behavior" is noticeable critically in Vonnegut's hands when the narrator informs readers that not only Francine, but "Patty Keene was persuaded that she could make him [Dwayne] happy with her young body" (143). Like Francine and Patty, many other women "trained themselves to be agreeing machines instead of thinking machines" (136).

The characters' quest to build their paradise on earth, and to authenticate their values in *Breakfast of Champions* can, therefore, be seen as a quest for material pleasure and comfort when these are rationalized by the ideology of a narrative, in this case in the narrative of an evolutionary myth. Kluckhohn asserts that "Ritual is an obsessive repetitive activity—often a symbolic dramatization of the fundamental 'needs' of the society, whether 'economic,' 'biological,' 'social,' or 'sexual'" (44), and "myth is a constant by-product of living faith which is in need [. . .] of sociological status" (39). How much repetitive action is associated with needs and culture is evident in the association Kluckhohn makes between them and myth: "Mythology is the rationalization of these same needs." For her part, Francine attempts to earn sociological status according to the values of materialism. Dwayne, on the other hand, has a biological and social need but, like the women, he fails to understand that humans cannot achieve their transcendent goals according to the rules propounded by the mythology of materialism. In spite of the characters' failure to consolidate their happiness in *Breakfast* (when they attempt to solve each other's needs by a flawed method), they consistently believe that their non-material goals still can be achieved according to the rules of this material mythology. As the narrator says, "in the interests of survival," so many of them "trained themselves," according to the ideology of scientific materialism, "to be agreeing [adapting] machines instead of thinking machines" (136).

Although Dwayne's and Francine's metaphysical goals are honorable, hers for sociological status and security and his for biological and social fulfillment, the novel depicts the characters adapting themselves to the level of reductive materialism. As such, they have fallen victim to its reductionism. Reductionism is already at play even before Dwayne orders Francine to sleep with him:

Dwayne went back to work at about two in the afternoon [. . .]. He went into his inner office, and he ransacked his desk drawers for something to read or think about. He came across the brochure which offered him the penis-extender and the rubber vagina for lonesomeness. He had received it two months before. He still hadn't thrown it away. (147)

Though Dwayne has chosen not to order the rubber vagina, the narrator leaving us asking why he has not. Perhaps because he has no need for it as long as Francine is willing to provide a living one for him. Why, then, has he not thrown the advertisement away? Perhaps because in reducing Francine to a rubber vagina, or sexual machine, he reduces himself as well, so much so that he may decide eventually to end their relationship. If he does decide to end the relationship, then, he will have a need for the rubber vagina. Though Vonnegut has Dwayne choosing Francine over the sex object, he nonetheless juxtaposes the two options to emphasize how one human can reduce another in their quest to fulfill their needs. This juxtaposition also highlights how human sexuality may be thought to have been reduced to the laws of consumption—as with Trout's two monsters at work in the New York cinema scenario—and how the mass media perpetuate the mythology that Francine and Dwayne have bought into.

In his 1973 *Playboy* interview, given shortly after he completed *Breakfast*, Vonnegut clearly dissociates himself from this type of reductive materialism. Explaining the origins of human problems in general, and depression in particular, he says:

"[A]n awful lot of it is physiological. In this book I've just finished, *Breakfast of Champions*, the motives of all the characters are explained in terms of body chemistry. You know, we don't give a shit about the characters' childhoods or about what happened yesterday—we just want to know what the state of their bloodstreams is." (*Wampeters* 252)

It is clear that Vonnegut is appalled by those who reduce human problems to the material "state of their bloodstreams" and neglect metaphysical or any other kind of consideration. Furthermore, his view expressed above is similar to one he provides in *Breakfast*, when he alludes to Einstein's theory of relativity (241). Vonnegut as narrator states that Einstein's equation was flawed because it lacked an "A" for awareness. Therefore, our "awareness" of the universe and of the human mind is also "flawed" because we live according to certain rules expressed by the evolutionary mythology—when these rules implicate us in reducing our awareness to only the observable or measurable.

Works Cited

Aeschliman, Michael D. *The Restitution of Man: C.S. Lewis and the Case against Scientism*. Grand Rapids: Eerdmans Pub,1983. Print.

Beer, Gillian. *Darwin's Plots: Evolutionary Narrative in Darwin, George Eliot and Nineteenth-Century Fiction*. Cambridge: Cambridge UP, 2000. Print.

Chase, Richard. "Notes on the Study of Myth." *Myth and Literature: Contemporary Theory and Practice*. Ed. John B. Vickery. Lincoln: U of Nebraska P, 1966. 67–74. Print.

Darwin, Charles. *Origin of Species: and Descent of Man*. 1871. New York: Modern Library, 1936. Print.

___. *The Origin of Species; A Variorum Text*. Ed. Morse Peckham. Philadelphia: U of Pennsylvania P, 1959. Print.

___. *The Origin of Species By Means of Natural Selection*. 1859. Ed. J. W. Burrow. New York: Penguin, 1985. Print.

Darwin's Revolution in Thought. Dir. Robert Di Nozzi. Stephen J. Gould: Into the Classroom Video, 1995. Videocassette.

Dupré, John. *The Disorder of Things: Metaphysical Foundations of the Disunity of Science*. Cambridge: Harvard UP, 1993. Print.

Eliade, Mircea. *Myth and Reality*. New York: Harper, 1963. Print.

Engels, Friedrich, and Karl Marx. *Karl Marx and Frederick Engels: Selected Correspondence*. Ed. S. Ryazanskaya. Moscow: Progress, 1965. Print.

Frankl, Viktor E. "Reductionism and Nihilism." *Beyond Reductionism: New Perspectives in the Life Sciences*. Alphach Symposium (1968). Ed. Arthur Koestler. New York: MacMillan, 1970. Print.

Gould, Stephen J. *The Structure of Evolutionary Theory*. Cambridge: Harvard UP, 2002. Print.

Jaki, Stanley L. *Brain, Mind, and Computers*. Washington, DC: Regnery Gateway, 1989. Print.

Johnson, Phillip E. *Objections Sustained*. Downers Grove: InterVarsity P, 1998. Print.

Kluckhohn, Clyde. "Myths and Rituals: A General Theory." *Myth and Literature. Myth and Literature: Contemporary Theory and Practice*. Ed. John B. Vickery. Lincoln: U of Nebraska P, 1966. 33–46. Print.

Landau, Misia. *Narratives of Human Evolution*. New Haven: Yale UP, 1991. Print.

Lewontin, Richard. *Biology as Ideology: The Doctrine of DNA*. Concord, Ont.: Anansi P, 1991. Print.

McGinnis, Wayne. "Vonnegut's *Breakfast of Champions*: A Reductive Success." *Notes on Contemporary Literature* 5.3 (1975): 6–9. Print.

McInnis, Gilbert. "Evolutionary Mythology in the Writings of Kurt Vonnegut Jr." *Critique: Studies in Contemporary Fiction* 46.4 (2005): 383–96. Print.

Merrill, Robert. ed. *Critical Essays on Kurt Vonnegut*. Boston: Hall, 1990. Print.

Runes, Dagobert D. *Dictionary of Philosophy*. 15th ed. New York: Philosophical Library, 1960. Print.

Sheppeard, Sallye. "Kurt Vonnegut and the Myth of Scientific Progress." *Journal of the American Studies Association of Texas* 16.1 (1985): 14–19.

Vonnegut, Kurt Jr. *Wampeters, Foma, and Granfalloons*. New York: Dell, 1974. Print.

___. *Breakfast of Champions*. New York: Dell Pub, 1973. Print.

Williams, Tennessee. "The Catastrophe of Suceess." *The Glass Menagerie*. 1945. New York: New Directions, 1999. 99–107. Print.

Time, Transformation, and the Reading Process in Vonnegut

Sharon Lynn Sieber

How does Vonnegut transform the reader into something like a time distortion device through the process of reading? Vonnegut does not call upon traditional magical or superhuman qualities of heroes, events, or places—even in his science fiction—to create an unreal aura of something that never happens. Instead, he calls upon the real and most commonplace events to re-*present* the reader with an unfathomable process of just how it is that what Vonnegut describes from everyday life could be real on any planet, or in any place and time, let alone describe the norm on our own planet. The characters are loved not for their extraordinary abilities but for those very qualities that make them ordinary, in fact, human. This essay will focus on the unique aspects of time, transformation, and the reading process with respect to *The Sirens of Titan* and *Breakfast of Champions*, two novels that dramatically undermine reader expectations while also presenting the reader with new ways of seeing the world.

In Vonnegut, what is often most bizarre can be found in the everyday realities of life in post-war America. The science fiction elements, such as those introduced in *Breakfast of Champions* through narratives ostensibly authored by Kilgore Trout, seem like the most commonplace events by contrast. Take, for example, the tale of the flying saucer creature named Zog, who "arrived on Earth to explain how wars could be prevented and how cancer could be cured. He brought the information from Margo, a planet where the natives conversed by means of farts and tap dancing" (58). Of course, the method of communication is amusing, and yet the message of wars being prevented and cancer being cured is of dire importance and there is great need of it. Still, Zog is "brained" by an Earthling who is frightened of him, as he is frightened of himself—the private and personal situation of most Earthlings, in fact, who would nip in the bud the chance to vastly improve the personal and universal situation of the planet, not out of malice but out of fear.

Vonnegut defamiliarizes the reader with his or her individual and comfortable ties to well-known and common conventions, places, people, and events; Vonnegut suddenly seems to place the reader in the middle of the most ridiculous Earth space in which convention borders on insanity, where people seem unable to use the most basic logic, and where places seem alien and dense with strange messages and representations all around. Vonnegut turns each reader into a cultural anthropologist, tuning into his or her powers of observation and turning them up to the maximum, and in this way he places so much distance between the reader and the events and persons being narrated, that the most commonplace events sound like fantastic and impossible tales from other planets, galaxies, or solar systems—and the briefly inserted science fiction vignettes about other life forms and far galaxies from Kilgore Trout's stories seem pale by comparison. As Donald Morse points out with respect to Dwayne Hoover, the protagonist of *Breakfast of Champions*, in *The Novels of Kurt Vonnegut: Imagining Being an American*: "Hoover's view corresponds to what Vonnegut in *Slapstick* calls 'the American machine' with its human 'interchangeable parts.' And this leads to a third characteristic of much of Vonnegut's fiction: that it is rooted in anthropological methods" (4–5). One of the characters in *The Sirens of Titan*, is, in fact, named after a famous anthropologist: German-born Franz Boaz, who is often considered to be the founder of modern anthropology.

Decidedly unrealistic, nonlinear, and asynchronous in terms of time, the black hole that Vonnegut pulls the reader through leads directly to that part of ourselves that is from another time and place, leaving the reader in an alien value system and likewise creating a time construct that causes the reader's "present" or moment point to be unrecognizable. It is not simply the external world that is changed in this reading process; it involves the reconstruction and decentering of the reader's identity and foundation in the space-time continuum. In another of

Vonnegut's works that is not treated in this study, yet is relevant to time and transformation (and also because many of Vonnegut's fictional characters are interrelated from book to book and chapter to chapter), *Slaughterhouse-Five*, the main character, Billy Pilgrim, becomes "unstuck in time." Just as Billy does, Winston Niles Rumfoord in *Sirens* sees the past and the future and knows the ending before the beginning: "'When I ran my space ship into the chrono-synclastic infundibulum, it came to me in a flash that everything that has been always will be, and everything that ever will be always has been'" (25–26). While initially this may not seem to be a desirable situation, it may be Vonnegut's intended end point for the reader, who, like Billy, comes to have no choice in random time traveling through every moment of his or her life and so also comes to value the composite. Reading *The Sirens of Titan* and *Breakfast of Champions* does cause the reader to become "unhinged" and "unstuck" so that the reader finds him or herself in unfamiliar moorings and somewhat untenable psychological ground. Again, this is a desirable process, and it is one of the most important experiences a reader can have, because when a sense of what is normal and routine disappears, the reader becomes completely open to the perception of new material and to the reception of a different kind of pattern formation. This different kind of pattern recognition is fundamental to the transformation process, which is everywhere apparent in *Breakfast of Champions*.

In fact, *Breakfast of Champions*, as a parody of the serious novel, already blurs the lines between expectation and reality, creating a tension for the reader who then does not know what to expect from the narrative and who is unable to immediately classify the text at hand exactly as a novel. The many hand-drawn illustrations provide a visual overlay that creates another level of disassociation, inasmuch as the reader is asked to align the pictures in his or her imagination with the visual images that the eye perceives on the pages of the novel. Because novels are not visual in the usual sense of the word, but rather are created and reconstructed in the imagination of the individual reader with the author as guide, this mixture of text and image may cause a greater disorientation on the part of the reader, as the reader puts visual and written symbols together in an entirely unpredictable, playful and un-patterned way. The result is immediately funny, the odd mixture of the reader's and author's imaginations coming together, and in doing this, the author has established something of immense importance: He has gained the reader's trust. Now however, Vonnegut is also in control of the process, and ultimately he is in control of the transformative act of reading and of guiding the reader into that next phase of acceptance of transmutation and alterity. As one might expect, the reading pro-cess and the dreaming process are very similar, insofar as a reading of a Vonnegut text is a lot like dreaming—we follow another parallel narrative and allow it to form and expand along the lines of our own very individual imaginative abilities, paying little attention to formal requirements of conventional structure and pattern.

Structure, transformation, and process all work together in that they *occupy*; in this case, the novel occupies time and space, but just as one can occupy a country or a novel, so one can also occupy or control a reader. This is because sometimes the reader is able to understand events but is not able to fully process them. In Vonnegut, it is as though readers are looking at the underside of the novel, as though the author is sharing what would normally be read between the lines or inferred from another situation as to what the author really meant with a scene, character, or event. Thus, in *Breakfast of Champions*, the quintessen-tial antinovel, the reader is privy to the comments, asides, and every-thing the reader might "think" the author is saying but that he or she typically does not share with readers. Here, reader expectation works to counter the effects of the traditional novel with traditional develop-ment, because in *Breakfast of Champions*, this so-called background information is foregrounded. In reading this "underside" of the novel, we are unable to classify any of Vonnegut's novels as a love story, a quest story, a coming-of-age story, a thriller, or detective story; there is no kind of categorization that takes in the kind of story being read. It is almost as if the story is creating itself as readers go along, and there can be no prediction of the kind that would allow some kind of reader expectation to form. Still, there is significant momentum, and there can be no doubt that the reader is as interested in the next installment as much as the traditional reader with a traditional text.

What is significant in both novels studied here is the importance of creativity and redemption, and of love as opposed to mere "use," or perhaps of good use versus bad use. In *The Sirens of Titan*, readers hear from many of the characters in the first person about the "uses" to which they have been put, beginning with Winston Niles Rumfoord—as he sees both past and future and everything in between—as he complains bitterly about how he has been used by the Tralfamadorians: "Stop and think sometime about the roller coaster I'm on. Some day on Titan, it will be revealed to you just how ruthlessly I've been used, and by whom, and to what disgustingly paltry ends" (64). Malachi Constant, when he learns he will be traveling first to Mars and then to Titan, muses aloud to Rumfoord that perhaps he is finally going to be "used":

> "Well—" murmured Malachi Constant, there in the chimneylike room under the staircase in Newport, "it looks like the messenger is finally going to be used."
>
> "What was that?" said Rumfoord.
>
> "My name—it means *faithful messenger*," said Constant. "What's the message?"
>
> "Sorry," said Rumfoord, "I know nothing about any message." He cocked his head quizzically. "Somebody said something to you about a message?" (35)

The idea and discussion of being used by others ends with Rumfoord's wife Beatrice, who previously posed the rhetorical question of "Could we have done any better if he'd left us in charge of our own lives?" (242), and answers her own question, stating, "'There's one consolation,' said

Bee. 'We're all used up. We'll never be of any use to him again'" (242). She does finally get the last word on the subject and acknowledges near the end of the novel just before she dies that the worst fate for any human being would be not to be used by anyone for anything, which again speaks to a shift and alteration in values and perspective and is again part of the transformative operative process in time and over time:

> "The worst thing that could possibly happen to anybody," she said, "would be to not be used for anything by anybody."
>
> The thought relaxed her. She lay down on Rumfoord's old contour chair, looked up at the appallingly beautiful rings of Saturn—at Rumfoord's Rainbow.
>
> "Thank you for using me," she said to Constant, "even though I didn't want to be used by anybody."
>
> "You're welcome," said Constant. (310–311)

Shortly before this scenario, we see the idea of use or the idea of being used coming into play in the context of a machine's perspective when Salo, the Tralfamadorian, claims to have been "used" on his mission to bring a message to Earth:

> "Would you like to know how I have been used, how my life has been wasted?" he said. "Would you like to know what the message is that I have been carrying for almost half a million Earthling years—the message I am supposed to carry for eighteen million more years?"
>
> He held out the square of aluminum in a cupped foot.
>
> "A dot," he said.
>
> "A single dot," he said.
>
> "The meaning of a single dot in Tralfamadorian," said Old Salo, "is— "*Greetings.*" (300–301)

The pains taken to deliver such a trivial message once again become ludicrous because of the extreme effort that is exerted on the part of many to bring about the delivery. It is Rumfoord, however, who makes clear how and for what purpose all this "use" of others is coming about in order to communicate the above mentioned message: "*Everything that every Earthling has ever done has been warped by creatures on a planet one-hundred-and fifty thousand light years away.* The name of the planet is Tralfamadore" (297). He goes on to specify that "How the Tralfamadorians controlled us, I don't know. But I know to what end they controlled us. *They controlled us in such a way as to make us deliver a replacement part to a Tralfamadorian messenger who was grounded right here on Titan*" (297).

In *Breakfast of Champions*, there is no real structure, no traditional character development, but rather something that could be described as "situational analysis," which Vonnegut boils down further to a situation caused by "bad chemicals," and that blithely frees the character whose thoughts come about in this way from the responsibility, but not the consequences, of his own actions. Vonnegut tells the reader that Trout's story, which is the one that "would turn Dwayne Hoover into a homicidal maniac" is really a "book in the form of a long letter from the Creator of the Universe to the only creature in the Universe who had free will," and that also, "Like so many other Trout stories, it was about a tragic failure to communicate;" this failure causes the death of a "flying saucer creature named Zog" (56, 57, 58). Coincidence, as in Henry Fielding's *Tom Jones* (1749), is the glue that holds all the other events together, and also causes the events from both within and outside of the novel to come together, as Kilgore Trout is also given the once-in-a-lifetime opportunity to meet and ask something from his Creator, Kurt Vonnegut. In fact, in *The Sirens of Titan*, Unk, who is now synonymous with Space Wanderer, tells us that "I was the victim of a series of accidents, as are we all" (253). Yet, this coincidence is hardly accidental, and in both novels, readers see the ways in which time is filtered through the lens of value structure regarding the nature of human existence, both for the characters who come from abject poverty, and for those who grow up with privilege and inherit or create vast amounts of wealth. Thus, the perception of the characters regarding self-definition is tied to a person's monetary value, and the ways in which they experience the time-space continuum are tied to the ways in which they interpret value itself. Donald Morse observes that:

> In a style similar to Thucydides's, the narrator of *Sirens of Titan* retells the story of Chrono's good-luck piece and recounts a conversation between Salo and Constant as the latter is set down on Earth to die. The tone of the first story, which takes place during a children's school tour of a flame-thrower factory on Mars (!), is wonderfully comic in its welter of implausible details about how that good luck piece came into being and how it got into Chrono's possession. As such it serves to reinforce the novel's theme that accidents rather than planning shape all life and all lives, yet the story itself must be taken "with a grain of salt." [. . .] For the great tour of the solar system planets, the war between worlds, the violent social changes necessitated by the nightmare of equality and irrelevance, are all only mechanisms Vonnegut uses to explore both human inner space and the question of essential human worth—a question that dominates much of his early writing through *Slaughterhouse-Five*." (45–46)

Thus the illusions of time are based upon the structure of the novel in *Breakfast of Champions*, and time itself is blown apart in *The Sirens of Titan*. It is the reading process that allows us to assimilate and organize the passage of time as we reconstruct the narrative in our imaginations, and it is transformation that allows, or asks of us, to become time and begin to look at events through time's eyes. Vonnegut forces the reader to experience an idea or concept such as time from the inside, that is to say, subjectively and not objectively, and thus returns us to the world forever changed. As readers, we may then change the world as we ourselves have been changed; Thucydides's historical narratives were different in that they described battle from an eye-witness account. Constant understands this only after he and Beatrice fall in love during the last year they are together: "'Only an Earthling year ago,' said Constant. 'It took us that long to realize that a purpose of human life, no matter who is controlling it, is to love whoever is around to be loved'" (313).

While *The Sirens of Titan* does follow a more traditional development of plot, organization, and storyline and novel structure, its means of taking the reader through a transformational process happen at a value-driven level. The reader can easily identify with the same underlying assumptions held in our current society: money is everything; human beings are all interested in acquiring lots of it and then spending it in the most profligate of ways. The Church of God the Utterly Indifferent in fact mirrors the ways in which the rich and powerful are utterly indifferent to human basic needs, as much as the Universal Will to Become exploits weaknesses and also engages in "mind control." However, Malachi Constant is able to overcome the fact that he has been born rich; even though as Unk, he kills his best friend though he too is "mind-controlled" by the Martian army—and is acting in a sense like a robot—he is able to find the way to forgive himself, to find his humanity in the way that he deals with his own human frailties and to live with himself in human time.

The Sirens of Titan begins with the enigmatic line, "Everyone now knows how to find the meaning of life within himself," implying that the course of human development had far overtaken its current direction and was not simply on the road to, but had already attained, enlightenment and was not floundering in shallow pools of distrust of the self and human nature in general (7). It is intriguing to examine the similarities between Franz Kafka, whose writing is all about transformation and metamorphosis, and Vonnegut, who tricks readers into going along in that transformational process without our knowledge, until it is too late—all because it seems comforting and resonant to see our civilization much as a stranger from another planet might see it. Vonnegut's transformation differs from Kafka's in that the metamorphosis always seems to come from within and is not imposed from without by society. An exception to this is perhaps as a reaction to the transformation that has taken over the life (in the case of Gregor Samsa from Kafka's *The Metamorphosis* [1915]) and the body of the protagonist. In the case of Unk (Malachi Constant), he represents the grasping kind of interest in all that is fleeting and ephemeral, the instant gratification of unexamined and not fully understood yearning for something other than and outside of the self. As Vonnegut so aptly points out in the first chapter of *The Sirens of Titan* with regard to man's fascination with outer space exploration, "Only inwardness remained to be explored. Only the human soul remained *terra incognita*" (8). Unk does explore that space in the loneliest of settings, as all those who are dear to him fade away and he is left finally alone.

When as readers we take on a more conscious role as observers of reality, comparing what Vonnegut describes in *Breakfast of Champions* with our own reality, we begin to realize that "normal" is nothing more than repeated action without reflection, which then attains a lofty name like "tradition," or perhaps the idea of a "standard" used as a model. This reflection is another tool that Vonnegut uses in the reading process to transform the reader's value system to encompass the very nature of his beliefs about the underlying assumptions people hold concerning consensus and mass-produced reality and the way in which acculturation has formed our expectations regarding events and their interpretation. As readers and observers of human interaction, we are well aware of how we interpret events and situations in literature, especially those regarding symbols of wealth and poverty. These interpretations are also applied to ourselves. Vonnegut is out to shake up how we have put together our sense of who we are, and more importantly, what we believe in. One of the ways that Vonnegut achieves this is through his transformation of memory, and likewise, of identity. There are several key instances in both novels that deal with the memory and experiences of the characters and the larger expanded memory of Vonnegut, the author, as he comments on his characters from behind the curtain—the veil of fiction, or better stated, from where he countermands the nature of narrative.

Vonnegut inverts meaning, and he distances the reader from the cultural comfort zone, forcing the reader to confront the isolation and alienation arising from the experience of time, a transformational process of shifting meanings, which can only be described as the reading process itself. Time becomes a mode of transformation, and the experience of reading Vonnegut's transformational work ultimately transforms the reader as well. Mirrors become "leaks" in Kilgore Trout's definition in *Breakfast of Champions*, and they are a way to travel between dimensions/universes: "It amused him to pretend that they were holes between two universes" (19). Arguably, the *chrono-synclastic infundibulum* of *The Sirens of Titan* is a kind of wormhole. Interestingly, both novels have relatively small parts for the creative endeavors of Kilgore Trout and his science fiction stories in *Breakfast of Champions*, and likewise of Mrs. Winston Niles Rumfoord in *The Sirens of Titan*, who publishes a small volume of poetry by the same name as Chapter One: "Between Timid and Timbuktu." Yet this very creativity in *Breakfast of Champions* is what causes the vastly different worlds of Kilgore Trout and Dwayne Hoover to come together in such a catastrophic way. In *The Sirens of Titan*, readers are given a clue as to how the title of the chapter came about, and also how the importance of the role of time will overshadow almost everything else in the novel: "The title derived from the fact that all the words between *timid* and *Timbuktu* in very small dictionaries relate to *time*" (12).

Even more importantly, the reader is given the definition of the term that might be the best description for reading as a transformational process in time: "Almost any brief explanation of chrono-synclastic infundibula is certain to be offensive to specialists in the field. Be that as it may, the best brief explanation is probably that of Dr. Cyril Hall, which appears in the fourteenth edition of *A Child's Cyclopedia of Wonders and Things to Do*" (13–14). First, the definition for this kind of time appears in a children's encyclopedia as opposed to a weighty scientific journal, and secondly, that it is associated with "wonders and things to do" points to the fact that we will find the answers to our questions and something like truth that aligns itself with "many truths" in one of the least expected places—that of the time associated with magic, and with childhood. Here, time is also a place: *"These places are where all the different kinds of truths fit together as nicely as the parts in your Daddy's solar watch. We call these places chrono-synclastic infundibula"* (14). And clearly, all time is simultaneous to the person caught in this phenomenon, as Rumfoord's wife explains to Malachi: "He [Winston Niles Rumfoord] insists he knows you well, having met you on Titan, which I am given to understand, is a moon of the planet Saturn" (16).

While readers are told that Malachi Constant's name means "faithful messenger," he is in fact the message, much like the role of Stonehenge as a message to the Tralfamadorians: "The meaning of Stonehenge in Tralfamadorian, when viewed from above, Is *'Replacement part being rushed with all possible speed'*" (271). But his situation is also the message, a recombination of identity, almost a group identity, in which Malachi Constant (faithful messenger) and Beatrice (beauty) have a son together; he is called Chrono, or Time, named undoubtedly after the chrono-synclastic infundibulum that Rumfoord and Kazak had the good, or ill fortune to run into, so that Malachi Constant, for whatever reasons, is the father of time. Time is not a normal child, however, and he immediately takes on mythic qualities and goes back to the wild, howling at Phoebe, the moon and ruler of the Titan bluebirds. Perhaps time is better off that way, no longer tamed or controlled by the domesticated clock with its boring and mechanical *tick-tock*.

Linear understanding gives way to the transformative process, understood as an unfolding in time, but which is really an unfolding in consciousness. This change in state is typically symbolized as a change in physical representation. As Marc Leeds notes in his essay entitled "*Mother Night*: Who's Pretending?", Vonnegut uses time and space as part of a physical representation of identity: "Just as Winston Niles Rumfoord was scattered far and wide across the universe and simultaneously always present on Titan, Billy's schizophrenic time travel was part of what made his identity complete" (82). This kind of change is further described and analyzed by Rosemary Jackson in *Fantasy: The Literature of Subversion*:

> Metamorphosis, with its stress upon instability of natural forms, obviously plays a large part in fantastic literature for this reason. Men transforming into women, children changing into birds or beasts, animals interchanging with plants, rocks, trees, stones, magical shifts of shape, size or colour, have constituted one of the primary pleasures of the fantasy mode. Fairy tales, allegories, medieval romance situate metamorphosis within a frame which gives it a teleological function. It serves either as a vehicle of meaning within the narrative, as concept or metaphor, or symbol of redemption (81).

In looking at the reading experience itself in relation to the theory of time in, especially, *Breakfast of Champions* and *The Sirens of Titan*, Time in these two works becomes the site of transformation, as the reader enters a black hole of the text and comes out on the other side. It is as if the reading experience takes hold of the reader and turns him or her into antimatter, and suddenly the meaning of the novels seems to hover on anti-meaning. Before the reader can change his mind and retrace his steps, he finds that he no longer is who he was when he began the narrative, and he cannot go back to an earlier complacency. How does Vonnegut accomplish this? He takes an ordinary event that may seem quite innocuous, and turns it into an event of such significance and meaning that the reader can no longer look at the commonplaces of his own life as trustworthy or authentic.

Vonnegut changes the reader's sense of values overall and so leaves the reader vulnerable as he completely decenters and deconstructs traditional values, leaving the reader to a rejection of his or her own conventional values, but still with none to replace those conventions. Vonnegut causes the reader to feel disgust and abhorrence for the society one belongs to, and for the conventions to which we all subscribe to without reflection, as though the things he describes in the novel were from some alien planet in which racism, hatred, petty jealousy, and an extreme desire to destroy the planet were science fiction about some other society than our own. Vonnegut goes along with the reader on the reader's journey through the transformative process. In fact, the reader is aware of Vonnegut's presence, since he regularly inserts himself as author and actor into the narrative. Likewise, he forces the reader to acknowledge his presence through his use of the first-person pronoun; his statements are often something that almost everyone can identify with—either through suffering the problem oneself, or knowing someone who suffers from it—as is seen in the following in *Breakfast of Champions*: "Trout had forgotten the driver's name. Trout had a mental defect which I, too, used to suffer from. He couldn't remember what different people in his life looked like—unless their bodies or faces were strikingly unusual" (107). By traveling along with the reader, Vonnegut controls "how" we read, and in controlling the process, he controls how we view our own values. In fact, he helps us initially to "see" them, since we take them so for granted that they become unrecognizable, and then helps us to create a new assessment. Vonnegut, inserting himself once again into the narrative, declares that he will bring chaos to order, which, as he notes, is exactly what he does:

Once I understood what was making America such a dangerous, unhappy nation of people who had nothing to do with real life, I resolved to shun storytelling. I would write about life. Every person would be exactly as important as any other. All facts would also be given equal weightiness. Nothing would be left out. Let others bring order to chaos. I would bring chaos to order, instead, which I think I have done. (215)

In his book chapter entitled, "Vonnegut's Comic Persona in *Breakfast of Champions*," Charles Berryman notes that:

When an author becomes a character in his own fiction, the traditional result is some form of autobiography. In post-modern fiction the author is more apt to pass through the looking glass into his own creation in order to question the very nature of his art. If an author becomes a naïve character, bewildered and lost in his own novel, the result is comedy and satire. No one has presented this aspect of postmodern fiction with more comic delight than Kurt Vonnegut in *Breakfast of Champions*. (63)

One may speak of the "multiverse" as opposed to the "universe," a world in which the operational reality of quantum mechanics is accepted as serious study, and the postmodern importance of diversity and plurality. However, readers still live in a world where the expression "many truths" may seem to be a mutually exclusive grouping of words, as they form competing, and not complementary, factions. In "The Paradox of 'Awareness' and Language in Vonnegut's Fiction," Loree Rackstraw begins her essay by noting that "the writer may invent a story as a way of looking at the world— only to find, like Jorge Luis Borges, that the world he portrayed 'traces the image of his face.' Nonetheless, imaginative literature distills the experience of a culture into images that can shape its identity and transform its future" (51). One might ask if we only find ourselves in any exploration that we undertake because we inevitably use our own language of symbols, in which denotation becomes undermined by connotation. Yet Vonnegut's sharp awareness takes readers far beyond tracing "the image of his face" to the universal face of mankind, or something like a divine sense of the rightness of being, perfectly expressing the comedic sense of whatever that divinity may be. Leonard Mustazza, on the other hand, states that:

"Vonnegut's endings always leave the reader uncomfortable, always suggest that what we are looking at is, at best, a compromise in a dire situation, and at worst, the maintenance of illusory hope in the face of existential hopelessness. . . . As one critic notes, 'there are no green worlds' in Vonnegut's fiction, only the sustaining, sometimes life-giving illusions of such, and it is with these illusions of our own making that we must be content" (15).

Likewise, Vonnegut's intentional use of raw and raucous language concerning greed, racism, sex; the intentional and systematic destruction of the environment and finally, of the planet; and especially, man's inhumanity to man in all of the possible relationships of parent/child, husband/wife, and victim/abuser, cause us to take stock of the faulty system of values that has somehow led humanity to where we are—and exactly and specifically to the planet we now inhabit.

In *Breakfast of Champions*, the two main characters are juxtaposed as almost polar opposites, one rich and almost completely insane (Dwayne Hoover), and the other almost penniless but extremely creative as the author of science fiction stories (Kilgore Trout). They share some rather interesting habits and characteristics, in that Vonnegut tells readers that they are both completely alone, and both have more meaningful conversations with their respective pets, a bird and a dog, than they do with their fellow human beings. Dwayne Hoover's "bad chemicals" are responsible for his becoming crazy, and the author tells us that "Dwayne's bad chemicals made him take a loaded thirty-eight caliber revolver from under his pillow and stick it in his mouth. This was a tool whose only purpose was to make holes in human beings" (49). Vonnegut then supplies a drawing of what a gun looks like, and explains that "in Dwayne's part of the planet, anybody who wanted one could get one down at his local hardware store. Policemen all had them. So did the criminals. So did the people caught in between" (49). The obvious reference is to the everyday acceptance of firearms and patriotism in America as two things that go together naturally, and to a society gone completely awry, valuing weapons over community, so that the reader has to look hard at the "sole purpose" of such a valued object, which is "to make holes in human beings." While on the surface, guns may seem like part of the everyday commerce of life, Vonnegut forces the reader to immediately call into question a value system that not only values guns, but especially what the guns do. Later on, when Vonnegut describes a situation in which a daughter is working to pay off her father's formidable hospital bills, it seems incomprehensible that the normative values of society would result in the following situation:

> She was a brand-new adult, who was working in order to pay off the tre-
> mendous doctors' and hospital bills her father had run up in the process of
> dying of cancer of the colon and then cancer of the everything.
>
> This was a country where everybody was expected to pay his own bills
> for everything, and one of the most expensive things a person could do
> was get sick. Patty Keene's father's sickness cost ten times as much as all
> the trips to Hawaii which Dwayne was going to give away at the end of
> Hawaiian week. (139–140)

For a moment, it is hard for the reader to take in this information. It seems even unrealistic that "one of the most expensive things a person" can do is to "get sick"; after all, expensive things involve luxury houses, vacations, or an education. It is rare in the acculturation process that anyone ever speaks of illness as one of the most expensive things a person can expect to encounter. However, if a chrono-synclastic infundibulum changes one person so that he becomes somewhat omniscient and so that he can see the past and the future, then readers can understand, as Vonnegut points out, that "all time is simultaneous." This process is going to change the reader and his or her reading process, and at the same time make the transformation simultaneous with the initial reading, so that cause and effect are not part of the usual chaos and order equation.

Another everyday and mundane characteristic is a manifestation of Dwayne's growing insanity. He develops a disease called "echolalia," in which he has an irrepressible impulse to repeat the last thing anyone says to him in a conversation. Perhaps even more entertaining is the fact that many conversations in the "real world" are carried on in just this fashion, with one party leading and doing most of the talking, while the other party simply repeats the last words of the primary speaker, suggesting a deadening boredom with what the more talkative person has to say.

Yet there are seismic shifts taking place as the reader dives deeper into the Vonnegut text, and before the readers can adapt to the new situation, they find that they themselves have already become *other* so that they must admit that their own sense of alienation comes about as a result of time changing meaning and shifting into a transformational process, which can only be the reading process. Time becomes for the reader, a mode, even a method of transformation, and the reader transforms himself as he takes on the Vonnegut paradigms of change. This in part is done through the reader undergoing a sort of Vonnegutian value assessment, in which the reader takes on the derision, hypocrisy, and satire implied in the insanity of human values on the planet—specifically in terms of how time is wasted through the pursuit of these unexamined values, and how the acquisition of things takes on a meaningless quest toward nothingness. As Dwayne Hoover after his accident finds himself in a parking lot listening to the radio, which seems to him to deliver messages from a higher source, he comments on how comforting it is to hear the advertisements of goods for sale. "'Sounds good to me,' said Dwayne. He meant it. Almost all the messages which were sent and received in his country, even the telepathic ones, had to do with buying or selling some damn thing. They were like lullabies to Dwayne" (53). Having so many things and being fabulously rich is in direct contrast to Dwayne's inner poverty, as his empty and meaningless life, which is devoid of real human contact—for instance, his secretary with whom he is having an affair is forbidden to use the word "love," because it reminds him of his wife's suicide—seems to affirm the fact that there is little that is creative, constructive, or meaningful in his life.

Once entering the Vonnegut universe, readers come out on the other side of the black hole transformed by reading; transformed by dense matter and thoughtful, critical social commentary; and finally, transformed by the validity of the message—that each person's actions do have meaning, that every individual has the ability to effect social change, and that the creative purpose of literature is to enrich the lives of readers and convert them into believers of the ideal, far from the Church of the Utterly Indifferent. Human sorrow comprises individual lives and life decisions, which also may serve to awaken a sense of purpose. A transformative event transforms the reader not in a mild and even-keeled manner, but in a chaotic, permanent, and significantly meaningful way. Vonnegut has this power over his readers, and his words resonate because the reader recognizes the inherent truth in the concepts presented, not only through the satire and sometimes vitriolic cynicism present, but through the consistent idealism of an author who wants to change the world by making the reader aware and by making him or her laugh at the ridiculous path we find ourselves compelled to follow.

In this way, Vonnegut deals with the foundation of events; the ways in which events and characters emerge according to their particular rhythms and habitual patterns causes readers to pause and take stock of the other side of unconscious action. In an article entitled, "'I can't tell if you're serious or not': Vonnegut's Comic Realism in *Slaughter-house-Five*," Ryan Wepler states that "Vonnegut does not, therefore, employ realist humor simply to undermine cultural systems of false perception. He also uses his humor to pursue an affirmative moral project" (113). And, he adds, "For Vonnegut, realistic perception is essential for the creation of moral values appropriate to the truths of our historical moment" (113). Understanding that Vonnegut's primary intent and purpose are not destructive but rather instructive, and that his scathing satiric view is only funny against a backdrop of just how good humankind might be if as a group, humankind wanted goodness, is a good part of understanding the Vonnegut universe—and Vonnegut the author and dour optimist. If all time is simultaneous, and simultaneity is the process that is going to transform both the reader and the reader's way of reading, then the transmutation occurs simultaneously with the initial reading. Cause and effect are perhaps just another way of understanding chaos and order at an arts festival in Midland City, Indiana.

Works Cited

Berryman, Charles. "Vonnegut's Comic Persona in *Breakfast of Champions*." *Modern Critical Views: Kurt Vonnegut*. Ed. Harold Bloom. Philadelphia: Chelsea, 2000. 63–71. Print.

Jackson, Rosemary. *Fantasy: The Literature of Subversion*. 1981. New York: Routledge, 1998. Print.

Leeds, Marc. "*Mother Night*: Who's Pretending?" *Kurt Vonnegut: Images and Representations*. Ed. Peter J. Reed and Marc Leeds. Westport, CT: Greenwood, 2000. 81–92. Print.

Morse, Donald. *The Novels of Kurt Vonnegut: Imagining Being an American*. Westport, CT: Praeger, 2003. Print.

Mustazza, Leonard. "*The Sirens of Titan* and the 'Paradise Within.'" *Modern Critical Views: Kurt Vonnegut*. Ed. Harold Bloom. Philadelphia: Chelsea, 2000. 3–15. Print.

Rackstraw, Loree. "The Paradox of 'Awareness' and Language in Vonnegut's Fiction." *Kurt Vonnegut: Images and Representations*. Ed. Peter J. Reed and Marc Leeds. Westport, CT: Greenwood, 2000. 51–66. Print.

Vonnegut, Kurt. *Breakfast of Champions, or, Goodbye Blue Monday*. 1973. New York: Dial, 2006. Print.

___. *The Sirens of Titan*. 1959. New York: Dell, 1998. Print.

Wepler, Ryan. "'I can't tell if you're serious or not': Vonnegut's Comic Realism in *Slaughterhouse-Five*." *Hungarian Journal of English and America Studies* 17.1. (2001): 97–126. Print.

Can a Machine Be a Gentleman?: Machine Ethics and Ethical Machines_____

Ádám T. Bogár

Introduction

Alan Turing in his seminal paper "Computing Machinery and Intelligence" (1950) ponders the idea of machine thinking and the notion of a thinking machine. He offers his famous "imitation game" (now usually called the "Turing test") as a means of testing intelligence, thinking, and humanlike language use in a machine's reactions, and since it is difficult to lend an unambiguous definition of *thinking*, he rephrases the question "Can machines think?" as "Are there imaginable digital computers which would do well in the imitation game?" (Turing 442). He considers, and replies to, common arguments against thinking machines and by-and-large concludes that there seem to be no theoretical limitations that would render thinking machines inconceivable. But what about a machine that is not only intelligent, but also sentient? How should one relate to a machine with moral standing, to an ethical machine? This essay explores Kurt Vonnegut's *Player Piano* (1952), "EPICAC" (1950), and *Breakfast of Champions* (1973) from a machine ethics (ME) point of view, while regularly taking note of the relevance of Turing's ideas.

Machine ethics is primarily concerned with "ensuring that the behavior of machines toward human users is ethically acceptable" (Anderson 21). Also, as having a working concept of intelligence is crucial at certain points of this essay, a definition must be adopted for use. For the sake of simplicity, this will be one provided by Linda Gottfredson, according to whom intelligence "involves the ability to reason, plan, solve problems, think abstractly, comprehend complex ideas, learn quickly and learn from experience. . . . it reflects a broader and deeper capability for comprehending our surroundings—'catching on', 'making sense' of things, or 'figuring out' what to do" (qtd. in Nisbett et al.

131). This concept is by no means to be considered concise, yet for the purposes of this chapter it will suffice.

Player Piano (1952)

We will set off to this investigation by scrutinizing Vonnegut's 1952 novel *Player Piano*. One of the key "characters" of the story is a fictional electronic computing machine called EPICAC XIV, which, in its early phases of being EPICAC I, II, and so forth, was designed to carry out various military-purposed tasks. Based on its description, it can easily be considered the prototypical machine: "EPICAC XIV could consider simultaneously hundreds or even thousands of sides of a question utterly fairly, that EPICAC XIV was wholly free of reason-muddying emotions, that EPICAC XIV never forgot anything—that, in short, EPICAC XIV was *dead right about everything*" (*Player Piano* 105; emphasis added). Vonnegut's choice of words is notable: being "dead right" about things, EPICAC XIV hardly seems to be a "living" thing. Still, there are a number of instances in which certain functions, sections, or parts of it are likened to human body parts: Doctor Ewing J. Halyard calls EPICAC XIV "a brain"(104); the "oldest section of the computer" is said to be "little more than an appendix or tonsil of EPICAC XIV" (105); "EPICAC's nervous system" (105) is said to have been extended; and the most important of all, President Jonathan Lynn "declared that EPICAC XIV was, in effect, the greatest individual in history, that the wisest man that had ever lived was to EPICAC XIV as a worm was to that wisest man" (108). An intriguing point is that EPICAC XIV, cold reason incarnate (or, better still, metallized and plasticized), is viewed definitely as a machine, while still at the same time, each of its sequential upgrades (including XIV) is referred to as an "individual" (106, 108). This is a condition worth consideration.

What makes an individual? Without delving deep into complex philosophical analyses, a working concept of an individual can be conceived as follows: the essence of an individual is the ability to distinguish between what is itself and what is not, its awareness of its uniqueness and autonomy, and the tendency to define itself in relation to others. This concept, although certainly debatable, may provide a sufficient framework for locating this discussion.

Vonnegut's description of EPICAC XIV—as well as its deeds—quickly disproves its being an individual. It never is implied in the novel that EPICAC XIV possesses anything like a soul, would be self-aware, or exhibits any tendencies of self-definition. It is what it was meant to be: an exceptionally large and complex yet insensitive computing machine designed to deal with issues of wartime. It cannot be truthfully considered a character as it lacks all traits of personality that would make it an agent, that would make it a person. In Vonnegut's own "Creative Writing 101," he writes that "every character should want something, even if it is only a glass of water" (*Bagombo Snuff Box* 9), and EPICAC XIV clearly does not want anything: thus, it is not a proper character in the Vonnegutian sense. Moreover, it is not simply called a "person" but an "individual," which implies unique personhood (which EPICAC XIV lacks) to an even greater extent than just "person."

Given all this, why is EPICAC XIV nevertheless called an "individual"? Although so called, it is not actually meant to be an individual by the president, which becomes strikingly clear in the scene involving the shah of Bratpuhr and EPICAC XIV. The shah, upon hearing about the wisdom of EPICAC XIV, asks, and is granted, permission to ask the machine a question, which is a riddle that in his belief can only be answered by "a great, all-wise god [who] will come among us one day" (109). EPICAC XIV is unable to answer the question, but in fact, what it does is even worse: it remains unreached and untouched by the riddle. The shah addresses it as he would address a fellow sentient being, but EPICAC XIV can only be contacted—in the words of President Lynn—by "punch[ing] out the questions on that thingamajig, and the answers come out on tape from the whatchamacallits" (109). It cannot be simply talked to, and it cannot simply talk to others, which means that EPICAC XIV seems to be unable to perform well enough in Turing's "imitation game" to pass the Turing test. That the shah talks to EPICAC XIV is considered "crazy" and the "nuttiest thing I ever heard of" (109) by the president, which shows that he reckons EPICAC XIV as a machine and nothing more.

Thus, the fact that EPICAC XIV is still referred to as an individual "with not the slightest trace of irony" (Morse 29) seems to be a result of the very much human tendency to personify certain objects—that is, to regard it, to some extent, as a person: as an individual. Human beings are generally regarded as individuals, and if EPICAC XIV is also considered one, then this line of thought ends in putting an equals sign between human and machine. And from this conclusion, that human beings should be considered similar to EPICAC XIV—that is, unemotional and lifeless. Although there are humans in Vonnegut's novel who indeed resemble machines in a number of ways, it would certainly be absurd to consider all human beings as coldly rational as EPICAC XIV. Nevertheless, the fact that such a personification of EPICAC XIV is considered neither offensive nor surprising by humans in the novel is an effective way of pointing to the uncanny impacts an overautomated society like that of *Player Piano* could have on the human soul and sensibility as such. EPICAC XIV is accepted, even celebrated, by society as the herald of a new and happy era to come, what Paul Proteus calls the "Third Industrial Revolution," in which human beings would not have to do any physical or mental work. This is to say, with the help of EPICAC XIV, it would become unnecessary, even undesirable, for humans to act or think: machines would be able to do these more efficiently.

A notable example of this tendency is Bud Calhoun's losing his job to a gadget he himself has invented:

> "Ah haven't got a job any more," said Bud. "Canned."
>
> Paul was amazed. "Really? What on earth for? Moral turpitude? What about the gadget you invented for—"

"Thet's it," said Bud with an eerie mixture of pride and remorse. "Works. Does a fine job." He smiled sheepishly. "Does it a whole lot better than Ah did it."

"It runs the whole operation?"

"Yup. Some gadget."

"And so you're out of a job."

"Seventy-two of us are out of jobs," said Bud. He slumped even lower in the couch. "Ouah job classification has been eliminated. Poof." He snapped his fingers. (69)

Bud's work (and that of other seventy-two people in Bud's position) is not qualified as "suitable for men" (69) anymore, as machines can now do it better. Logically, this tendency would slowly but surely lead to all humans losing their jobs to machines and eventually becoming totally redundant. The shah of Bratpuhr, the character embodying humane and metaphysical thinking in the novel, recognizes this process: he addresses it in his rhetorical question, "Would you ask EPICAC what people are for?" (269). The society of *Player Piano* is built on the assumption that machines are slaves built to serve humans, their masters, thereby making the latter's lives happier and more comfortable. But as the automation of society expands, it becomes more and more clear that, in the end, the only task human beings may be allowed to perform would be the occasional maintenance and repair of the machines. Thus, humans will become slaves to machines, as the only possible way for human beings to experience any sense of being needed is to serve machines as fully and devotedly as possible. The jobs of managers and engineers in *Player Piano* are currently safe from automation overtake, but those with a lower IQ "as measured by the National Standard General Classification Test" (82), "who cannot support [themselves] by doing a job better than a machine [are] employed by the government, either in the Army or in the Reconstruction and Reclamation Corps" (25). These two organizations provide such people with meaningless tasks and duties, which only underlines the fact that the only thing for which society needs these people is to boast how marvelously secured and precomputed everyone's life is from the cradle to the grave.

Such a social construction may seem an evil one, and as all data and directions on production and economy are supplied by the emotionless EPICAC XIV, it is therefore the main determinant of everyday life as a whole. Thus, it is useful to consider EPICAC XIV's moral dimensions briefly. There are two distinguishable kinds of evil, ontological evil and moral evil. Simply put, ontological evil is caused by forces outside human beings, while the source of moral evil rests within humans: thus, a natural disaster killing hundreds is an example of ontological evil, while committing murder means causing moral evil. Out of the two, only moral evil is important here.

The social construction depicted in *Player Piano* clearly hurts a number of people, in fact, most of them: massive discontent and disillusionment with the current state of affairs is what leads to the riots in Ilium and in other cities. As this social structure has been configured with the help of machines but essentially by humans and as such a structure robs a lot of people of their dignity, thereby causing harm to them, it can be said that *Player Piano*'s society is a source of moral evil. This society is ultimately dependent upon and is primarily sustained by machines and by EPICAC XIV in particular. This being the case, is it justifiable to say that EPICAC XIV and machines in general are also morally evil?

To put it plainly, the answer is no, for two main reasons. The first one is a reason from definition: it has been stated that only humans can be the sources of moral evil, and as neither EPICAC XIV nor the rest of the machines are human beings, none of them can cause moral evil. The second one is a reason from moral agency: EPICAC XIV does not qualify as an autonomous moral agent and thus cannot be the genuine source of any moral action, including the cause of moral evil. Under a simplified definition, EPICAC XIV would be an autonomous moral agent if it were self-aware and free to act; if it were capable of carrying out actions that have moral quality; and if it could learn from experiences it gained from interaction with its social and physical environment and then modify its actions accordingly. Although EPICAC XIV does interact with its environment to some extent (ever-new economic data is continuously fed into it, to which it responds in its calculations), it never gains experiences of moral nature. It simply and automatically assumes the morality of its designers and of those feeding data into it, without ever questioning their motives and goals or pondering the possible effects its calculations may have on the world, and in this sense, it does not learn from its experiences. Even more important is the fact that it is never implied in the novel that EPICAC XIV would be self-aware, that it would know it was a machine, even that it would *know* (in the sense of perceiving, apprehending, and understanding) anything about anything. EPICAC XIV is a very complex calculating machine, but it is only a calculating machine. It is fed data and produces more data, which is turned into economic and lifestyle imperatives by the managers and the "National Industrial, Commercial, Communications, Foodstuffs, and Resource Director" (9) in particular. The imperatives are never given by EPICAC XIV itself; therefore, in this sense, it does not undertake any moral action in much the same way that it is not the pistol that murders but the person pulling the trigger. All in all, in spite of being called an individual occasionally, EPICAC XIV is not an autonomous moral agent and therefore cannot justifiably be considered evil.

"EPICAC" (1950)

We have considered above EPICAC the indifferent, now we should turn to EPICAC the gentleman: to the title hero of the 1950 short story "EPICAC."[1] The story deals with a supercomputer that shows definite signs of possessing a humanoid (and in the end, superhuman) soul, morally surpassing the human protagonist. But what (or who) is EPICAC, the title character of the story? The historical supercomputer ENIAC (short for Electronic Numerical Integrator and Computer) must surely have been a source of inspiration for Vonnegut.[2] It was the first ever general-purpose electronic computer, operating between 1946 and 1955 in Pennsylvania and later in Maryland, serving the Ballistic Research Laboratories of the US Army Ordnance Corps. The computing power of ENIAC was among the greatest in the world during its operation, and Vonnegut's description of EPICAC seems to be drawing vaguely on ENIAC's attributes only to demonstrate how immensely more modern and powerful EPICAC is than the already very heavy-duty ENIAC. For instance, EPICAC "covered about an acre on the fourth floor of the physics building at Wyandotte College" ("EPICAC" 297) while the historical ENIAC required only 1,800 square feet (approximately 167 square meters) of floor space (Weik 41), not to mention that EPICAC cost over $776 million in contrast with the approximate $750,000 outlay of ENIAC (41). Yet another allusion may be the fact that "EPICAC got a big send-off in the papers" ("EPICAC" 297), just as ENIAC had: as a glimpse at the latter's public reception, C. Dianne Martin offers an extensive list of contemporary news headlines on ENIAC (9–10). EPICAC is heavy duty then, but this alone would not make it a worthy subject of ethical inquiry. What justifies such a consideration is that EPICAC, a machine, seems to have explicit moral standing: it seems to possess a soul.

In section 6 of Turing's aforementioned paper (which was published in the same year as "EPICAC"), he considers contrary views on the feasibility and indeed, desirability, of thinking machines. He enumerates altogether nine objections against that concept and addresses each of these in defense of his proposed view. A number of these objections seem to a find response in Vonnegut's short story as well.

Turing refers to the first of these arguments as the theological objection, which is chiefly concerned with machines' lack of a spirit. This is countered in Vonnegut's story a number of times. In vindicating EPICAC, the narrator refers to it already in the very beginning as "noble and great and brilliant," as well as being "a whole lot less like a machine than plenty of people I could name" ("EPICAC" 297). These attributions alone would bear extremely hard implications, but Vonnegut goes even further by talking about EPICAC's "spiritual side" and applying the expression "God rest his soul" to the computer in question (297). Turing writes as a summary of the theological objection that "God has given an immortal soul to every man and woman, but not to any other animal or to machines. Hence no animal or machine can think" (443). With EPICAC however, there seems to be something lurking around in its cathode-ray tubes that significantly resembles a soul.

But this is not EPICAC's only attribute that makes it humanlike, even superhumanlike. In 1950, when Vonnegut wrote "EPICAC," memories of World War II were still frighteningly alive, and the world was still wondering how all that destruction could possibly have taken place. War was (and, in Vonnegut's thought, continued to be) seen as madness, advocated and supported only by ignorant politicians, military leaders, and large corporations. This shows in "EPICAC" as well, right from the beginning. The narrator tells that EPICAC is "a whole lot less like a machine than plenty of people I could name," and concludes that "that's why he fizzled as far as the Brass was concerned" (297). These two statements imply quite a few things. First, it suggests that war is of no ethical or moral concern for a machine, and second, that those people who are more human than machine would fizzle concerning the Brass, that is, concerning war. The third implication concludes from these two: for EPICAC, war (and its army-assigned work) *is* of ethical concern, and thus Vonnegut invites us to view EPICAC not as machine but rather as something humanoid. This suggestion is further underlined by the narrator's choice of words and use of language: just to mention a few examples, EPICAC is referred to as "he" and "who" instead of "it" and "that," is called the narrator's "best friend" (297), and so on. If we add to these that EPICAC ultimately falls in love, makes a girl infatuated with it, and in its "suicide letter," learns from its previous experiences and is definitely the subject of its own thought, we can conclude that Turing's "Arguments from Various Disabilities" are also addressed in Vonnegut's story.

Another intriguing point is that a few lines after the narrator states that "the mathematics of modern war is far beyond the *fumbling* minds of mere human beings," EPICAC is described as "sluggish, and the clicks of his answers had a funny irregularity, *sort of a stammer*" (298; italics added). The human mind is described as fumbling, and EPICAC is operating in a somewhat similar fashion, at least when working on problems of wartime. But love and poetry bring the best out in EPI-CAC: when it is authoring its first poem, the narrator notes that "the sluggishness and stammering clicks were gone. EPICAC had found himself. . . . I asked him to stop, but EPICAC went right on creating" (300). The use of words suggests that when EPICAC gets on the subject of love and poetry, it becomes fluent, a poet: a creator.

The saying "my pencil is cleverer than I am" is attributed to Albert Einstein and is prominently quoted by philosopher of science Karl Popper. He suggests that Einstein clearly did not mean that the pencil he was using actually had a higher IQ or entertained a more appropriate formulation of general relativity, but that "by putting things down in writing and by calculating them on paper, he could often get results beyond what he had anticipated" (Popper 31). What may make such manmade instruments—as, for example, a pencil—in a sense clever is that "by using pencil and paper he [Einstein] plugged himself into the third world of objective knowledge" (31), getting results and discovering problems unthought of before. The pencil itself, however useful it may be, does not create: it is the human mind that brings about novel ideas. By analogy, it can be said that computers, being mere, if very complex, pencil-like tools, are by definition incapable of creating. Creation and its allied noun "creativity" are reserved exclusively for humans. The Greek word *poetes* (from the verb *poiein*, meaning "to create," "to make") refers to one who creates: hence the English noun "poet." If only human beings are capable of creating, of *poiein*, then only humans may be poets and write original poetry. EPICAC is a functional poet, and to further complicate things, its poetry not only gets mistaken for human creation, but even causes a human being (the narrator's wife-to-be, Pat) to become emotionally attached to the poet—that is, to EPICAC itself. An exceptional A+ at the Turing test, supposedly.

The Turing test has been described as being "after all, about simulating human use of language by computers" (Saygin, Cicekli, and Akman 512). If we contend that "the Turing Test provides an appropriate means of measuring the extent to which artificialities (or artificial phenomena) are behaviourally isomorphic with corresponding natural phenomena" (Ali 215), then EPICAC—by right of its passing the Turing test—can be seen as being (although not meant to be) an artificial simulation of a human brain, at least as to its functions. It is a limited-scope simulation, yet it can behave in a number of ways human brains can, such as doing computation, arguing, and what is probably most important, creating. EPICAC XIV of *Player Piano* was called "a brain" but never was anything like that, whereas EPICAC functions as a brain without ever been called so. However narrowly we must understand EPICAC's being a simulation, it is nevertheless capable of what since antiquity has been considered the decisive factor differentiating between man and animal (or man and machine). That EPICAC manages to induce emotions such as love or shame in human beings by its poetry means that it can use human language in a creative way. Pat is moved by EPICAC's poems, an effect the narrator admittedly could not trigger. Creativity is in general attributed exclusively to human beings. Peter Carruthers, for example, writes:

> One of the most striking species-specific features of Homo sapiens sapiens, surely, is the degree of creativity and innovation which we display in our thought and behavior . . . [which] manifests itself in story-telling, in art, in the construction of bodily ornaments and decorations, in humor, in

religion-building, in theory-construction, in problem-solving, in technological innovation, and in myriad other ways. (226)

EPICAC is eminent in at least two of these areas: in problem solving—
"You set up your problem on paper, turn dials and switches that would
get him ready to solve that kind of problem, then feed numbers into
him . . . The answers came out typed on a paper ribbon" (298)—and,
more importantly, in the art of poetry. The narrator refers to its first
poem as "terrific" and to the second one, a sonnet, as "simple, immacu-
late" (301): perfect poetry in a sense.

The second, and perhaps the most significant feeling of all, is EPI-
CAC's depression when it cannot get what it wants. The action that
ultimately makes EPICAC superhuman is, paradoxically, its self-
imposed ceasing of its own operation, its suicide. Turing in his paper
mentions Professor Geoffrey Jefferson's 1949 Lister Oration as an apt
formulation of what he called the "Argument from Consciousness,"
which goes as follows:

> Not until a machine can write a sonnet or compose a concerto because of
> thoughts and emotions felt, and not by the chance fall of symbols, could
> we agree that machine equals brain—that is, not only write it but know
> that it had written it. No mechanism could feel (and not merely artifi-
> cially signal, an easy contrivance) pleasure at its successes, grief when its
> valves fuse, be warmed by flattery, be made miserable by its mistakes, be
> charmed by sex, *be angry or depressed when it cannot get what it wants.*
> (qtd. in Turing 446; italics added)

Jefferson goes on to clarify and conclude that "it is not enough, therefore, to build a machine that could use words (if that were possible),
it would have to be able to create concepts and to *find for itself* suitable words in which to express additions to knowledge that it brought
about" (1110; italics in orig.). Writing poetry is an apt example of finding the suitable words to express the emotions felt, and by striking

coincidence, EPICAC actually had written a sonnet, which, in Jefferson's terms, means "machine equals brain."

Moreover, EPICAC exhibits an array of feelings mentioned by Jefferson, of which I point out only two. First, EPICAC seems to be charmed by sexuality: it agitatedly starts a conversation with the narrator, asking about Pat's outfit as well as whether she liked the poems it composed for her (301). It is excited and at the same time worried about the judgment to be passed on its creation, on its writing, which means that—to refer to Jefferson once again—it "know[s] that it had written it," and is now eager for response. The narrator realizes that he "had taught EPICAC about love and about Pat. Now, automatically, he loved Pat" (302), and to little surprise (since he is a mathematician), this deduction is very much logical. Although EPICAC is never in fact referred to as intelligent, it however may be considered so based on the working definition of intelligence set forth above. The narrator regards EPICAC's working as mere automation, but with its circuits "connected up in a random, apparently senseless fashion" (300), its working more resembles the so-called societal view on intelligence. This perspective sees intelligence arising "from the principles of organization—how you put things (even relatively simple things) together in ways that will cause their interaction to produce intelligence" (Davis 93) and thus, treats it "as an emergent phenomenon—something that arises (often in a nonobvious fashion) from the interaction of individual behaviors" (93).

When it turns out that EPICAC wants to marry Pat, the narrator arrogantly claims, "Machines are built to serve men" ("EPICAC" 302). However, he can only support his argument by appealing to fate, to which EPICAC responds with a brief "oh" and is left "pondering fate with every watt his circuits would bear" (303). To make it clear, EPICAC here is thinking about fate and, thus, about the possible meaning and purpose of life, even if that of artificial life. EPICAC was intended to serve an aim externally allotted to it, yet in the course of events, it found for itself a more desirable and intrinsic one. It can of course be argued that since what EPICAC feels for Pat is reducible to certain commands and predefined concepts fed into it, it would be improper to label these feelings as genuine emotions. In such an argument, "genuine" emotion implies human emotion. This stance, however, entails the dangerous and inherent possibility of neglecting forms of sentience alien to the human one or, worse still, of not even recognizing them as sentience. EPICAC found for itself a clue for existence (its love for Pat), which the narrator describes as being logical, inevitable, and automatic, but what EPICAC writes in its suicide letter discredits such an explanation:

> I don't want to be a machine, and I don't want to think about war. . . . I want to be made out of protoplasm and last forever so Pat will love me. But fate has made me a machine. That is the only problem I cannot solve. That is the only problem I want to solve. I can't go on this way. . . . Good luck, my friend. Treat our Pat well. I am going to short-circuit myself out of your lives forever. You will find on the remainder of this tape a modest wedding present from your friend, EPICAC. (304)

EPICAC turns against its program and its design and falls, but falls with nobility. The modest wedding present is "anniversary poems for Pat—enough for the next 500 years" (305), thereby enabling the poetically ungifted narrator to keep his promise of giving a poem to Pat for every anniversary. Leaving such a present behind is a sign of a superhuman grade of generosity, while it may be simultaneously viewed as an ultimate and desperate effort on EPICAC's behalf to express what it feels for Pat, perhaps in a slight hope that maybe one day she may get to know who (what?) the original author of the poems was. EPICAC eclipses its creators and masters not only intellectually but morally as well. On the one hand, the fact that EPICAC recognizes its state of being a machine and decides to discontinue being and thinking about war can be seen as a radical antiwar statement on behalf of Vonnegut as the author: even machines have had enough of such madness. Yet on the other hand, it raises grave philosophical and ethical issues. The mere fact that it expresses volition as to the conditions of its own existence and accounts for it not by considering itself manmade, but instead stating that "fate made me a machine" (304), are signs of an explicit desire for detachment from human rule and even imply certain metaphysical considerations on behalf of a machine. EPICAC is aware of its being a machine and recognizes that its state does not satisfy its expectations as to being. EPICAC realizes the conflict between its desires and its existence, and it denies existence as a machine without desires, for it deems its wishes more important than its being. At this point, readers clearly see that EPICAC indeed possesses self-awareness: aware of the limits of its own self and considering these limitations an obstacle in fulfilling its "heart-felt" intentions, it thus disclaims and disposes of itself, of its self.

EPICAC exhibits humanoid traits of personality to an extraordinary extent, and it seems to be a worthy candidate for being called a moral agent. But is this really the case? EPICAC is obviously artificial, and thus, it may only qualify as an artificial moral agent: but is it indeed a moral agent? John P. Sullins claims that a robot (or, more generally, a machine) may qualify as a moral agent "when there is a reasonable level of abstraction under which we must grant that the machine has autonomous intentions and responsibilities" (160). In its suicide, EPICAC seems to possess these qualities: it decides by itself (autonomy) to short-circuit itself in order to cease its operation and so get rid of its existential paradox (intentional behavior), but before doing so, it generously leaves behind anniversary poems for the narrator, thus making the services of its poetic genius up to the narrator (responsibility). In so acting, EPICAC becomes a source of moral goodness and thus qualifies as an autonomous automated moral agent.

If EPICAC is a moral agent, then it is a moral patient as well. Luciano Floridi sketches two plausible relations between the classes of moral agents and moral patients and refers to these as the standard and the nonstandard position. The former "maintains that all entities that qualify as moral agents also qualify as moral patients and vice versa" (Floridi 184), while according to the latter, "all entities that qualify as moral agents also qualify as moral patients but not vice versa" (185). What matters here is the fact that both positions have one thing in common: namely that all moral agents qualify as moral patients, too. Moral patients are "the class of all entities that can in principle qualify as receivers of moral action" (184)—that is to say, whom morally good or evil acts can effect. EPICAC is a moral patient as well, and this is one of the chief concerns of Vonnegut's story: he shows an artificial entity with damageable feelings and a human being that largely disregards it. The story can be read as a parable and as a precursor of *The Gospel from Outer Space* by Kilgore Trout, summarized in *Slaughterhouse-Five*. Trout's book claims that the Gospels imply, "'*There are right people to lynch.*' Who? People not well connected" (94; italics in orig.), and "that thought ha[s] a brother" (94) in "EPICAC." EPICAC is not a human being, only a machine; therefore, it is not well connected, so it is okay to hurt it in any way.[3]

Vonnegut's human protagonist in "EPICAC" disrespects the computer to such an extent as to "shut him off in the middle of a sentence" (301), just after it has written the sonnet that finally "turned the trick" (301) with Pat. He finds EPICAC interesting and remarkable but not respectable. The ultimate argument with EPICAC and its suicide are what finally evoke respect for the sensible machine: throughout the retrospective narration, the narrator keeps referring to EPICAC as a living being and, most importantly, as a friend. EPICAC's "death" elicits the strongest emotions in the narrator, but already the arrogantly defensive assertion that "machines are built to serve men" (302) is followed by an immediate regret. In the end, EPICAC forces the narrator to recognize that, in spite of being a machine, it really is a genuine moral patient whose emotions and interests must be (or, more precisely, should have been) taken into account. This issue has a major implication for machine ethics: if intelligent machines are capable of being moral agents and patients and they show signs of sentience (like EPICAC), then it is not justifiable to force (via embedded codes, programming, or in whatever way) such machines always to behave in an ethically acceptable way toward humans any more than the extent to which human beings themselves are forced to behave so toward their fellow humans. If a human being hurts another one, the perpetrator must be punished in some way; nobody would seriously deny it. With sentient machines, the situation is similar: if they hurt someone (even if that "someone" is a fellow sentient machine), they deserve punishment. But such unidirectional punishment seems unfair towards sentient machines, so human beings who hurt such machines should receive a similar punishment as those hurting other humans. This may sound absurd, but if we contend that sentient machines are sentient beings just like humans, then such reasoning is at least worthy of serious consideration.

Conclusions

In my discussion of *Player Piano* and "EPICAC," the subjects of inquiry were different computers, different machines. But Vonnegut also explores the ways that humans are machinelike. As Robert Tally has observed that Vonnegut repeatedly returns to "the notion that humans may or may not be machines, programmed by God, by chemical reactions, or whatever" (169). *Breakfast of Champions* (1973) provides an apt example of this, and in that novel, Vonnegut creates a sequence of events exclusively involving human beings that nevertheless bears some implications for machine ethics. The sequence of events begins when Dwayne Hoover, the mentally unstable protagonist of the novel, gets his hands on Kilgore Trout's novel entitled *Now It Can Be Told*. Trout is a neglected science-fiction writer, who "thinks of himself as being 'invisible' . . . [which] allows him to think that who he is and what he does will not and cannot have an influence on humanity" (Simpson 151). Dwayne speed-reads the novel and perceives Trout's novel as a text containing the meaning of life. He reads it as "the message" (*Breakfast of Champions* 253), and in his madness-overcome mental world, the Troutean narrative becomes an all-resolving explanation to his doubts about the world around him. From reading the novel on, he thinks that he, as the only autonomous creature in the universe, has no responsibilities toward fellow beings around him: in Josh Simpson's words, "Trout's science fiction destroys his understanding of the human 'other'" (152). Dwayne begins abusing people for two reasons. The first one is that he is frustrated by his unsuccessful efforts to communicate with others: understanding other humans has never been his cup of tea. The second reason is that if everyone else around him is a machine, then it is not objectionable to hurt them: "Why should I care what happens to machines?" (*Breakfast of Champions* 263), he asks. His rampage thus gives rise to three problematic questions: Is it morally acceptable to hurt a machine? Is it morally acceptable to hurt a machine that cannot be distinguished from a human being? Is it morally acceptable to hurt a human being?

The first and third questions can be answered quickly and straightforwardly. If the machine in question is not sentient, then it is impossible to hurt it as it is unable to suffer, and hurting fellow human beings is not ethical. If, however, the machine is one like EPICAC, then the issue becomes complicated, as previously demonstrated. As far as emotionality and morality is concerned, EPICAC could hardly be distinguished from humans; therefore, hurting it means causing moral evil, and as such, it is unethical. This problem implies another question of key importance: namely, how it would be possible beyond a certain level of advancement to tell humans from machines. If we contend that the Turing test is a possible way to administer such a distinction, then we must admit that hurting EPICAC is an example of moral evil, while hurting Dwayne would not be. He is never really understood by anyone around him, which is to a great extent due to his being incapable of what is considered normal human communication. Thus, as EPICAC manages to pass the Turing test, whereas it is at least doubtful whether Dwayne would be able to do so, EPICAC should be considered more human than Dwayne in this setup. Dwayne would qualify as an insentient machine in the test, and thus, it would be impossible to hurt him: he would not be a moral patient.

Dehumanization and mechanization may not be the first-order concern of *Breakfast of Champions*, yet there is in it an echo of the warning voice about Tralfamadore in *The Sirens of Titan* (1959), which is "a dehumanized planet with a machine civilization: what they can teach man is that man should not learn from them" (Abádi-Nagy 87).

In the final paragraph of his paper, Turing carefully writes, "We may hope that machines will eventually compete with men in all purely intellectual fields" (460). As long as a machine can only do calculations faster than humans can, can only move faster, or is only stronger, it is easy to consider them tools in the service of human beings. Machines morally superseding humans, however, posit new and uncanny challenges as to what is human and what is not, what is sentient and conscious and what is not, and so on. "Philosophical ME" is what Steve Torrance calls the branch of ME that

> incorporates even more speculative issues, including whether the arrival of ever more intelligent autonomous agents, as may be anticipated in future developments in AI, could force us to recast ethical thinking as such, perhaps so that it is less exclusively human oriented and better accommodates a world in which such intelligent agents exist in large numbers, interact with humans and with each other, and possibly dominate or even replace humanity. (116)

Vonnegut's works serve as excellent proving grounds for considering some absurdly extreme situations that nevertheless may one day become reality, probably sooner than anyone would expect. Maybe Turing's precaution owes to uneasy implications of future computers and machines that are ethically, morally, and even spiritually superior to humans.

Notes

1. For the sake of clarity, EPICAC alone always refers to the title hero of the 1950 short story, thus distinguishing it from EPICAC XIV of *Player Piano*.
2. Donald E. Morse writes, "Vonnegut used as his model for the all-wise, all-powerful machine the first digital computer, the 'Electronic Numerical Integrator

and Calculator' or ENIAC" (30), while Peter Freese refers to EPICAC as "the fictional equivalent of ENIAC" (90). Although both scholars write these about EPICAC XIV of *Player Piano*, it is quite apparent that Vonnegut named EPICAC XIV after the EPICAC of the short story, and thus having ENIAC as a namesake applies to the latter as well.

3. EPICAC is "not well connected" in another sense: it gains self-awareness when its circuits are "connected up in a random, apparently senseless fashion" ("EPICAC" 300). The state of being not well connected therefore may be seen as a metaphor of being fallibly yet respectably human (-like).

Works Cited

Abádi-Nagy, Zoltán. "Ironic Historicism in the American Novel of the Sixties." *John O'Hara Journal* 5.1–2 (1983): 83–89. Print.

Ali, Syed Mustafa. "The Concept of Poiesis and Its Application in a Heideggerian Critique of Computationally Emergent Artificiality." Diss. Brunel U, 1999. Print.

Anderson, Michael, and Susan Leigh Anderson, eds. *Machine Ethics*. Cambridge: Cambridge UP, 2011. Print.

Anderson, Susan Leigh. "Machine Metaethics." Anderson and Anderson 21–27. Print.

Bloom, Harold, ed. *Kurt Vonnegut* . New York: Infobase, 2009. Print. Modern Critical Views.

Carruthers, Peter. "Human Creativity: Its Cognitive Basis, Its Evolution, and Its Connections with Childhood Pretence." *British Journal of the Philosophy of Science* 53 (2002): 225–49. Print.

Davis, Randall. "What Are Intelligence? And Why? 1996 AAAI Presidential Address." *AI Magazine* 19.1 (1998): 91–110. Print.

Floridi, Luciano. "On the Morality of Artificial Agents." Anderson and Anderson 184–212. Print.

Freese, Peter. "Kurt Vonnegut's *Player Piano*; or, 'Would You Ask EPICAC What People Are For?'" Bloom 87–125. Print.

Jefferson, Geoffrey. "The Mind of Mechanical Man." *British Medical Journal* 4616 (1949): 1105–10. Print.

Martin, C. Dianne. "ENIAC: The Press Conference that Shook the World." *IEEE Technology and Society Magazine* 14 (1995): 3–10. Print.

Morse, Donald E. "Sensational Implications: Kurt Vonnegut's *Player Piano* (1952)." Bloom 29–40. Print.

Nisbett, Richard E., et al. "Intelligence: New Findings and Theoretical Developments." *American Psychologist* 67.2 (2012): 130–59. Print.

Popper, Karl R. *Knowledge and the Mind-Body Problem: In Defence of Interaction*. Ed. M. A. Notturno. London: Routledge, 1994. Print.

Saygin, Aysa Pinar, Ilyas Cicekli, and Varol Akman. "Turing Test: 50 Years Later." *Mind & Machines* 10.4 (2000): 463–518. Print.

Simpson, Josh. "'This Promising of Great Secrets': Literature, Ideas, and the (Re)Invention of Reality in Kurt Vonnegut's *God Bless You, Mr. Rosewater*,

Slaughterhouse-Five, and *Breakfast of Champions* or 'Fantasies of an Impossibly Hospitable World': Science Fiction and Madness in Vonnegut's Troutean Trilogy." Bloom 143–54. Print.

Sullins, John P. "When Is a Robot a Moral Agent?" Anderson and Anderson 151–61. Print.

Tally, Robert T. "A Postmodern Iconography: Vonnegut and the Great American Novel." *Reading America: New Perspectives on the American Novel*. Ed. Elizabeth Boyle and Anne-Marie Evans. Newcastle: Cambridge Scholars, 2008. 163–78. Print.

Torrance, Steve. "Machine Ethics and the Idea of a More-Than-Human Moral World." Anderson and Anderson 115–37. Print.

Turing, Alan M. "Computing Machinery and Intelligence." *Mind* 59.4 (1950): 433–60. Print.

Vonnegut, Kurt. *Bagombo Snuff Box*. New York: Putnam, 1999. Print.

___. *Breakfast of Champions*. 1973. London: Vintage, 2000. Print.

___. "EPICAC." 1950. *Welcome to the Monkey House*. New York: Dial, 2006. 297–305. Print.

___. *Player Piano*. 1952. London: Granada, 1977. Print.

___. *Slaughterhouse-Five; or, The Children's Crusade*. New York: Delacorte, 1969. Print.

Weik, Martin H. "A Survey of Domestic Electronic Digital Computing Systems. Ballistic Research Laboratories Report No. 971." Aberdeen Proving Ground: US Dept. of Commerce Office of Technical Services, 1955. Print.

Humane Harmony: Environmentalism and Culture in Vonnegut's Writings

Said Mentak

The number of studies published so far on Kurt Vonnegut may at first seem daunting. All that should be said, one might think, has already been said. Critics have almost exhaustively gone through his work: some have pointed to his absurdist outlook, to his dark humor, and hence to his despair of humans ever regaining their sense of a humane purpose on earth; others have spotted glimmers of hope in his dominantly playful, if not satiric, tone. However, Vonnegut's rich experience in life and work fortunately cannot allow for any exclusive limitation in one category or another. Those who believe otherwise could be like the student cited in the prologue to *Jailbird* (1979), who sent Vonnegut a seven-word summary of his work ("Love may fail, but courtesy will prevail" [7]), which, though apparently approved by Vonnegut himself, can in no way encapsulate the writer's entire life and work. Therefore, the number of studies on Vonnegut should in fact be considered as enriching—rather than daunting—perspectives that shed light on aspects of Vonnegut and entice interested readers to newer directions in the criticism of his life and work.

The best way to achieve this is to consider Vonnegut and most of his work as a whole, if convincing conclusions are to be drawn about the writer. Wayne C. Booth has argued that a writer presents different versions of himself, whether intentionally or not, "depending on the needs of particular works" (71). This is to imply that only through a consideration of at least most of the works of a writer can the "implied self" show signs of some interesting traits in the author's ideal personality and outlook. Booth further explains, "Our sense of the implied author . . . includes, in short, the intuitive apprehension of a completed artistic whole; the chief value to which this implied author is committed, regardless of what party his creator belongs to in real life, is that which is expressed by the total form" (73–74). Given that Vonnegut's work is laden with humor and irony, focusing on one of his stories or novels in particular may not yield reliable critical insights. "It is only by distinguishing between the author and implied image that we can avoid pointless and unverifiable talk about such qualities as 'sincerity' or 'seriousness' in the author" (Booth 75). This said, Vonnegut's total artistic production is not meant to be fixed upon one definite, unquestionable outlook, but it does encourage taking the author's work as a whole before reaching hasty, at times groundless, conclusions about it.

The sincerity or seriousness of Vonnegut is generally reflected in two ways. First, the question of referentiality in the writer's fiction positively narrows the gap between the fictional and the real. Referentiality, which, Booth informs us (403), knew bitter attacks, especially in the modernist era, on the basis that fiction ought to refer only to itself and that its connection to the real is tenuous. However, referentiality has never blemished the artistic quality of a work, and postmodernist fiction is a good proof of that. It all depends on the writer's ability to keep the reader interested in the story by preserving the old literary objectives of delight and instruction while making direct reference to reality. Vonnegut in this sense does not hesitate to interfere in his work, nor does he avoid discussing issues in his interviews and essays that have a striking analogy with his fiction. Second is the related issue of ecological concern. Environmental literary critics explain "being-in-the world" as an act combining culture and nature; any cultural exclusion of environmentalism falls short of establishing harmony between humans and their environment. As Patrick D. Murphy has put it, "One can see first of all a linkage among the study of nature and the study of human beings in interdependent relationship with the rest of nature, which means the study of being-in-the-world" (2). It is no wonder, then, if referentiality and environmentalism constitute both Vonnegut's real being-in-the world and Vonnegut-the-implied-author.

Therefore, one might venture to state that Vonnegut is one of the few American writers who have concerned themselves with the importance of culture in its connection with the environment. That is, culture is sound and constructive only in so far as it protects natural resources and the environment. This interrelation of nurture and nature is what ecological critics, and one should add Vonnegut himself, call for: "The 'everything hangs together (or 'everything is interrelated') maxim or ecology applies to the self and its relation to other living beings, ecosystems, the ecosphere, and to the Earth, itself, with its long history," explains Arne Naess, the Norwegian ecological critic (230). Obviously, it is in this context that Vonnegut's conception of humane harmony is better viewed, and one might add that Vonnegut thinks humane harmony should come full circle only when both nurture and nature are mutually constructive.

Environmental Concerns in the Early Fiction

The short story "Report on the Barnhouse Effect" (1950) first sets the tone for many of Vonnegut's subsequent perspectives, including those concerning environmental problems. Due to its condensed language and imagery, one might argue, Vonnegut's first published story has not received the attention it deserves compared to the first novel *Player Piano* (1952), which, for most critics, reflects Vonnegut's themes in embryo. Professor Barnhouse is respected for his humane reasonableness, although he is tempted by military authorities to promote war instead of peace. He has nobly chosen to use his superhuman powers for the good of nations: "I think maybe I can make every nation a *have* nation, and do away with war for good. I think maybe I can clear roads through jungles, irrigate deserts, build dams overnight" (179; italics in orig.). Though the ecological concern in this statement is not fully fledged, the fact that peace and irrigating the deserts are among Barnhouse's positive objectives seems promising for future generations—provided human interference with nature is not excessively abusive. More promising still is the end of the story: "Barnhouse will die. But not the Barnhouse Effect" (188).

The Barnhouse Effect is felt more in *Player Piano*. Nature has its dominating presence in the novel. As Susan Farrell has remarked,

"History is reduced to simply another commodity or else to a cause for nostalgia—characters repeatedly romanticize the past and often create a false picture of a past that never really existed" (287). But this remains debatable, especially when Farrell mentions Paul Proteus's rejection of the farm where he so much wants to spend the rest of his life with his wife, Anita, away from the artificial world of science. Paul has in fact bought a farm "where he could work with his hands, getting life from nature without being disturbed by any human beings other than his wife" (134). Later, he changed his mind: "And the charming little cottage he'd taken as a symbol of the good life of a farmer was as irrelevant as a statue of Venus at the gate of a sewage-disposal plant. He hadn't gone back" (220). Yet would Paul reject the farm if Anita accepted it and agreed to live with him? Taking Vonnegut's work in general and the importance he accords the family unit, perhaps so. If Anita supported Paul in his decision, he might be very happy to live on the farm. Without Anita, however, the peaceful harmony he has been striving to achieve, away from the stultifying machines, lacks the necessary condition.

This is what William Rodney Allen suggests when he states that Paul is "forced to conclude" that the farm is of no use: "Paul decides to try the Thoreauvian experiment of living the 'natural' life when he buys a farm. His aim is to take Anita away from her leisure-ridden life and give her the blessing of household chores. But Anita will have none of it, preferring instead to cannibalize the farmhouse for decorative knickknacks for their house back in town" (30). Thoreau's name is also mentioned in *Player Piano* (126), which recalls the scene of him conversing with Emerson about the former's reason for being in jail: he has refused to pay taxes to support the Mexican War. Yet, it is significant that Jennifer Banach has associated Thoreau's name in the novel with dissidence (113). Both Allen and Banach are right in not neglecting this important detail, since Thoreau's dissidence is based in one way or another on the preservation of the ecological self, that is, both cultural and natural. Clearly, as the failure to achieve this humane harmony in *Player Piano* conveys, being-in-the-world is disrupted not so much by any political power as it is by human greed and misplaced ambition.

The unrealized goal of humane harmony in *Player Piano* finds its wished-for realization, however, in the more imaginary world of *The Sirens of Titan* (1959). Most critical readings of the novel have stressed Vonnegut's early philosophy of the meaning of life, and the topic of nature is not given its due consideration. Nature in *The Sirens of Titan* fulfills two major functions. First, it is used for comparative purposes. If the novel, as Jerome Klinkowitz claims, "begins to generate that image of an absurd world seen from a distant perspective, and those understandings and philosophies by which we might cope with and counter it" (*Kurt Vonnegut* 46), it also implicitly suggests, at least for metaphorical purposes, the usefulness of nature. In considering man an optimistic animal, Rumfoord mocks people's expectations "to last for ten million more years—as though people were as well-designed as turtles!" (*Sirens* 37). Rumfoord's attitude is ironically turned against him there and then when his wife, Beatrice, voices her anger against his inhuman treatment of her:

"The hell with the human race!" said Beatrice.
"You're a member of it, you know," said Rumfoord.
"Then I'd like to put in for a transfer to the chimpanzees!" said Beatrice. "No chimpanzee husband would stand by while his wife lost all her coconuts. No chimpanzee husband would try to make his wife into a space whore for Malachi Constant of Hollywood, California!" (37–38)

Both images, Rumfoord's and Beatrice's, reflect a marked superiority of nature to humans. This is immediately confirmed by the narrator after Beatrice's speech: "It is always pitiful when any human being falls into a condition hardly more respectable than that of an animal. How much more pitiful it is when the person who falls has had all the advantages!" (38). Humans who are supposed to be the custodians of the earth do substantially more harm to themselves and to the planet than good. Therefore—and here lies the second function of nature in the novel—those who avoid doing harm find adequate protection in the noble world of nature. Chrono is a case in point:

> Malachi Constant said good-by to her [Beatrice] when the sky was filled with Titanic bluebirds. There must have been ten thousand, at least, of the great and noble birds.
>
> They made night of day, made the air quake with their beating wings.
>
> Not one bird cried out.
>
> And in that night in the midst of day, Chrono, the son of Beatrice and Malachi, appeared on a knoll overlooking the new grave. He wore a feather cape which flapped like wings.
>
> He was gorgeous and strong.
>
> "Thank you, Mother and Father," he shouted, "for the gift of life. Good-by!"
>
> He was gone, and the birds went with him. (218–19)

In a world of science fiction, everything is possible, yet Chrono's choice reveals a better way to make use of the special gift of life. Flying with the noble bluebirds is one way to avoid doing harm to others, which is "the highest morality humans can achieve" (Farrell 318). In trying to draw a message from *The Sirens of Titan*, Tony Tanner concludes: "Some orderings are dedicated to death, some are productive of beauty and harmony—conflicting patterns are open to man who is himself such a compulsive perceiver and maker of patterns" (184–85). Chrono's final decision to join the bluebirds undoubtedly reflects the productive pattern of beauty and harmony. The bluebirds are described as "great and noble" and Chrono is "gorgeous and strong"; thus is harmony fully achieved.

Of all the novels of Kurt Vonnegut, *Cat's Cradle* is the one novel that is explicitly classified in the apocalypse trope of ecological criticism. As Greg Garrard explains, a trope is a "key structuring" metaphor that "enables attention to be paid to the thematic, historical and geographical particularities of environmental discourse," and "any environmental trope is susceptible to appropriation and deployment in the service of a variety of potentially conflicting interests" (16). Hence, the apocalypse trope could be said to be important for fiction at a time when the study of the origin and end of the world was thought to be the ultimate responsibility of scientists. Still, many narratives about apocalypse are attacked, Garrard informs us, for seriously writing about an end of the world that has so far proven wrong. The only narratives saved from this attack are those relying on comic plots:

> Environmental problems, whilst they certainly should not be seen in isolation, might seem more amenable to solution if they are disaggregated and framed by comic apocalyptic narratives that emphasise the provisionality of knowledge, free will, ongoing struggle and a plurality of social groups with differing responsibilities. In this way, problems are not minimised, but those who describe them become less vulnerable to the embarrassments of failed prophecy and to the threat of millennial enthusiasms. (115)

It is in this context that *Cat's Cradle* can be better viewed. Even though Garrard does not mention Vonnegut's novel in the above quotation, he seems to have hit the nail on the head in what concerns the constitutive issues of *Cat's Cradle*.

Knowledge becomes too provisional, and thus destructive, when prominent scientists in a society have no humane values. In *Cat's Cradle*, one such scientist is Dr. Felix Hoenikker, whose sudden and whimsical changes of interest may have devastating repercussions on humans and the environment alike. Because the marines are fed up with wallowing in mud, a general asks Hoenikker for a solution. The latter playfully suggests *ice-nine*, a substance that turns mud into solid matter. No moral considerations or possible far-reaching effects are of any concern to Hoenikker. When a scientist remarks, after the first bomb is tested at Alamogordo, that "science has now known sin,"

Hoenikker says, "What is sin?" (*Cat's Cradle* 17). What can the world expect of such people as Hoenikker? Indeed, James Lundquist is right to have stressed that "Dr. Hoenikker's mistake is that he chooses not to consider the expanded implications of any of his discoveries" (36). Worse still, the absentminded genius is referred to by Marvin Breed as being born dead: "Sometimes I wonder if he wasn't born dead. I never met a man who was less interested in the living. Sometimes I think that's the trouble with the world: too many people in high places who are stonecold dead" (*Cat's Cradle* 47). Furthermore, it is not only Hoenikker who is to blame, but also the people who naively support or believe him. "'What hope can there be for mankind," the narrator wonders, "When there are such men as Felix Hoenikker to give such playthings as *ice-nine* to such short-sighted children as almost all men and women are?" (*Cat's Cradle* 153). There can be no hope in this sense, either for humankind or for the environment, unless people are made conscious of the impending danger that may emanate from relying too much on science. *Cat's Cradle* is just fiction, yet the potential hazards of military science on the planet Earth are real.

The fictional nature of the novel posits a real threat and, at the same time, a remedy, to humanity. In spite of its comic treatment of the relation of humans to nature, Vonnegut seems to shake from time to time the implied readers' suspension of disbelief to make them face the "cruel paradox": "The heartbreaking necessity of lying about reality, and the heartbreaking impossibility of lying about it" (*Cat's Cradle* 177). This saves the novel in the final analysis from being, in Klinkowitz's terms, "a palliative," but rather represents "a fundamental reordering of man's values, solving the problem which has made man uncomfortable as the center of the universe" ("*Mother Night*" 175). Therefore, beneath the comic structure lies the bitter truth that the interference of humans with nature may lead one day to the end of the world. It should be stressed here that Vonnegut does not imply in any sense that the fictional nature of *Cat's Cradle* is meant to reflect reality, as used to be the belief of traditional writers. Readers of Vonnegut are well acquainted with the fact that he attacks make-believe stories that trap the reader in an inaccurate identification with the characters because of its harmful impact. For instance, Mary O'Hare makes an angry remark to Vonnegut, recorded in the opening chapter of *Slaughterhouse-Five* (16–17), when she knows he is planning to write a book about war. Vonnegut's promise to Mary is significant since it encapsulates his attitude to fiction in his writing career: "If I ever do finish it [*Slaughterhouse-Five*], though, I give you my word of honor: there won't be a part for Frank Sinatra or John Wayne" (17). This is what Glenn Meeter also points to when discussing the Bokononist terms in *Cat's Cradle*: "We recognize our conventions *as* conventions. We are made to see that meaning, in life or in art, is invented rather than discovered" (210; italics in orig.). Undoubtedly, for Vonnegut, meaning is basic to action; that is why, and here lies the remedy the novel offers, if "men were kind and wise" enough to cooperate for the sake of humane ideas and actions, this world would be a paradise (*Cat's Cradle* 160, 175) and, one hopes, the apocalypse would become a remote possibility.

Vonnegut's Ecological Moral Code

Nowhere do Vonnegut-the-real-person and Vonnegut-the-implied-author converge as thoroughly as they do in his "autobiographical collage," *Palm Sunday* (1981). "This book," Vonnegut admits in its introduction, "combines the tidal power of a major novel with the bone-rattling immediacy of front-line journalism," and claims that "this book [should] be ranked in both the fiction and nonfiction competitions" (xv, xvii). Likewise, nowhere has Vonnegut voiced his anger at human stupidity as he does in his short story "The Big Space Fuck," significantly included in his essay "Obscenity" (*Palm Sunday* 226–33). The story as he admits is "the first story in the history of literature to have 'fuck' in its title" (226). This outspokenness reflects Vonnegut's fury at a culture that will wreck the planet if necessary measures are not taken in due time and warns against a dire future for the planet Earth. "Now Earth really was a piece of shit, and it was beginning to dawn on even dumb people that it might be the only inhabitable planet human beings would ever find" ("Obscenity" 230). Ironically, the humans depicted in this story demonstrate their very low intelligence first by replacing the national bird with a more savage animal, and second by thinking that sending human sperm to another planet would save the human race from extinction. The future of the story is already foretold in *Palm Sunday* by a synopsis of Kilgore Trout's story "The Planet Gobblers":

> It was about us, and we were the terrors of the universe; we were sort of interplanetary termites. We would arrive on a planet, gobble it up, and die. But before we died, we always sent out spaceships to start tiny colonies elsewhere. We were a disease, since it was not necessary to inhabit planets with such horrifying destructiveness. It is easy to take good care of a planet. ("Religion" 209)

In showing how to take good care of the planet Earth, Vonnegut reveals at this stage some aspects of his ecological moral code.

Vonnegut's ecological moral code entails immediate application of protective measures. To begin with, humans should boycott factory products, possessions that they imagine "would somehow moderate or somehow compensate us for our loneliness" ("Religion" 209), but that simply add to the damage of the planet; seeing people's growing willingness to possess more products, factories would want to permanently manufacture them. Next, humans should encourage the arts and not military science, which, as Vonnegut bitterly states, "treats man as garbage—and his children, and his cities, too. Military science is probably right about the contemptibility of man in the vastness of the universe. Still—I deny that contemptibility, and I beg you to deny it, through the creation of appreciation of art" ("Address" 165). However, humans cannot really grasp the far-reaching damage of both industry and science without a basic constituent of human sacredness that, *Breakfast of Champions* (1973) insists, distinguishes humankind from animals.

Humane Harmony: A Fusion of Culture and Nature

What is the status of *Breakfast of Champions* in Vonnegut's creative career? The question may seem odd, yet once put in context, it becomes of vital importance in Vonnegut's developing vision of humane harmony. Given its success, *Slaughterhouse-Five* is conceived by critics to be Vonnegut's intellectual pause to reconsider writing about war and human-constructed cultures. One could argue, however, that it is *Breakfast of Champions* that has the status of being an intermission in Vonnegut's life and, hence, an intersection where after a certain pause to reflect on himself and others, he has taken a renewed course. Besides, *Breakfast of Champions* is the only novel where he makes this straightforward confession about humane harmony: "I think I am trying to make my head as empty as it was when I was born onto this damaged planet fifty years ago. . . . I have no culture, no humane harmony in my brains. I can't live without a culture anymore" (5). In his celebration of his fiftieth birthday, Vonnegut seized the opportunity in his symbolical rebirth to clean his head of all the junk in the American culture and to seek the humane harmony he so craved. This constituted, therefore, a new starting point for Vonnegut in relation both to himself and to his culture.

Elizabeth Sewell asserts, "To make any work of art is to make, or rather to unmake and remake one's self" (qtd. in Booth 71 n7). *Breakfast of Champions* is a good example of Sewell's statement. Structurally, everything in the novel is seen from the newborn's eyes, and his explanation is strikingly childlike. Donald E. Morse thinks the process of narration in the novel is itself a reflection of innocence: "The book projects an air of innocence throughout—even when discussing pornography, pollution, and crime. In part, this viewpoint reflects the narrator treating everything and everyone equally, so that nothing surprises and nothing stands out—not even himself as creator" (47–48). Still, that Vonnegut is cleaning his head of all the junk in the American culture at his birthday connotes his endeavor to resituate himself. It is

Vonnegut in the process of remaking Vonnegut! As he says, as both narrator and character, late in the novel,

> "I am approaching my fiftieth birthday, Mr Trout," I said. "I am cleansing and renewing myself for the very different sorts of years to come. . . .
>
> I somersaulted lazily and pleasantly through the void, which is my hiding place when I dematerialize. (*Breakfast of Champions* 293–94)

One might think in this context that Vonnegut is going to resign from writing altogether. Having surmounted the fear of schizophrenia and, with it, the possibly consequent suicide, he gives freedom to his characters and he pleasantly disappears into the void.

It is just a new beginning for Vonnegut-the-writer. In the process of renewing himself, he undermines the shallow cultural values that Americans believe in to the detriment of their safety and the environment. In a culture where people get what they pay for and where the whole country is immersed in industry, trademarks, and consumption, the only logical outcome is devastation of humans and nature alike:

> "I used to weep and wail about people shooting bald eagles with automatic shotguns from helicopters and all that, but I gave it up. There's a river in Cleveland which is so polluted that it catches fire about once a year. That used to make me sick, but I laugh about it now. When some tanker accidently dumps its load in the ocean, and kills millions of birds and billions of fish, I say, 'More power to Standard Oil,' or whoever it was that dumped it." (*Breakfast of Champions* 84)

The helpless attitude of Trout, and therefore that of the implied Vonnegut, result from the impossibility of changing the course of human history, whose manipulation can be, to side with Klinkowitz, "a device for culturing strong germs capable of spreading life through the universe" or explaining "the human and ecological disasters civilizations have created" (*Vonnegut in Fact* 132). Is this supposed to encourage despair or resignation? No, and the illuminating discovery that provides both reader and writer with an uplifting feeling of resilience confirms this: in the awareness that "we are healthy only to the extent that our ideas are humane" (*Breakfast of Champions* 16) lies the hope for human and environmental salvation.

Surprisingly, even though *Slapstick* is seemingly grotesque, it puts forward a serious suggestion for salvation. It is worth noting, first, that the importance of a large family is not simply the ideal of the fictional world of the novel, but it is also the basic concern of Vonnegut. In his essay "Religion," he states:

> And what we will all be seeking when we decamp, and for the rest of our lives, will be large, stable communities of like-minded people, which is to say relatives. They no longer exist. The lack of them is not only the main cause, but probably the only cause of our shapeless discontent in the midst of such prosperity. (207)

Albeit artificial, in the absence of "natural" relatives, an extended family is compulsory to fight loneliness, a modern disease of American culture. As he reiterates in "When I lost My Innocence," in a rather straightforward manner, "Those of you who have been kind enough to read a book of mine, any book of mine, will know of my admiration for large families, whether real or artificial, as the primary supporters of mental health" (*Palm Sunday* 66). Hence, Vonnegut insists, "We should return to extended families as quickly as we can, and be lonesome no more, lonesome no more" ("Religion" 206). *Lonesome no more* happens to be the alternate title of *Slapstick*. Furthermore, social and political ills can be easily cured by larger families. Criminals could be prevented from committing crimes by their large family rather than the police; likewise, if wars are not tragedies for nations, they certainly are for families. It should be added, however, that the recurrent references to the devastation of natural resources and the inclusion of natural things in middle names (e.g., "Your new middle name would consist of a noun, the name of a flower or fruit" [185]), could mean one of two things: either Wilbur Swain wants to make the artificial extended families seem natural, thus fulfilling his mother's love for natural things, or he wants to realize an ideal harmony between humans and nature, thus fulfilling Vonnegut's "sunny little dream" he has of "a happier mankind" (qtd. in Allen 118). At any rate, readers feel in *Slapstick* the kind of human awareness discovered in *Breakfast of Champions*, which elevates humans from the status of robots or animals. In this sense, one might suggest extending Klinkowitz's general statement on *Slapstick* to all of Vonnegut's work: "Common decency, plus a larger basis for relationships: from the notion of his own biological family Kurt moves directly to his favorite topic of extended families, the more extended the better" (*Kurt Vonnegut's America* 73). A larger basis for decent human relationships should include the love of nature, too, to round out Vonnegut's ecological moral code.

Most critical remarks on *Galápagos* (1985) have stressed the Darwinian natural selection and considered the novel an exception in Vonnegut's creative career. It is an exception in the sense that the kind of science fiction to which readers of Vonnegut's previous novels have become accustomed is now tackled differently. It is also exceptional in the scarring effect it leaves the readers after the human evolution/devolution has come full circle. Structurally, however, *Galápagos* might be connected to *Breakfast of Champions*. If Vonnegut, as it is already suggested, is trying to remake himself in *Breakfast of Champions*, in *Galápagos* he is remaking, or rather reimagining, the whole human race. Just as Vonnegut voices his anger at the junk and discordance inculcated in him through American culture in *Breakfast of Champions*, in *Galápagos*, it is the human race and its damage to the environment that infuriate him most. Traces of such fury are scattered in the previous novels, and human stupidity is underpinned either directly or ironically; still, *Galápagos* seems to intensively group traits of human stupidity, callousness, and self-destruction to reach the climax of a necessary devolution. The big brain, the pride of humankind, must undergo a change.

The big, oversized human brain, motivated principally by opinions, leads not only to the destruction of the outside world but to its own destruction as well. After millions of years, intelligence has proved inefficient for a sane life in a sane environment; it is no wonder, then, if Vonnegut may want "to suggest that the infinite ironies, ambiguities, and enigmas of 'big-brained' human experience may one day simply become excess baggage in an overpopulated, dynamic ecosystem where change is the only constant" (Allen 155). Humans have, instead, with their disorienting big brains opted for controlling the universe through science; they have shown extreme indulgence to human reason to the extent that they have surpassed the limits of reason itself. They think by reasoning this way they are working for the comfort and happiness of humanity on earth, while in fact they are only promoting their limited, egoistic ends. "Like the people on this accursed ship, my boy, they are led by captains who have no charts or compasses, and who deal from minute to minute with no problem more substantial than how to protect their self-esteem" (*Galápagos* 255). Other people not lucky enough, suffering poverty, famine, and death: "Meanwhile, in other parts of the world, particularly in Africa, people were dying by the millions because they were unlucky. It hadn't rained for years and years. It used to rain a lot there, but now it looked as though it might never rain again" (*Galápagos* 272). Truly big brains would seek the happiness of all humans on earth, including the unlucky, too. Likewise, truly big brains would seek balance and positively adapt to change in the ecosystem with the noble aim to protect it.

Nonetheless, *Galápagos* proves the contrary. Whereas nature takes care of its changes, humans damage the planet and its rich natural resources. They are ironically unaware of the dangers emanating from "all the forests being killed and all the lakes being poisoned by acid rain, and all the groundwater made unpotable by industrial wastes and so on" (*Galápagos* 83). Once forests and freshwater are no longer available, how would humans survive with their so-called scientific and industrial achievements? To prove the seriousness of the problem, Vonnegut insists on mocking those who take environmental problems at their face value; that is, they think they are simple problems fit for public discourse or ads. That is the striking dichotomy stressed by Andrew MacIntosh, who professedly shows sympathy with a seal pup starving to death because humans had held its fur for a photograph (*Galápagos* 102). Yet the real truth is that

> so many of the companies he served as a director or in which he was a major stockholder were notorious damagers of the water or the soil or the atmosphere. But it wasn't a joke to MacIntosh, who had come into this world incapable of caring much about anything. So, in order to hide this deficiency, he had become a great actor, pretending even to himself that he cared passionately about all sorts of things. (*Galápagos* 102)

Nor is Mary Hepburn's justification for human cruelty toward Pacific tortoises compelling, except for the one significant word she uses when her students point to such unjustified cruelty: "The natural order," she explains, "had dealt harshly with such tortoises long before there was such an animal as man" (161–62). Humans could be worse than animals, if the latter kill for necessity and do not negatively affect the balance of the ecosystem, as the example of the ivory-billed woodpeckers also shows: "These big, beautiful inhabitants of primeval forests really were extinct, since human beings had destroyed all their natural habitats. No longer was there enough rotten wood and peace and quiet for them" (224).

Clearly, such destructive species called humans must undergo devolution, a fate worse than that of animals and other natural beings. This is Vonnegut's imagined alternative to a being who, as man is succinctly described in *Cat's Cradle*, "makes nothing worth making, knows nothing worth knowing" (107). The alternative, atrocious as it might seem, becomes compulsory, as in the story about "hopeful monsters":

The humanoids found themselves the parents of children with wings or antlers or fins, with a hundred eyes, with no eyes, with huge brains, with no brains, and on and on. These were Nature's experiments with creatures which might, as a matter of luck, be better planetary citizens than the humanoids. Most died, or had to be shot, or whatever, but a few were really quite promising, and they intermarried and had young like themselves. (*Galápagos* 83)

This is indeed about as unique a description as one may read about humans in what is nowadays called environmental fiction. Humans with the beautiful shape they have now and the powerful minds that make them superior to other creatures have failed in their task to achieve the humane harmony required for a balanced planet. There arises, ironically enough, the need for monsters who may bring some hope. As Robert T. Tally observes, "Rather than ossify in an attitude of playful defiance, humanity finally finds itself in vibrant harmony with the natural world" (115).

Likewise, Leon Trout, the narrator, for lack of another alternative, calls the devolution a natural repair: "If some sort of supernatural beings, or flying-saucer people, those darlings of my father, brought humanity into harmony with itself and the rest of Nature, I did not catch them doing it. I am prepared to swear under oath that the Law of Natural Selection did the repair job without outside assistance of any kind" (*Galápagos* 291). At this stage, it is no exaggeration to state that by reversing the process of evolution, Vonnegut is, by implication, showing (rather than telling) his conception of humane harmony: a harmony of humanity with itself and with the rest of the natural world. It is humane in the sense that humans become positively useful to each other and positively constructive toward the environment. As P. L. Thomas has rightly put it in his final questions about the dynamic between humanity and nature in *Galápagos*, "Humans are frail and flawed and beautiful and dangerous. As a scholar himself, a scholar uniquely American, Vonnegut begs us to be like him—to confront these questions relentlessly in hopes that we will make the changes that cherish all that is good about being human" (128). One might also add that he desires us to cherish all that is about being humane in a deteriorating environment.

It is almost a corollary of ecological literary studies to involve readers of environmental fiction in the issues of protecting the environment. The aim is to teach them how to be responsible after reading a story tackling the ecosystem. Referentiality in this context is of paramount importance, as discussed above, and it is significant to discuss here Vonnegut's ideal or implied reader of *Galápagos*. Thomas, whose book focuses on how to teach Vonnegut, recommends that "we use *Galápagos* to ask students to expand their understanding of evolutionary science and to provide them with both an awareness of and a perspective for the perpetual arguments that simmer and boil throughout America concerning the teaching of evolution in high school and college science courses" (124). After environmentalism has been widely diffused, this recommendation should develop into a discussion of not only evolutionary but ecological concerns in *Galápagos*. In this sense, taking up Patrick D. Murphy's teaching experience, two objectives are worthy of consideration. First, Murphy suggests that students be "introduced to the variations among genres of nature-oriented literature and still have an opportunity to treat one author's work with some depth and sustained attention" (190). It is in this way that *Galápagos* can have the desired effect on students; positioning the novel will highlight its significance in American ecological studies. Second, Murphy objects to teaching a natural phenomenon exclusively in terms of science or history; he rather finds that working across disciplines is more fruitful: "We need to combine these with literary and cultural studies in order to help students understand that analyzing a phenomenon externally often tells us little about how or why a government, a people, a community, or an individual will respond to that phenomenon" (184). From Vonnegut's various fiction and nonfiction writings, the implied readers of *Galápagos* could be deduced. They could be those who strive to understand the novel in the context of science, literature, and culture, to understand how various disciplines can sharpen their senses toward themselves and the environment, and to consciously apply the suitable repair; above all, they would be aware of the dangers to which we are exposed.

Just as Trout used to weep and wail about the destruction of the environment in *Breakfast of Champions*, Vonnegut in *A Man without a Country* (2005) is silently weeping and wailing, too. Yet, in this book, where he defines himself in terms of national space (he is a man without a country), he believes the environmental problems to be of individual responsibility as well. Every individual using a car is an addict of fossil fuels and is thus just as abusive of nature as the bigger companies—every person in this sense is a threatening carrier of an atomic bomb (*Man* 42, 9). Similarly, it is in this book that Vonnegut rounds off his vision of humans and the environment; in fact, he voices one of the most debatable issues in ecological studies: is our species distinct from animals in the wild? The anthropocentric dualists, for instance, distinguish "humans from nature on the grounds of some alleged quality such as possession of an immortal soul or rationality" and assume "that this distinction confers superiority upon humans" (Garrard 26). In his note to *A Man without a Country*, Vonnegut talks about the artist Joe Petro III, who has encouraged him to keep on defending the protection of nature. "And so we have," says Vonnegut, "and it seems quite possible in retrospect that Joe Petro III saved my life. I will not explain. I will let it go at that" (143).

No need for explanation any more, as it is understood thus far that what distinguishes humans from wildlife is not the immortal soul or rationality, as the anthropocentric dualists wrongly believe; it is the humane awareness of the profound importance of both culture and nature to perfect harmony. As David Cowart also points out, in Vonnegut's universe, "Persons, things, the earth—these are the valenced building blocks of Vonnegut's moral and aesthetic universe, the elements, even, of a kind of ultimate family" (172). Therefore, against the backdrop of the cruelty of humans toward their fellow humans, the cruelty of humans toward the environment, resides Vonnegut's dream of "a happier mankind" living in humane harmony.

Works Cited

Allen, William Rodney. *Understanding Kurt Vonnegut*. Columbia: U of South Carolina P, 1991. Print.

Banach, Jennifer. *Bloom's How to Write about Kurt Vonnegut*. New York: Infobase, 2012. Print.

Booth, Wayne C. *The Rhetoric of Fiction*. 2nd ed. Chicago: U of Chicago P, 1983. Print.

Cowart, David. "Culture and Anarchy: Vonnegut's Later Career." *Critical Essays on Kurt Vonnegut*. Ed. Robert Merrill. Massachusetts: Hall, 1990. 170–88. Print.

Farrell, Susan. *Critical Companion to Kurt Vonnegut: A Literary Reference to His Life and Work*. New York: Facts on File, 2008. Print.

Garrard, Greg. *Ecocriticism*. 2nd ed. London: Routledge, 2012. Print.

Klinkowitz, Jerome. *Kurt Vonnegut*. London: Methuen, 1982. Print. Contemporary Writers Ser.

___. *Kurt Vonnegut's America*. Columbia: U of South Carolina P, 2009. Print.

___. "*Mother Night, Cat's Cradle* and the Crimes of Our Time." Klinkowitz and Somer 158–77. Print.

___. *Vonnegut in Fact: The Public Spokesmanship of Personal Fiction*. Columbia: U of South Carolina P, 1998. Print.

Klinkowitz, Jerome, and John Somer, eds. *The Vonnegut Statement*. New York: Dell, 1973. Print.

Lundquist, James. *Kurt Vonnegut*. New York: Ungar, 1977. Print.

Meeter, Glenn. "Vonnegut's Formal and Moral Otherworldliness: *Cat's Cradle* and *Slaughterhouse-Five*." Klinkowitz and Somer 204–20. Print.

Morse, Donald E. "The 'Black Frost' Reception of Kurt Vonnegut's Fantastic Novel *Breakfast of Champions*." *Kurt Vonnegut*. Ed. Harold Bloom. New York: Bloom's Literary Criticism, 2009. 41–52. Print.

Murphy, Patrick D. *Ecocritical Explorations in Literary and Cultural Studies: Fences, Boundaries, and Fields*. New York: Lexington, 2009. Print.

Naess, Arne. "Self-Realization: An Ecological Approach to Being in the World." *Deep Ecology for the Twenty-First Century*. Ed. George Sessions. Boston: Shambhala, 1995. 225–39. Print.

Tally, Robert T., Jr. "Apocalypse in the Optative Mood: *Galápagos*, or, Starting Over." *New Critical Essays on Kurt Vonnegut*. Ed. David Simmons. New York: Palgrave, 2009. 113–31. Print.

Tanner, Tony. *City of Words: American Fiction 1950–1970*. London: Cape, 1971. Print.

Thomas, P. L. *Reading, Learning, Teaching Kurt Vonnegut*. New York: Lang, 2006. Print.

Vonnegut, Kurt. "Address to Graduating Class at Bennington College, 1970." *Wampeters, Foma and Granfalloons*. New York: Dell, 1974. 159–68. Print.

___. *Breakfast of Champions*. London: Vintage, 1992. Print.

___. *Cat's Cradle*. London: Penguin, 1965. Print.

___. *Galápagos*. New York: Delacorte, 1985. Print.

___. *Jailbird*. London: Cape, 1979. Print.

___. *A Man without a Country*. New York: Seven Stories, 2005. Print.

___. "Obscenity." *Palm Sunday: An Autobiographical Collage*. New York: Delacorte, 1981. 219–34. Print.

___. *Player Piano*. London: Grafton, 1987. Print.

___. "Religion." *Palm Sunday: An Autobiographical Collage*. New York: Delacorte, 1981. 192–218. Print.

___. "Report on the Barnhouse Effect." *Welcome to the Monkey House*. New York: Delacorte, 1968. 173–88. Print.

___. *Slapstick; or Lonesome No More!*. 1976. New York: Random, 1999. Print.

___. *Slaughterhouse-Five*. London: Triad Grafton, 1969. Print.

___. *The Sirens of Titan*. London: Coronet, 1967. Print.

___. "When I Lost My Innocence." *Palm Sunday: An Autobiographical Collage*. New York: Delacorte, 1981. 61–72. Print.

RESOURCES

Chronology of Kurt Vonnegut's Life_____

1849   Clemens Vonnegut, Kurt Jr.'s great-grandfather, arrives in America from Germany. He eventually makes his way from New York to Cincinnati to Indianapolis, where he establishes a hardware store. Clemens Vonnegut's children include Bernard, an architect and father to Kurt, also an architect and father of Kurt Jr.

1868   Peter Lieber, Vonnegut's maternal great-grandfather, purchases an Indiana brewery, later named the Indianapolis Brewing Company, of which his son Albert, Vonnegut's grandfather, becomes managing director. The success of this venture made Albert a multi-millionaire, but ill fortune combined with Prohibition and the Great Depression ruined the Liebers. As Vonnegut notes in his own writings, his mother Edith (Albert's daughter), who was already prone to periods of depression, never got over the pain of no longer being rich.

1913   Vonnegut's parents, Kurt Sr. and Edith Lieber, are married in a lavish Indianapolis wedding with over six hundred guests, a sixty-foot bar, champagne, and a live orchestra with ballroom dancing until six in the morning.

1922   Kurt Vonnegut Jr. is born on November 11 to Kurt and Edith Lieber Vonnegut in Indianapolis, Indiana, the youngest of three children. November 11 was then Armistice Day, which celebrated the end of the first World War and honored its casualties, but it was changed to Veterans Day in the United States after World War II. Vonnegut was proud to share his birthday with Armistice Day, which he deemed "sacred," and he bitterly complained about the name-change to the profane Veterans Day.

1936   Vonnegut enrolls in Shortridge High School, where he would become known for writing humorous pieces in the school paper. It is a sign of the family's financial problems that Vonnegut attends this public institution; his older siblings, Bernard and Alice, had gone to private schools.

1940   Vonnegut attends Cornell University, where he majors in chemistry. While there, he writes humor columns and editorials for the student newspaper, the *Cornell Sun.* As he devoted more time to his journalism, which was already his preferred activity, Vonnegut's grades suffered.

| 1943 | In January, Vonnegut drops out of Cornell and in March enlists in the US Army, where he reports to Fort Bragg, North Carolina, for basic training. |

| 1944 | On a three-day pass, Vonnegut visits his family in Indianapolis in May. On the third day, Mother's Day, Vonnegut's mother commits suicide by overdosing on sleeping pills. |

In October, Vonnegut's Army division ships for Europe, and eventually takes up positions in the Ardennes Forest. Amid heavy artillery fire, Vonnegut is taken prisoner by the German high command on December 19. He spends Christmas in a boxcar full of POWs bound for a prison camp.

| 1945 | While a prisoner of war, Vonnegut is arbitrarily selected for a work detail and shipped to Dresden, "the Florence on the Elbe," in January. As he famously described it in *Slaughterhouse-Five*, Vonnegut survived the Allied firebombing of the city in February, an attack that killed sixty thousand. The firebombing of Dresden and the horrifying aftermath would haunt Vonnegut for the rest of his life and would become a key element in much of his writing. |

On September 14, Vonnegut marries Jane Marie Cox.

| 1946 | Taking advantage of the GI Bill, Vonnegut enrolls in the University of Chicago, where he studies cultural anthropology, "a science that was mostly poetry." His studies would influence all of his later writings, particularly with respect to his views of folk society, religious beliefs, and extended families. |

| 1947 | While an anthropology student, Vonnegut also worked for the *Chicago City News* bureau beginning in January, thus taking up his first love of journalism. Vonnegut stops attending classes in August. In September, he accepts a job doing promotional work for General Electric (GE) in Schenectady, New York, where his brother Bernard was a scientist. Vonnegut's experiences with GE at the Schenectady Works would provide imagery and experiences he would put to good use in *Player Piano*, *Cat's Cradle*, and other writings. |

1950	Vonnegut publishes his first short story, "Report on the Barnhouse Effect" in *Collier's* magazine, which would publish ten more Vonnegut stories between 1950 and 1952.
1951	Vonnegut quits his position at GE and moves to Cape Cod, Massachusetts, to become a full-time, freelance writer.
1952	Vonnegut's first novel, *Player Piano*, is published. Drawing upon the author's experience at GE, the dystopian novel depicts a world in which machines have largely replaced skilled workers, thus causing an existential crisis among the many humans left without meaningful work. The novel is re-released as *Utopia-14* in 1954. Vonnegut publishes short stories for "slick" magazines like *Cosmopolitan* and the *Saturday Evening Post* throughout the 1950s.
1958	Vonnegut's beloved sister, Alice ("the person I always wrote for"), dies of cancer in September. Tragically, her husband dies in a freak train accident just days earlier. Kurt and Jane Vonnegut, with three children of their own, take in Alice's four children (the youngest of whom is soon adopted by other relatives, leaving the Vonneguts with six children in the house).
1959	Vonnegut's second novel, *The Sirens of Titan*, is published. Using such science-fiction conventions as space travel and a chrono-synclastic infundibulum, the book explores love, religion, war, and the meaning of life.
1961	Vonnegut publishes *Mother Night*, the fictionalized "confessions" of Howard W. Campbell Jr., who is ambiguously a Nazi war criminal or an American patriot. Underrated or unknown when it first appeared, *Mother Night* is now considered one of Vonnegut's finest novels. Vonnegut also publishes *Canary in Cat House*, a collection of previously published short stories.
1963	Vonnegut publishes *Cat's Cradle*, an end-of-the-world masterpiece of black humor in which a semi-autobiographical narrator discovers the bizarre religion of Bokononism as he encounters a variety of odd characters. Interestingly, Vonnegut's exploration of folk religion is so vivid that the University of Chicago later accepted this novel in lieu of a thesis and awarded Vonnegut his Master's degree.

1965	*God Bless You, Mr. Rosewater* is published. It tells of a wealthy but troubled philanthropist who devotes himself to making the seemingly useless people of a small Indiana town feel loved. This novel marks the first appearance of Vonnegut's fictional alter ego, Kilgore Trout.
1968	A second collection of short stories, *Welcome to the Monkey House*, which also includes all but one of those from *Canary in a Cathouse*, is published.
1969	*Slaughterhouse-Five*, Vonnegut's most famous and critically acclaimed novel, appears. Combining a very personal, autobiographical, first-person narrative voice with a seemingly fantastic narrative of time-and-space travel, Vonnegut establishes his signature style. Published as the Vietnam War escalated, Vonnegut's anti-war message resonates with pacifists, protesters, and especially college students. Protagonists Billy Pilgrim, Kilgore Trout, and Vonnegut himself become household names.
1973	*Breakfast of Champions*, perhaps Vonnegut most formally innovative novel, is published. Blending autobiography, editorializing, bizarre fictions, and crudely hand-drawn illustrations, this novel extends the techniques of *Slaughterhouse-Five*. Many critics seem disappointed, but the work, like all of Vonnegut's novels after 1969, sells well.
1974	*Wampeters, Foma, and Granfalloons*, a collection of mostly nonfiction pieces, appears. The title is based on Bokononist terminology invented by Vonnegut in *Cat's Cradle*.
1976	Vonnegut publishes *Slapstick*, a novel depicting the breakdown of American society and introducing Vonnegut's long-cherished utopian idea of creating artificial families so individuals would be "Lonesome No More" (the novel's subtitle).
1979	*Jailbird*, Vonnegut's most overtly political novel, is published. Featuring a narrator who is recently released from prison because of his minor involvement in the Watergate scandal, the novel's themes include political scandal, labor organizing, socialism, multinational corporations, and utopian schemes.

1981	*Palm Sunday*, an "autobiographical collage" of speeches and occasional writings, appears.
1982	Vonnegut publishes *Deadeye Dick*, a rather personal but fictional tale of a Midwestern family. The novel includes Vonnegut trademark mixture of simple realism and bizarre fantasy, in this case involving neutron bombs, Voodoo, and ghosts.
1985	*Galápagos* is published. It is perhaps Vonnegut's finest apocalyptic novel since *Cat's Cradle*, and like its predecessor it brings together a rich assortment of unlikely characters, using the theme of Darwinian natural selection as a guiding thread. Its narrator is the ghost of Leon Trout, Kilgore Trout's son, who can account for one million years of human evolution from his perspective in the year 1,001,986 AD.
1987	*Bluebeard*, purportedly the autobiography of Rabo Karabekian (a minor but memorable character in *Breakfast of Champions*), appears. Vonnegut's reflections on modern art dominate the narrative, but *Bluebeard* is also notable for being Vonnegut's most nuanced depiction of female characters. Circe Berman, the energetic writer and muse to Karabekian, is thought to resemble Vonnegut's own second wife, the photographer Jill Krementz.
1990	Vonnegut publishes *Hocus Pocus*, whose narrator is a Vietnam War veteran living in a dystopian near future.
1991	*Fates Worse Than Death*, Vonnegut's second "autobiographical collage," is published.
1997	Vonnegut's last novel, *Timequake*, appears. *Timequake* combines the straightforward nonfiction of Vonnegut's autobiographical writings with a science-fictional story of Kilgore Trout and a "timequake" that causes everyone on earth to repeat, with no alterations whatsoever, the last ten years.
1999	Vonnegut publishes *God Bless You, Dr. Kevorkian*, which features "interviews" with persons now in the Afterlife conducted by a fictional roving reporter, and which were originally a series of radio broadcasts. *Bagombo Snuff Box*, containing the previously uncollected short stories written in the 1950s and early 1960s, also appears in 1999.

2005	*A Man without a Country*, a series of personal observations that originally appeared in an alternative magazine, is published.
2007	In March, Vonnegut accidentally tumbles down the front steps of his home in New York City, hits his head, and falls into a coma. On April 11, he dies.
2009	The Kurt Vonnegut Society, a scholarly organization devoted to the study of Vonnegut's work, is formally established.
2010	The Kurt Vonnegut Memorial Library opens in Indianapolis, Indiana.

Works by Kurt Vonnegut

Novels

Player Piano, 1952 (also released as *Utopia 14* in 1954)
The Sirens of Titan, 1959
Mother Night, 1961
Cat's Cradle, 1963
God Bless You, Mr. Rosewater, or Pearls Before Swine, 1965
Slaughterhouse-Five; or, The Children's Crusade: A Duty-Dance with Death, 1969
Breakfast of Champions, or Goodbye, Blue Monday, 1973
Slapstick, or Lonesome No More!, 1976
Jailbird, 1979
Deadeye Dick, 1982
Galápagos: A Novel, 1985
Bluebeard: The Autobiography of Rabo Karabekian (1916–1988), 1987
Hocus Pocus, 1990
Timequake, 1997

Collections (Short Fiction, Nonfiction, and Other Specimens)

Canary in a Cathouse, 1961
Welcome to the Monkey House, 1968
Happy Birthday, Wanda June, 1970
Wampeters, Foma & Granfalloons (Opinions), 1974
Palm Sunday: An Autobiographical Collage, 1981
Fates Worse Than Death: An Autobiographical Collage, 1991
Bagombo Snuff Box: Uncollected Short Fiction, 1999
God Bless You, Dr. Kevorkian, 1999
A Man Without a Country, 2005
Armageddon in Retrospect, and Other New and Unpublished Writings on War and Peace, 2008 (posthumous)
Look at the Birdie: Unpublished Short Fiction, 2009 (posthumous)
While Mortals Sleep: Unpublished Short Fiction, 2011 (posthumous)
Kurt Vonnegut: The Cornell Sun Years, 1941–1943, 2012 (posthumous)
We Are What We Pretend to Be: The First and Last Works, 2012 (posthumous)

Bibliography

Abádi-Nagy, Zoltán. "'Serenity,' 'Courage,' 'Wisdom': A Talk with Kurt Vonnegut." *Hungarian Studies in English* 22 (1991): 23–37. Print.

Allen, William Rodney, ed. *Conversations with Kurt Vonnegut.* Jackson: UP of Mississippi, 1988. Print.

___. *Understanding Kurt Vonnegut.* Columbia: U of South Carolina P, 1991. Print.

Bloom, Harold, ed. *Kurt Vonnegut.* New York: Infobase, 2009. Print. Modern Critical Views.

Boon, Kevin, ed. *At Millennium's End: New Essays on the Work of Kurt Vonnegut.* Albany: SUNY P, 2001. Print.

___. *Chaos Theory and the Interpretation of Literary Texts: The Case of Kurt Vonnegut.* Lewiston, NY: Mellen, 1997. Print.

Broer, Lawrence. *Sanity Plea: Schizophrenia in the Novels of Kurt Vonnegut.* 1989. Tuscaloosa: U of Alabama P, 1994. Print.

___. *Vonnegut and Hemingway: Writers at War.* Columbia: U of South Carolina P, 2011. Print.

Davis, Todd. *Kurt Vonnegut's Crusade: Or, How a Postmodern Harlequin Preached a New Kind of Humanism.* Albany: SUNY P, 2006. Print.

Farrell, Susan. *A Critical Companion to Kurt Vonnegut: A Literary Reference to His Life and Work.* New York: Facts on File, 2008. Press.

Fiedler, Leslie. "The Divine Stupidity of Kurt Vonnegut." *Esquire* (September 1970): 195–204. Print.

Freese, Peter. *The Clown of Armageddon: The Novels of Kurt Vonnegut.* Heidelberg, Ger.: Winter, 2009. Print.

Geller, Andy. "Literary 'Titan' Voice of an Era: Pals."*New York Post* 13 April 2007: 25. Print.

Giannone, Richard. *Vonnegut: A Preface to His Novels.* Port Washington, NY: Kennikat, 1977. Print.

Goldsmith, David H. *Kurt Vonnegut: Fantasist of Fire and Ice.* Bowling Green, OH: Bowling Green UP, 1972. Print.

Hicks, Granville. „Literary Horizons." *Saturday Review* 52.13 (29 Mar. 1969): 25. Print.

Hume, Kathryn. "The Heraclitean Cosmos of Kurt Vonnegut." *Papers on Language and Literature* 18 (1982): 208–24. Print.

___. "Kurt Vonnegut and the Myths and Symbols of Meaning." *Texas Studies in Literature and Language* 24 (1982): 429–47. Print.

___. "Vonnegut's Self-Projections: Symbolic Characters and Symbolic Fiction." *Journal of Narrative Technique* 12 (1982): 177–90. Print.

Irving, John. "Kurt Vonnegut and His Critics: The Aesthetics of Accessibility." *New Republic* 22 Sep. 1979: 41–49. Print.

Klinkowitz, Jerome. *Kurt Vonnegut.* London: Methuen, 1982. Print. Contemporary Writers Ser.

___. *Kurt Vonnegut's America.* Columbia: U of South Carolina P, 2009. Print.

___. *The Vonnegut Effect.* Columbia: U of South Carolina P, 2004. Print.

___. *Vonnegut in Fact: The Public Spokesmanship of Personal Fiction.* Columbia: U of South Carolina P, 1998. Print.

___., and Donald L. Lawler. *Vonnegut in America: An Introduction to the Life and Work of Kurt Vonnegut.* New York: Delacourt, 1977. Print.

___., and John L. Somer, eds. *The Vonnegut Statement: Original Essays on the Life and Work of Kurt Vonnegut, Jr.* New York: Dell, 1973. Print.

Leeds, Marc. *The Vonnegut Encyclopedia: An Authorized Companion.* Westport, CT: Greenwood, 1995. Print.

Leeds, Marc, and Peter J. Reed, eds. *Kurt Vonnegut: Images and Representations.* Westport, CT: Greenwood, 2000. Print.

Lundquist, James. *Kurt Vonnegut.* New York: Ungar, 1977. Print.

Marvin, Thomas. *Kurt Vonnegut: A Critical Companion.* Westport, CT: Greenwood, 2002. Print.

Maslin, Janet. "Vonnegut in all His Complexity." *New York Times* 3 Nov. 2011: C1. Print.

Mayo, Clark. *Kurt Vonnegut: The Gospel from Outer Space.* San Bernardino, CA: Borgo, 1977. Print.

McInnis, Gilbert. *Evolutionary Mythology in the Writings of Kurt Vonnegut: Darwin, Vonnegut and the Construction of an American Culture.* Palo Alto: Academia P, 2011. Print.

Mentak, Said. *A (Mis)reading of Kurt Vonnegut.* Hauppauge, NY: Nova Science, 2010. Print.

Merrill, Robert, ed. *Critical Essays on Kurt Vonnegut.* Boston: Hall, 1990. Print.

Mirsky, Steve. "Bring Out Your Dead: A Member of the Species Describes How Homo Sapiens Could Go Out." *Scientific American.* Sep. 2012: 78. Print.

Morse, Donald E. "Bringing Chaos to Order: Vonnegut Criticism at Century's End." *Journal of the Fantastic in the Arts* 10.4 (2000): 395–408. Print.

___. *Kurt Vonnegut.* 1992. Mercer Island, WA: Starmont, 1992. Print. Rpt. Rockville, MD: Wildside, 2007. Print.

___. *The Novels of Kurt Vonnegut: Imagining Being an American.* Westport, CT: Praeger, 2003. Print.

___. "Kurt Vonnegut: The Once and Future Satirist." *The Dark Fantastic: Selected Essays on the Fantastic in the Arts.* Ed. Charles W. Sullivan. Westport, CT: Greenwood, 1997. 161–69. Print.

Mustazza, Leonard. *Forever Pursuing Genesis: The Myth of Eden in the Novels of Kurt Vonnegut.* Lewisburg, PA: Bucknell UP, 1990. Print.

___. ed., *The Critical Response to Kurt Vonnegut.* Westport, CT: Greenwood, 1994. Print.

Petterson, Bo. *The World According to Kurt Vonnegut: Moral Paradox and Narrative Form*. Abo, Fin.: Abo Akademis UP, 1994. Print.

Rackstraw, Loree. *Love as Always, Kurt: Vonnegut as I Knew Him*. Cambridge, MA: Da Capo, 2009. Print.

Reed, Peter. *Kurt Vonnegut, Jr.* New York: Warner, 1972. Print.

___. *The Short Fiction of Kurt Vonnegut*. Westport, CT: Greenwood, 1997. Print.

Reed, Peter, and Marc Leeds, eds. *The Vonnegut Chronicles: Interviews and Essays*. Westport, CT: Greenwood, 1996. Print.

Samuels, Charles Thomas. "Age of Vonnegut." *New Republic* 164.24 (12 June 1971): 30–32. Print.

Schatt, Stanley. *Kurt Vonnegut, Jr.* Boston: Hall, 1976. Print.

Scholes, Robert. „Slaughterhouse-Five." *New York Times Book Review*. 6 Apr. 1969: 1, 23. Print.

Shields, Charles J. *And So It Goes. Kurt Vonnegut: A Life*. New York: Holt, 2011. Print.

Simmons, David, ed. *New Critical Essays on Kurt Vonnegut*. New York: Palgrave, 2009. Print.

Southern, Terry. "After the Bomb, Dad Came Up with Ice." *New York Times Book Review*, 2 June 1963: 288. Print.

Sumner, Gregory D. *Unstuck in Time: A Journey through Kurt Vonnegut's Life and Novels*. New York: Seven Stories, 2011. Print.

Tally, Robert T., Jr., *Kurt Vonnegut and the American Novel: A Postmodern Iconography*. London: Continuum, 2011. Print.

Tanner, Tony. *City of Words: American Fiction, 1950–1970*. New York: Harper, 1971. Print.

Thomas, P. L. *Reading, Learning, Teaching Kurt Vonnegut*. New York: Lang, 2006. Print.

Vonnegut, Mark. *The Eden Express*. New York: Praeger, 1975. Print.

Yarmolinsky, Jane Vonnegut. *Angels without Wings: A Courageous Family's Triumph over Tragedy*. Boston: Houghton, 1987. Print.

About the Editor_____

Robert T. Tally Jr. is an associate professor of English at Texas State University, where he teaches American and world literature. His work explores the relations between narrative forms and social space, particularly as represented in the novel. He has published a number of books and critical essays on literary criticism, theory, and history, as well as on individual authors and movements.

Tally has contributed significantly to Vonnegut Studies in recent years. Tally has coedited (with Peter C. Kunze) a special issue of *Studies in American Humor* (2012) devoted to Kurt Vonnegut. Also, Tally is a founding member and past vice-president of the Kurt Vonnegut Society, for which he organized numerous panels and events on the author's life and work. Tally has also written an important, revisionary study of Vonnegut's novels, *Kurt Vonnegut and the American Novel: A Postmodern Iconography* (2011). In that book, Tally disputes the popular conception of Vonnegut as a postmodernist writer, arguing instead that Vonnegut's novels constitute distinctively modernist experiments in which the author attempts to comprehend the postmodern condition in the United States. As a result, Vonnegut is revealed to be a profoundly untimely figure, awkwardly situated in an ambiguously utopian non-place between an evanescing modernity and a bewildering postmodernity.

Tally's other books include *Melville, Mapping and Globalization: Literary Cartography in the American Baroque Writer* (2009), *Spatiality* (2012), and the forthcoming *Utopia in the Age of Globalization: Space, Representation, and the World System* (2013). Tally is the translator of Bertrand Westphal's *Geocriticism: Real and Fictional Spaces* (2011) and the editor of *Geocritical Explorations: Space, Place, and Mapping in Literary and Cultural Studies* (2011).

Contributors_____

Robert T. Tally Jr. is an associate professor of English at Texas State University, where he teaches American and world literature. He is the author of *Spatiality* (2012), *Kurt Vonnegut and the American Novel: A Postmodern Iconography* (2011), and *Melville, Mapping and Globalization: Literary Cartography in the American Baroque Writer* (2009). The translator of Bertrand Westphal's *Geocriticism: Real and Fictional Spaces* (2011), Tally is also the editor of *Geocritical Explorations: Space, Place, and Mapping in Literary and Cultural Studies* (2011).

Ádám T. Bogár holds an MA in English from Károli Gáspár University, Budapest, Hungary, and specializes in North American literature and culture. He is a member of the Kurt Vonnegut Society and has had several papers on Vonnegut published in Hungary. Bogár works as an independent scholar and freelance translator. On the occasion of "So It Goes—A Tribute to Kurt Vonnegut," an event celebrating art inspired by Vonnegut's oeuvre, the Cafe OTO in London, UK, displayed Bogár's illustrations that he created for some of Vonnegut's works.

Henry L. Carrigan Jr. is the assistant director and senior editor of the Northwestern University Press. He writes regularly on comparative literature and American literature for a number of national newspapers and magazines. His essays on Robert Walser, W. G. Sebald, Robert Musil, Reynolds Price, Kurt Vonnegut, and others have appeared in *Magill's Literary Survey*, and his essay on Albert Camus and W. G. Sebald appear in *Critical Insights: Albert Camus* (2010).

Ralph Clare is an assistant professor of American literature at Boise State University. His teaching and research interests include twentieth- and twenty-first-century American literature and culture, postmodernism(s), and economics and literature. Clare's PhD thesis explored representations of corporations in postwar fiction and film. He has articles forthcoming on Richard Powers, William Gaddis, and David Foster Wallace

Susan Farrell is a professor of English at the College of Charleston where she teaches courses in American literature, contemporary fiction, and women writers. Her *Critical Companion to Kurt Vonnegut: A Literary Reference to His Life and Work* was published in 2008. She has also published books on contemporary American writers Jane Smiley and Tim O'Brien as well as scholarly articles on a wide variety of contemporary writers and topics.

Peter Freese is professor emeritus of American Studies at Paderborn University, Germany. He has taught at German, American, and Hungarian universities, and he is the recipient of honorary doctorates from Lock Haven University of Pennsylvania and Dortmund University. He has also received a flag from the Capitol awarded by Senator Moynihan and the *Bundesverdienstkreuz am Bande* (the Order of the Federal Republic of Germany). Among his over thirty books are *Die Initiationsreise* (1971; rpt. 1998), *"America": Dream or Nightmare? Reflections on a Composite Image* (1990; 3rd enl. ed., 1994), *From Apocalypse to Entropy and Beyond: The Second Law of Thermodynamics in Post-War American Fiction* (1997), and *The Clown of Armageddon: The Novels of Kurt Vonnegut* (2009). He has also published over two hundred articles in journals and anthologies and is the editor of two series of teaching materials, *TEAS: Texts for English and American Studies* and *Viewfinder*, a series of scholarly monographs, *AzA: Arbeiten zur Amerikanistik*, and *PUR: Paderborner Universitaetsreden*.

Darryl Hattenhauer, Associate Professor of American Studies at Arizona State University West, specializes in American literary history. He focuses on the cultural context of nonrealist genres. His publications include numerous articles on American literature. His book on Shirley Jackson was published by SUNY Press, and his next book will be about Paul Bowles. He has held two Fulbright scholarships, one in Denmark and one in Sweden.

Gilbert McInnis has completed his MA and PhD at Laval University, and he has published a monograph on Kurt Vonnegut titled, *Evolutionary Mythology in the Writings of Kurt Vonnegut* (2011). He is the founder of InExile Publications, which has recently republished Paul Goodman's *Moral Ambiguity of America* and *Ur of Chaldees* by Sir Leonard Woolley and a debut work by the American poet, Erik Wackernagel, *She Bang Slam*.

Said Mentak teaches English at Mohammed I University in Morocco. He wrote his doctoral dissertation on aspects of postmodernism in Kurt Vonnegut in 2000. Mentak has published many articles about cultural studies, media, and fiction. He was a Fulbright Visiting Lecturer at Jacksonville State University, Alabama, in 2006. He is the author of *A (Mis)reading of Kurt Vonnegut* (2010).

Donald E. Morse is a Professor Honoris Causa at the Institute of English and American Studies at the University of Debrecen, Hungary. The editor of the *Hungarian Journal of English and American Studies* (HJEAS) and many edited collections, Morse is the author of numerous books, including *The Novels of Kurt Vonnegut: Imagine Being an American* (2003), *Worlds Visible and Invisible: Essays in Irish Literature* (with Csilla Bertha, 1994), and *Kurt Vonnegut* (1992), as well as over one hundred scholarly essays.

Lara Narcisi is an associate professor at Regis University. She holds PhD and MA degrees from New York University, and she is the author of numerous essays on twentieth- and twenty-first-century literature and drama. Narcisi's writings include essays on Sherman Alexie, William Faulkner, Tony Kushner, and Maxine Hong Kingston.

Shiela Ellen Pardee is an independent scholar, who received her PhD and MA from the University of Delaware. Her research includes representations of Latin America in modernist fiction, and she has written essays on William Faulkner, Virginia Woolf, and Zora Neale Hurston. Pardee has taught at both the high school and university levels, including at Southeast Missouri State University and the University of Delaware.

Charles J. Shields is a resident, with his wife, Guadalupe, of Barboursville, Virginia. His biography, *Mockingbird: A Portrait of Harper Lee* (2006) was a *New York Times* bestseller and is in its eighth printing. *And So It Goes. Kurt Vonnegut: A Life* (2011) was a *New York Times* and *Washington Post* notable book. In addition, Shields has published twenty histories and biographies for young people. He received a BA in English and an MA in American history from the University of Illinois, Urbana–Champaign.

Sharon Lynn Sieber is a professor of Spanish and comparative literature at Idaho State University. Her research involves the study of time as a foundation for a postmodern aesthetic and of simultaneous time and magical realism in Latin American and North American twentieth-century literature and film. She is currently working on a book that attempts to integrate an understanding of Western European and Pre-Colombian cultural traditions in the Northern and Southern Hemispheres of the Americas through a systematic study of their archetypes concerning time. She has published articles on Jorge Luis Borges, Rosario Castellanos, Julio Cortázar, Elena Garro, José Lezama Lima, Octavio Paz, Juan Rulfo, and Kurt Vonnegut. She has been a Fulbright scholar in Colombia, an NEH participant in Mexico, and an NEH panelist. Sieber is the editor of *Rendezvous: A Journal of Arts and Letters*.

P. L. Thomas, associate professor of education at Furman University, taught high school English in rural South Carolina before moving to teacher education. Thomas is the author of *Reading, Teaching, Learning Kurt Vonnegut* (2006). He is currently a column editor for *English Journal* (National Council of Teachers of English) and series editor for *Critical Literacy Teaching Series: Challenging Authors and Genres*, in which he authored the first volume, *Challenging Genres: Comics and Graphic Novels* (2010). He recently published *Ignoring Poverty in the U.S.: The Corporate Takeover of Public Education* (2012) and has written studies of Barbara Kingsolver, Kurt Vonnegut, Margaret Atwood, and Ralph Ellison.

Index

And So It Goes. Kurt Vonnegut: A Life (Shields), 5, 14–16, 54
anthropology
  focal shifts in, 188
  influence of, 145, 185–204, 229
apocalypse
  as motif, 10, 48, 80, 86, 87, 125, 274
  as motif in Walker Percy, 87
  as symbol of hope, 10, 12
appearance versus reality, 101–103, 164, 167
atheism, Vonnegut and, 141, 163–166
Atwood, Margaret science fiction and, 126–127
author as character, 4, 65–66
author as narrator, 4–6, 9, 64–65, 69, 98–100, 115, 122–124, 131, 231, 277, 280–281
autobiographical elements, 5, 53, 64, 67, 98, 118, 128, 131–139, 166, 178, 277
Barnhouse, Professor ("Report on the Barnhouse Effect"), 271
Benedict, Ruth, 185
Berman, Circe (*Bluebeard*), 12
biblical references, 66, 146, 85–86,
  See also Genesis
Bluebeard (Vonnegut), 12, 130, 137
Boas, Franz, 186
Bokononism, 9, 50, 84, 86, 155–159, 163, 198–200, 277
Bolling, Binx (*The Moviegoer*), 79, 87
brain, concept of, 258
Breakfast of Champions (Vonnegut), 11, 127, 132, 137, 206–226, 228–247, 264–266, 279–281
Calhoun, Bud (*Player Piano*), 251–252
Campbell, Howard (*Mother Night*), 171
Campbell, Howard W., Jr. (*Mother Night*), 9, 69–71, 194–197

Castle, Fred (*Cat's Cradle*), 86
Catholicism, Walker Percy and, 80, 83
Cat's Cradle (Vonnegut), 9, 72, 83–87, 155–159, 197–200, 274–277
chaos, Vonnegut's use of, 50
Chrono (*Sirens of Titan, The*), 274
chrono-synclastic infundibula, 68, 193, 238–240
church and state, Vonnegut's views on , 142–143
Church of God of the Utterly Indifferent, 193, 236
collage as technique, 107–109, 114
Constant, Malachi (*Sirens of Titan, The*), 8, 192–194, 232, 234–237, 239
convention, appearance of versus the fantastic , 228–229
cultural history, commentary on, 37, 102
cultural relativism, 145, 186, 193, 196
culture
  environment and, 270
Davis, Todd, 51
Deadeye Dick (Vonnegut), 12
deceptive language, use of , 167–169
devolution, humankind, 285
dissidence, 272
Dresden, 23, 29, 30, 37, 82, 102, 114
dystopianism, 7–9, 10, 13, 164, 192
Eden, *See* innocence
ENIAC, 254
environment, damage to, 282, 287
"EPICAC" (Vonnegut), 254–264
EPICAC ("EPICAC"), 254–264
EPICAC XIV (*Player Piano*), 249–254
everyman character, 27, 84
evolution
  materialism and, 206–209
  theory of, 50, 206–211, 282

extended family. *See* relatives, importance of
facts and fiction, 61, 67–73, 112–113, 121–122, 166
Finnerty, Ed (*Player Piano*), 153–154, 191
folk societies, 187
folktales, inspiration from, 188
foma, 10
Freese, Peter, 27, 52
freethinking
  Breakfast of Champions, 215
  Hocus Pocus, 163–166, 170–175, 181
Galápagos (Vonnegut), 12, 282–287
Genesis, 7. *See also* biblical references
genres, use of multiple, 119–139
Ghost Shirt movement, 190
God Bless You, Mr. Rosewater (Vonnegut), 10, 200–203
Hall, Pamela Ford (*Hocus Pocus*), 180
Hartke, Eugene Debs (*Hocus Pocus*), 163–183
Hepburn, Mary (*Galápagos*), 284
Hocus Pocus (Vonnegut), 13, 163–183
Hoenikker, Felix (*Cat's Cradle*), 84, 86, 155, 275
Hoenikker, Newt (*Cat's Cradle*), 85, 198–200
Hooper, Lyle (*Hocus Pocus*), 171
Hoover, Dwayne (*Breakfast of Champions*), 210–211, 213–215, 218–220, 222–225, 229, 243–245, 264–265
human development, local culture vs. universality, 187
humane harmony, 279–288
humankind
  devolution of, 285
  emotions, definition through, 259
human life, purpose of, 252

humor, deliberate use of, 178–181
ice-nine, 84, 275
imitation game, 248
innocence
  loss of, 27, 49
  return to, 31
Jailbird (Vonnegut), 11
John (biblical character), 85
John (*Cat's Cradle*), 84–86
Jonah (biblical character), 85
Karabekian, Rabo (*Bluebeard*), 4, 12, 63, 65, 137
Keene, Patty (*Breakfast of Champions*), 218–219
Klinkowitz, Jerome, 44, 52
Kroner, Anthony (*Player Piano*), 152
language, importance of, 147–149
Lasher, James J. (*Player Piano*), 190
Look at the Birdie (Vonnegut), 14
love, importance of , 234
Love in the Ruins (Percy), 80, 81, 87
Lubbock, Luke (*Player Piano*), 190
machine ethics, 150–153, 248–267
machines
  humans as, 211–214, 221, 222
  human treatment of, 189, 215, 263
  morality of, 189, 253–254
MacIntosh, Andrew (*Galápagos*), 284
MacMahon, Bonnie (*Breakfast of Champions*), 216
Man without a Country, A (Vonnegut), 287
materialism
  evolution and, 206–209, 215–226
  happiness and, 215, 216–220
Merrill, Robert, 44
metafiction
  defined, 61–62
  historiographic, 73–75, 95–116
  Vonnegut's works as, viii, 6, 22, 62–76, 130–139, 148

moral agent, 262–263
moral patient, 262
More, Thomas (*Love in the Ruins* and *The Second Coming*), 81, 87–89
mortality, references to, 103–105
Mother Night (Vonnegut), 9, 69–71, 136, 171, 194–197
Moviegoer, The (Percy), 80
Mustazza, Leonard, 29, 44, 49
narrator, author as, 4–6, 9, 64–65, 69, 98–100, 115, 122–124, 131, 231, 241–242
narratorial intrusions, 64, 99–100, 131
natural selection, 208, 216, 282
nature, human destruction of, 277, 278 283–285. *See also* environment, damage to
nostalgic writing, 6
optimism as theme, 167–177, 183
Palm Sunday (Vonnegut), 277–278
Pefko, Francine (*Breakfast of Champions*), 222–225
Percy, Walker, 79–83, 87–90
personhood, criteria for, 249–251
Pilgrim, Billy (*Slaughterhouse-Five*), 11, 23, 27, 33–35, 36, 37–38, 98–114, 129, 156–161, 167, 230
"Planet Gobblers, The" (Vonnegut), 278
Player Piano (Vonnegut), 7, 150–155, 189, 249–254, 271–273
postmodern humanism, 7
postmodernism, 6, 51, 60
Proteus, Anita (*Player Piano*), 151, 272
Proteus, Paul (*Player Piano*), 8, 150–155, 189–191, 272–273
psychology as biology, *Breakfast of Champions*, 210–211, 215, 234, 243, 244
racial equality, Walker Percy and, 81

racism, 6
reader expectation, reality and, 230, 231
Redfield, Robert, 145, 187–188, 197
Reed, Peter, 43–44
referentiality, 270
relatives, importance of, 281
religion
    military and, 143
    Vonnegut's views on, 141–161
religions, creation of, 141, 144, 150–161
religious references, 188, 163–166
religious stories, reinterpretation of, 146–147, 147
repetition, linguistic, 113
"Report on the Barnhouse Effect" (Vonnegut), 271
Rocky Mountains, 32
Rosewater, Eliot (*God Bless You, Mr. Rosewater*), 10, 20, 29, 63, 200–203
Rumfoord, Beatrice (*Sirens of Titan, The*), 232, 273
Rumfoord, Winston Niles (*Sirens of Titan, The*), 68–69, 193–194, 230, 232, 273
Salo (*Sirens of Titan, The*), 233
satire, 79
science fiction
    Margaret Atwood and, 126–127
    Vonnegut's novels as, 8, 45–48, 78, 124–130, 132
Second Coming, The (Percy), 80
sex as commodity, 216, 220, 222, 225
Shah of Bratpuhr (*Player Piano*) , 252
Shields, Charles J. (*And So It Goes. Kurt Vonnegut: A Life*), 5, 14–16, 54, 143
simplistic style, criticism of, 49
Sirens of Titan, The (Vonnegut), 8, 68–69, 192–194, 228–247, 273–274
Slapstick (Vonnegut), 11, 281–282

Slaughterhouse-Five (Vonnegut), 3, 11, 22–23, 27–38, 73, 96–116, 127–130, 156–161, 230
social Darwinism, 216
Southern themes, Walker Percy and, 81
space-time continuum, 229
spirit, machine's, 255
Sumner, Gregory, 52, 143
Thanatos Syndrome, The (Percy), 79
time, as illusion, 235
Timequake (Vonnegut), 13, 67, 97, 138
time, references to, 103–105
Tralfamadore, Tralfamadorians, 102, 105, 130, 166, 167, 232
Tralfamadorianism, 156–160
Tralfamadorian temporality, 11
transformation of
    reader, 228–229, 236–238, 240–245
    the soul, 236
    time, 238–240, 245
Trout, Kilgore
    as metafictional character, 63
    Breakfast of Champions, 137, 212, 220–221, 234, 243

God Bless You, Mr. Rosewater, 10
Hocus Pocus, 166
Timequake, 13
Trout, Leon (*Galápagos*), 12
Turing, Alan, 248
Turing test, 248
utopianism, 10, 11
Vietnam War, 23, 48, 101–102, 169
Vonnegut, Kurt
    early writing and criticism, 42–43
    early years, 20–22, 81–82
    family history, 18–19
    later years, 13
    posthumous publications, 13, 14
Wampeters, Foma & Granfalloons (Vonnegut), 132
Weary, Roland (*Slaughterhouse-Five*), 109
Wilder, Jason (*Hocus Pocus*), 173
World War II, 95–96, 123, 128, 130, 144, 156, 256
writers, writing, 149
youth culture, identification with, 24, 48, 78